The Light House

Lynn Murrell

The Light House

Copyright © Lynn Murrell 2024

All rights reserved.

Typesetting and cover design by Michelle Emerson

www.michelleemerson.co.uk

This book is sold subject to the condition that it shall not, by way of trade or otherwise, be hired out, lent or resold, or otherwise circulated without the author's/publisher's prior consent in any form of binding or cover other than that in which it is published and without a similar condition including this condition being imposed on the subsequent publisher.

The moral rights of the author have been asserted.

This book is a work of fiction. All the names, characters, businesses, incidents and events in this book are either the product of the author's imagination or are used in a fictitious manner. Any resemblance to actual persons, living or dead, or actual events is purely coincidental and a work of the author's imagination.

Prologue

Hello.

"Fuck off." The skin around his jaw was slack and sallow. A patchy attempt at facial hair mostly disguised the teenage pockmarks that had never disappeared. His eyes, rheumy and pale with age, were staring into a darkness they couldn't see.

"Who the fuck are you, anyway?" he asked after a moment of silence, his voice gravelly with a hint of cruelty and anger. "Where's the usual little cunt?"

He hadn't realised yet. I took a step nearer, out of the shadows of his room and waited to see if he would. The badly hung curtains were drawn but didn't meet. It was dark outside. A small lamp burned gently in the corner behind the wingback chair in which he sat. The wings supported his body upright. The age-flattened, cushioned seat kept his body from sliding out of place.

My keen sense of smell could interpret every scent in the room. His last meal: roasted pork, mashed potatoes, peas, gravy – a cheap supermarket ready meal. The smell of the microwave. Alcohol. Cheap, from the corner shop that shut down two months ago. Mould from uncleaned walls and windows. Damp from the leaking roof and windows. An unflushed toilet. Milk in the fridge; at least a week old. Body odour. He hadn't washed for two weeks. Hadn't left the chair for almost as long.

"I know you!" he said suddenly cutting into my thoughts. A twinge of fear in his voice. "What are you doing here?" he tried to scoot back further into his chair. Further away from me. But his body didn't move.

"Hello, Tony." I smiled. Partly to reassure him that everything was okay. But partly because I was happy this moment had arrived. "How are you, Tony?" I asked. Because I did care. It's my job, you see. I took another step. Not that it made a difference. The light from the lamp threw far more shadows than light.

He was staring at me. Trying to work out who I was and why I was here. I could see how his memories were playing games with him. He wanted to believe I was here for good reasons. Maybe bringing him a hot meal. Maybe I was here to give him a bath. He liked it when the young ones bathed him. He would move so that they would touch him, then make out that they had touched him on purpose. He liked to see their faces. Liked to see them squirm with embarrassment. But he knew. He was trying to un-know. But he couldn't.

"What do you want?" he had a hint of panic in his voice now. "Piss off out of here. You aren't welcome. My care worker will be here any minute. She'll call the police."

I gave him a moment for understanding to hit. When it didn't, I told him, "She won't be coming, Tony." I waited to see if he remembered why she wouldn't be coming back. But he didn't want to remember. He wouldn't believe it was his fault. They never do.

I took another step forward and he gasped. Because he recognised me. He hadn't seen me since I was eight years old. But that was a meeting he would never forget.

"Fuck off," he said. Fear in his voice now.

I smiled but felt guilty.

"Fuck off, you fucking bitch." He was breathing heavily now, gulping in air. He knew why I was here.

"Fuck off. You fucking bitch," he repeated. Quieter. He knew there was nothing he could do. He knew why I was here. I had a choice now. HE had a choice now. He needed to make the choice before I offered him it, though.

I waited.

He was staring at me.

I continued waiting.

The sun began to rise. Weak light came in through the partially opened curtains. The dirty windows prevented the light and heat from penetrating too far into the room.

I waited.

The sun began to set. I took a step closer.

"Tony," I said quietly with a small amount of compassion in my voice. He started to cry. A small whimper initially, but it built to a loud wailing.

"It might not be as bad as you think," I said, smiling. But I hadn't forgotten what he tried to do. What he did do.

"I don't want to go," he sounded petulant, like a child. "I want to stay here."

There was a knock on the door. The sound of a key scraping around a lock, trying to find its home, then a click as it hit home and turned.

"Ha." Tony glared at me. "Now you can fuck off, you fucking bitch!" he smiled and called out to the person who had opened the door.

"Jeeee-suuuuus!" came a voice from the hallway. "Jesus fucking Christ. That stinks." Male voice. Young. Tony was still calling out, but they weren't listening.

"That's rank. What is it?" second voice. Female. Young.

"The old twat musta pegged it." Another male voice, also young. "Me gran's house smelled like this when she died."

The first male poked his head into the living room. Weak light from the lamp and the window showed him the room. The chair with Tony facing away from the door and toward the fireplace. The electric fire wasn't on.

"We should call the police," said the second male voice.

"Have a look round first," the female voice said. "He had some expensive jewellery. Let's get it and get out."

"Hey, you little bastards," Tony suddenly realised what they were doing. "Fuck off out of my house."

He looked at me as if to say, *help me*, get them out of here.

"Would you like my help, Tony?" I asked as the first male came around the chair and looked directly at him. The boy scrunched up his face and retched. Then he moved away toward me and continued looking through paperwork and objects on the sideboard and in the cupboards.

Tony looked again at me, realisation dawning. "They can't see you." It was a question and a statement all at the same time.

"They can't see you either," I returned. "Your body is decaying. They don't know you are still here."

"But …" he began and twisted in his chair so he was facing his physical body. He recoiled at the sight of his face. Every part of his face was sagging and beginning to decompose. "But … what? Why? How?"

"Your body died two days ago," I told him. "I came as soon as I could."

He was scared. I could tell. It is always the same. I have to be patient.

"I don't want to go to hell." The Soul had realised that he now had no choice. He had to make a choice!

"We don't go straight to hell," I told him. "We go somewhere quiet and we look at this lifetime. We see what you have done and we make a decision based on what we see."

"I'm sorry," he said. The part of him that still felt human released tears. "I'm sorry for what I did to you." And he meant it. But there was nothing I could do here.

"We need to leave now, Tony." I reached out to him. He flinched. Still worried.

"My things?" he looked around. The three teenagers had collected items from around his home and were putting them into a plastic supermarket carrier bag.

I touched the eldest on the shoulder. "Put them back and call the police," I told him. He shivered and threw the bag down. His companions began to complain, but he told them they needed to get out. He was getting the creeps, he told them.

"Thank you," said Tony. I could hear the gratitude in his voice. I didn't dislike this version of Tony, but I needed to get him out of there. The stench of his human body and the dark entities still crawling over it would continue affecting his Soul until he was in a better place.

"I'm ready," his Soul stood as tall as it was able to after years of being tainted. It was still attached to the physical body it had once resided in.

Part of my job was to remove the Soul from the body of those who didn't want to pass over, so I unhooked the cord that attaches Soul to body and wrapped him in the light and love of my Home.

*

The first time I went Home was a few weeks after my physical body was born. I was born to weak parents. They were easily manipulated by others. Considering the state of the world when I was born, it is surprising that I didn't take after them. But that was never my Soul's intention.

You see, I was born to die.

I was born in order to help you die.

It is true that every human being has a purpose. Mine was to get to know you. Humans. And then, when the time was right, I was to help you pass over into the forever life. The place where you originated. The place you occasionally visit when you sleep.

One of the places.

Because sometimes we visit the wrong place.

Accidentally.

*

You think you know me already. You have heard stories about me. You will have been told lies about me. It doesn't matter to me what you think of me. But when I come for you – and I will come for you – it's better for you if you aren't frightened.

When you are frightened, your energy lowers, and I have to take you to a lower level of the place you call heaven. To a place that matches the energy you are showing. When you are happy and relaxed, your energy is high and I can take you to a higher place – the place you currently think of as heaven.

Of course, if you are a bad human, like Tony, your energy is tainted by dark energies and entities and you go to an even lower place – some call it hell. But hell is made up of lots of levels, the same as heaven. If you think of the afterlife as a ladder, most of us start off about halfway up. The really loving, caring, giving humans usually start a couple of rungs higher. Those who live their lives being unkind and uncaring – trolls, bullies, murderers, abusers – end up a few rungs further down. Even those who end up in the lowest echelons of hell have the chance to climb higher.

God is all forgiving, after all.

It may take centuries to climb out of hell, but it has happened.

I am proof of that.

Now I sit with the Archangels, the Powers and the Virtues. And yes. I have met and spoken with God.

And now I try to help my fellow hell dwellers to climb out of their pits of despair. I have to get them there first, though. It is hard work. And I am trying to save humanity. That's why I'm talking to you today. I need to tell you something. But I have to start right at the beginning so that you will understand.

Are you ready?

Then let us begin ...

1

The First Time I Died

The first time I died, I was six months old. I didn't realise it at the time, of course, but just like visiting your favourite café or pub, the first time feels a bit daunting and confusing and you don't know where to sit or where to look – you worry that you might sit in the seat that belongs to the 'ard man of the village and he'll be all aggressive with you for sitting in his seat! Nonetheless, having visited a few times, you know the barman, the waitress, the locals by name, the colloquialisms, the way to act and to be. And people nod in your direction – they know you without knowing you. They might talk to you – "ooh, you've not been for a while. Remember when you were here before?" Hm! No, not really – and they enlighten you. That's how I know that …

At the time, my tiny human body was hungry, so it began to cry for its mother's milk. My father, a beast of a man with anger and control issues, had, moments earlier, ordered my mother not to move from the chair upon which she sat, with a threat that he would kill her if she did; so, she dared not come to console and feed me.

Fear is a wonderful thing for the controller. If you make another person scared enough of you, they will do anything that you say. The fear of retribution is enough to keep many humans and dogs under the control of their 'masters'. My mother, a tiny slip of a woman, had been married less than three years when I came along. She had already been beaten into submission and into hospital on far too many occasions, so she did her best to avoid escalating wherever possible. And, in all honesty, a baby isn't going to die for missing one feed, is it?

The squalling, hungry child was upsetting his mental balance, though, and my mother wasn't able to pacify her child in any way without moving – her bony knees visibly shook beneath her skirt and she was worried that that might constitute moving, so she closed her eyes and held her breath and tensed every muscle, nerve and atom in her body with the intention of stopping all movement. Fighting to keep the fear from causing her body to behave against her will took all the mental, emotional and physical strength that she had. He, on the other hand, was pacing nervously up and down the tiny room, heart beating fast, every muscle in his body pulsating, breath ragged with the stress of keeping control; he knew that if his wife picked up the child, it would calm the noise that was stopping him from being able to think straight and ease the discord that was flirting through his brain, but he couldn't take back the threat to his wife – that would be weak and unmanly – so he allowed the noise for possibly ten further seconds, maybe a little more before he picked up the tiny, fragile body and threw it forcefully back into the pram whilst screaming at it to shut up. Spittle flew from the edges of his mouth, landing on the baby's nose. He swiped absently to remove the spittle, then walked out of the room and slammed the door.

Neither father nor mother were aware of what happened next.

The Soul is a magnificent and gigantic force of pure energy. Moments before we are born, our Soul is squeezed funnel-like into this tiny delicate vessel of soft meat and bone – the force of which can cause infinitesimal mental and emotional damage to humans, but for most of them, the exertion and stress are forgotten once the conducting of spirit into physical has occurred. That means by the time the baby has popped out of its mother's body, it has forgotten that it ever was anything other than a squalling sac of poo!

The exit of the Soul from a tiny baby is a completely different kettle of fish! The trauma of my body being slammed down into the metal-based Silver Cross pram – a hand-me-down from two older siblings and god knows how many previous families – caused my heart to stop.

The aura surrounding the physical body doesn't like it when the body suffers any form of discord. It curves and comes away slightly from the body. Only a tiny amount. Hardly noticeable in the big scheme of things. If an aura reader were to look upon that tiny baby at that very moment, she probably would not have noticed anything amiss; so tiny was that fracture. The soul, though, sensing something was wrong but not having the understanding whilst in the body, attempted to flee, and the tiniest little split was a way out.

The soul, by the way, does not enjoy being trapped within a body. Most Souls come to earth to learn lessons and part of that lesson is to be encased, entombed by a physical pulsating, breathing bag of meat with senses to experience and explore this world and a body and brain to make sense of (most) of it. Usually, it is held in place by the physical and auric body.

On this particular day, my Soul saw that opening and went for it – let's be honest if you were left unfed, laying in your own excrement with an aggressively violent entity screaming what you later learned were obscenities directly into your face, you would do your best to escape too, wouldn't you?

If you were able to see the non-physical, the spiritual, the auric forms of other humans, with your own eyes, it would have looked like a silk scarf escaping from a deflating balloon beyond the speed of light. And ... POOOF ... there's nothing.

You see, the Soul doesn't belong on the earth plane. Without a body it has no purpose, no reason to exist. So it returns Home.

I – my Soul – opened my eyes in an endless room of shining whiteness. Some might call it heaven, but I know now that heaven, as humans have been trained to think, doesn't exist. Not in the form or the style that most humans currently alive will understand.

This was a waiting void – room, if you prefer if it makes you feel more comfortable.

I say, 'opened my eyes' for your benefit, but really, it was an awareness. One minute, I was crying with hunger, and the next, I was here – no hunger, no pain, no shouting, no fear. Warm. And there was something with me. Not a physical being. Not human, but like me – me the 'not a baby' me! We communicated and a decision was made that I would return to the body I had left. I didn't want to. I didn't like it. I liked being here. I liked the peace. The calm. The love. The at-homeness. The big-ness. The freedom. The warmth. The belonging. I had made the decision to be in a body on earth, myself. Before. Apparently. And it was my choice to return.

I understood everything. And nothing. My Soul was old but had spent time on the earth plane and was feeling confused. Understanding everything whilst knowing nothing is one of the strangest feelings and I sincerely hope you never have to feel that.

So, a second after my body landed back in the Silver Cross pram in a house in the north of England, in the United Kingdom, on earth, so did my soul. Time, it would seem, worked differently here and there. A tear formed in the corner of my tiny baby eye; my lips quivered ever so gently, but no sound escaped. Instead, my Soul lay quietly, waiting.

You may think she lay quietly waiting for her feed; the mother arrived at the same time as Soul and body reunited so the feeding was inevitable. But she knew now that there was more and that is what she would strive her whole life for. More. More than family. More than food. More than the earth. More than life.

Because once your Soul has stepped outside of your physical body it is never the same again. You are not the same again. It may forget where it has been and with whom it has communicated; but it never forgets the feel of Home. It never forgets the pull of Home. And quite often it encourages that which is not living to step a little too close so it can, once again, feel the sensation of Home.

2

Home is Where the Love is

Most of us have been babies at some time in our lives, so I think you will understand when I say that the preceding incident disappeared from my human consciousness very quickly. I grew a few years, we moved to a new house, and a new sibling came along. Nothing out of the ordinary for any ordinary family. But. The moment your Soul has its freedom, no matter how temporary, it cannot forget. It is like opening a door, seeing nicer wallpaper and a sofa in another room, and knowing that is where you want … no … NEED to be.

At the age of three, I would be allowed to wander outside our new home with my elder siblings while our pregnant mother ran the family home and cared for the youngest baby. To the back of our house were derelict blackened stone factories with broken windows, six storeys high in a long row, alongside functioning businesses. One day, while climbing in the giant bins of misshapen sweets from one factory, where we would sit and sniff the sugary delights – a scent that still to this day transports me back to my time and friendship with my siblings – I heard my name being called. I looked around, thinking it was my mum, but I knew it wasn't her voice. It was older and deeper, with a tinge of sadness that amazingly hadn't intruded on my mother's voice yet. But I heard it again and again and again. I say, 'I heard my name being called,' but it wasn't the sound of my name or the letters being pronounced that I heard. It was more of a feeling of the sound of my name if you can understand that. The feeling came from within and without, the sound like an echo of a stone being dropped into a rain-formed puddle three hundred miles away. I looked toward the tall buildings where standing at a window on the top floor, was a woman in a long grey dress with a high neckline and a touch of lace at the collar. I felt as though we were standing together, closer than I was to my siblings, but I knew she was quite a distance from me. Her hair was pulled tightly back from her face – a non-descript mousey colour framing a non-descript mousey face. "I don't know where to go," she said. Her voice was next to me, stood inside me, a resonance of a distant-ness that is both indescribable and not understandable. Yet as clear as day and as clear as the sound of my siblings' voices, I heard, "I think I fell and I'm alone now. Where should I go?"

Three-year-old children don't often have to give advice to adults. Especially adults who have been dead for a lot more years than the child has been alive. I did the only thing I could think of and pointed to the window next to her, where a bright light had suddenly appeared. I remember thinking someone must have turned a light on, but I knew it was too bright for a lightbulb. I remembered the light; it smelled of comfort, but I didn't know why it was so familiar. The woman smiled, nodded her head and disappeared.

3

The Second Time I Died

As I am sure you are aware, there are large parts of our childhood that we don't remember. Not for any particular reason. Not because we suffer enormous trauma and lock away the memories (although some of us do!). Not because we don't have the capacity to remember (although some of us don't!). Not for any reason other than a new moment brings a new activity, a new memory, and everything else slides out of conscious thought. But I mention this because I am fast-forwarding several years of my life, and I don't want you to think I have missed anything important in my story. Actually, I have missed out a gigantic chunk of information, which I'm leaving until later as it will make more sense then, but I haven't forgotten it. However, if you are reading this and have experience of childhood trauma and therapy, you might judge me. Or us. And I'm not ready for that yet!

So ... here we are. A family day out. The sun is shining. The adults are relaxed. There are five children at this point, all in their vests and knickers. We didn't have swimsuits then – and even if they were available to buy, we wouldn't have had them. Our family was not wealthy. Not in the financial sense, even though Beastman worked and at this point was running his own business. But we weren't wealthy in any sense – happiness is considered a measure of wealth and success, but ours was fleeting. One day of happiness would be both preceded and followed by several days of fear, anxiety and stress – the moods of a Beastman were not easy to comprehend and even less easy to predict.

But today. Yes, today we were all happy and we were in our underwear because we were having a day out at the reservoir. We had a picnic – sandwiches of meat paste and boiled egg. Not together, I hasten to add. We may have been poor, but we had taste – of some type, anyway! There were no biscuits, sweets or bottled pop – as I said, we weren't wealthy!

The reservoir was a giant lake used to supply drinking and utility water to the local towns and villages. Built less than ten years earlier, it covered a small local village, the church steeple of which could be seen on a dry, hot day, like today, when the water level was low. Although exceptionally deep in the centre, around the edge on one side was a stony, pebble 'beach'. This is where our happy family was sitting, eating our picnic on this hottest of hot days, this particularly happy summer day. Fully sated from our lavish picnic, the children were encouraged to paddle in the cool water. The elder children, having already had swimming lessons at school, were encouraged to go a bit further and swim in the still shallow waters. Now, seeing my elder siblings throw themselves flat onto the water, kicking their legs and screaming with glee, obviously affected me in some way, enough for me to want to feel that excitement, so I paddled out further. I had to skirt around my sister, who was splashing and splashing and screaming with joy – I was torn between not wanting to get wet and feeling the immense emotion that my sibling was enjoying … so I walked a bit further past my sister and past my brother. Thinking I was copying them, I threw myself into the water – just as an elderly gentleman in well-worn but very dry, blue-striped pyjamas walked past me, whistling, and I took a deep breath.

I love silence.

There are different types of silence, of course. The comfortable type is where you can be with one or a hundred people and all be sat quietly contemplating whatever you want without feeling the need to break the silence. Then there is the type where you are sitting with someone and feel uncomfortable with them and them with you, and you have no words to exchange! Then again, there is the silence you feel when you are in nature. The birds may be chirping, and the breeze may be gently blowing, but there is an absence of unfriendly 'noise'. And there is the silence one feels in one's own company – there is an absence of external 'peopled' noise, but you can hear your heartbeat or the ticking core of an antique clock.

Of course, on this particular occasion, I was not expecting silence. My physical body was expecting to feel the rapturous joy of splashing water and shrieking it out into the world. Instead, I abruptly became aware not of water and wetness but silence. Not of the blueness and movement of the liquid bliss. But a silence and bright whiteness of memory.

Not even an echo.

Of any time, past or present.

White.

Silence.

"You shouldn't be here," said a voice.

My voice but older. Wiser. Calmer. Happier.

Or maybe it was your voice? Coming from inside my head. And through my fingers. I remember that now. The sound was coming from everywhere and nowhere, from inside and outside. From the beginning of time to a future so distant, I can't even comprehend it now as I look back.

It was the voice of a woman. A girl. A man. A boy. All at once and yet separate. So kind and caring, like a hug in a warm towel after a bedtime bath – in other families, different to mine. And yet so apart that I couldn't even begin to contemplate it. I couldn't even begin to contemplate anything.

I wanted to ask a question. But there were too many questions, all fighting to escape my lips. But I didn't have lips. Or fingers. Or a body. I was a mass of light. The light emanating from the 'me' merged with the light of the other being, beings, multiple mes, the room, the void, space.

Stood apart, but looking toward me was the gentleman in the pyjamas, the edges of his body slightly smudged as though having been beautifully drawn in chalky pastels, the artist had begun to erase him, still whistling a nameless but silently beautiful tune. He nodded once, then turned and walked into bright nothingness.

I took a breath, but I had no lungs. I tried to sigh, but I had no physical-ness at all. I recall thinking this was a bit weird and I should be frightened. But it was Home, I realised. I was meant to be here and I wanted to be here. And I didn't have to go back to the other place because I belonged HERE.

"But you do," said the voice.

My voice but older. Wiser. Calmer. Happier. Outside of me, but within me. In silence and at full volume. I knew that she/he/it meant that I did belong here, but I had to go back.

"We'll talk again soon."

I felt myself falling, reducing, sinking … without any time to contemplate what had occurred. I began to feel the beginnings of my fingers and I clawed at the air, the void, the sky, desperate to cling on for one more minute. A moment. A nano-second …

"We love you more than you will ever comprehend, dearest child," said the silent air around me.

Then, with a deep intake of breath, my Soul swooped in as my body was hauled from the water and thrown unceremoniously onto the shingle beach. The Beastman shouted, "For fuck's sake, get in the fucking car," as the heavens opened and drenched every living and inorganic thing in the area. "Will you all get in the fucking car, NOW?"

I don't know how long I was out of my body. I don't know if my parents or siblings noticed that my body was empty of the 'person' they knew and loved. I don't know if they loved me. Or if they even knew me. Because there's something else I forgot to mention!

4

Talking to Myself

As a child I loved, above all other things, reading and playing with my dolls. Both of these activities took me away from 'people'. Even the people within my family. Reading was such a joy, an escape from everything and everyone, especially Beastman and the ineffectual care of my mother. Now, before I continue, I don't want you to think badly of either of my parents. Beastman had a mental illness which, thirty years later, may have been seen and taken care of with the right medication and several rounds of effective therapy. Back in the old days, as I now like to call them, there wasn't much to be done with a man who kept himself away from doctors, dentists, hospitals, churches and priests. Particularly priests. I think that maybe he knew deep down that not everything was the way it should be, mentally speaking, and perhaps he thought he may have been evil, demonic or satanic. He may have been right, but I haven't yet managed to meet his Soul form on the 'other side', so I can't ask him. And it makes me think that his Soul is on a lower plane than mine has the opportunity to reach. More on that later!

As a child I spent most of my time on my own in my bedroom – a bedroom shared with at least two other of my siblings, I might also add. Our parents didn't have the means to give each child a bedroom of their own and for me every moment away from the noise of a seven-person family was a nugget of gold. But not for the reasons you may think.

Reading was my escape. I was well above the reading age of every other child in my class at every school I attended (and we moved a lot, so there were a lot of schools!). I needed to be able to read, you see because I was looking for something. I didn't know what. I didn't understand. But there was something I was looking for, and the more books I read, the more likely I was going to be able to find it. But additionally, when I read, I was able to block out the external stuff: four other siblings vying for food and attention, competing for a moment of their own self, a kind word; adults shouting at one another; the noise of blame, anger, fear, frustration, fear, anger, sadness, guilt. Fear. Anger. Guilt.

These were the major emotions that circled our home as we grew as a family. Not the love, happiness and joy of storybook families, Christmas film families, or what-we-thought-we-saw-in-our-neighbours' families. These emotions are very difficult to handle as an adult. Even a stable, well-brought-up adult will struggle with emotions of this type if they are regularly offered as normal. As a child growing up in this atmosphere, they are all you know. The happy emotions, the calm emotions, the laugh-out-loud-without-getting-shouted-at-or-beaten emotions are rare and difficult to understand.

As a child with a chink in her Aura, with her Soul hanging out like a chihuahua's tongue, they were even harder to comprehend because somewhere deep inside, I knew there was something else. I knew that this was not 'normal', but I didn't know why. I didn't have the knowledge to place it and to say it and to own it. But I knew that 'something' else existed and was meant for me.

It was that summer that my favourite doll, a baby doll made of dark brown plastic with black nylon hair and wearing a red cord dress, began to speak!

Okay, she didn't actually speak – that would be crazy, right? And although I didn't feel 'normal' like other children, I knew I wasn't crazy. But as a small child, when you hear a grown-up voice that doesn't seem to be coming from an adult that you can see, you have to do whatever you can to make sense of it. And although I knew that the voice wasn't coming from the piece of plastic I was holding in my arms, it made sense to pretend that it was for that moment. And then you forget that it doesn't make sense and just accept that it's the doll. But we don't tell anyone else because even though we are very small and young, we do understand that what is happening here isn't quite the thing you discuss with anyone else!

Most often, the doll would tell me stories when I was tired or upset. She would advise me what to say if a sibling was being mean or was upset. She would tell me when I should speak up for myself or if doing so would cause disruption to the peace. But it was always when I was alone. The voice was both inside my head and outside, in space. It could have been my own voice. I would be alone and in my room. With my doll. Until …

I was in the downstairs room of the family home. Mother was at the sink preparing vegetables for tea and the other children were quietly playing their own games.

"You should go upstairs, child," the voice said.

The voice was inside, outside, throughout every living and non-living thing in the room. I looked around at my mother, but she hadn't turned when the voice spoke. I looked at my siblings – either the voice was very quiet, or they were very loud, but they hadn't heard it, either.

I sat looking at my doll. I knew that voice. I felt that voice. It was part of me and apart from me. A memory that I couldn't quite reach was tickling the back of my mind.

"Who are you?" I asked inside my head because I didn't want my family to hear, just in case I was going mad! I thought I heard her respond, 'My … Aaaa,' but I can't remember. If she was going to tell me her name, my physicalness stopped the sound as I suddenly felt the urgent need to leave this room, to flee, to go upstairs. Not a fear. A prickling of the skin on my scalp, arms, legs, and face, a burning sensation deep in my gut and within the room.

So I stood up and left, closing the room door behind me. The steps leading upstairs faced directly onto the front door and as I reached the first floor and entered my room, an almighty bang came from the front door.

I heard splintering as the door banged again, then the screaming voices of Mother and siblings. I clung on to Myaa, shaking. Unsure what to do or what had just happened. If you have ever been terrified, truly terrified, you will know that your body relaxes a lot of your muscles – this is an unconscious thing – you don't know it is happening until you feel it or smell it. The smell of urine released through fear is probably one of the worst possible smells that you can imagine – and I have smelled enough bad smells in my time to know what I am talking about! As the warmth of the liquid makes its way to the floor, down your legs, soaking your socks and filling your shoes, a kind of recognition occurs in your brain that puts you into a state of suspense. You are neither here nor anywhere else.

I was abruptly shaken from my inertia as one child, I don't remember which one, escaped from the melee downstairs and practically flew up the stairs toward me; a bruise the size of a tennis ball had already begun to travel across his white face. His eyes, wide and staring, terrified me even more. Slowly, one after the other, my other siblings made their way upstairs. One silent and wide-eyed, one whimpering and bewildered, one screaming down the house with a large bleeding gash on her arm, holding the youngest to her chest. Then, for the next few hours, there was just the sound of Mother's whimpers, followed occasionally by screams as another kick or blow was aimed recklessly at her motionless body.

When Beastman had returned home the latch was down on the door, locking it. Locking him out. We only ever locked the door when the house was going to be empty or we were going to bed. Being locked out of his own house is not something Beastman appreciated. Knocking on the door to request entry would have been the sane thing to do, but when you are Beastman you don't know who is in the house being nice to your wife and children, so you have to get in before anyone knows you are there and take appropriate action. Ask questions later. Accuse everyone. Never apologise.

Sleep that night was difficult. Partly because my siblings and I were all in the one room with the one bed and we all had to sleep together. We were grateful for that. We had never believed in the old adage 'there's safety in numbers' because we knew through bitter experience that that wasn't true. For the cold and damp of the old room, we were grateful; for the two shared itchy, threadbare wool blankets, we were grateful. For the other bodies around us, we were grateful. The sniffles from the crying that hadn't stopped since the attack, the yelps as someone moved and accidentally touched someone else's bruised leg, arm, face. The dark heaviness in the air smelled of fear and pain and a longing soooo desperate I still feel it today as I sit at my blue Smith Corona typewriter with the fading ribbon in a warm, comfortable room. That was part of the difficulty that night. I can't yet tell you why else it was difficult. Not for my siblings; they were all inside their own stories just then. But about an hour after the storm of Beastman had calmed, I heard the door downstairs open and the splintered pieces of wood groaning quietly as someone left the house. The door was left open, the hinges creaking gently … holding tightly onto Myaa, I tentatively put my foot on the top step and listened.

Was I lucky? Was I warned? Why didn't I warn my siblings? Why didn't I stay and take the beating alongside them? Was there an experience, just waiting, that would be mine and mine alone? I sit here today with tears rolling down my cheeks. Memories cost so much. Physically, emotionally and psychologically.

I took to spending more time alone in my room after that. Because of the psychological and emotional stuff? No, absolutely not. Because of the voice. It came more frequently until it was most days, most of the day. And there were others, too. Male-sounding, female-sounding, child-sounding voices. And they would speak with me and laugh with me and play with me. And when they weren't there, I would read. Whatever story I could get my hands on, both children's and adolescent stories and occasionally adult stories.

It never stops surprising me how much you can learn about people from a story book. I know that all the stories I read were figments of someone's imagination, but in order to make a story believable, your characters have to have some real-life attributes – they have to remind you of someone you know or aspects that prompt memories of people you know. It's what makes us linger a little longer over the pages. We want to know that the princess will be saved by a dashing knight on a shining steed; the evil sovereign will get his comeuppance – or preferably his head chopped off; and the characters will all live happily ever after, preferably in a warm castle with diamonds and gold falling at their feet and endless plates of delicious food to eat surrounded by people they love and who return that love.

The truth isn't quite so wonderful as a fictional happy ending, but once you start reading about the characters, you quickly learn about people. Every character is based on a real person, whether the character is a vampire, a scullery maid, a Gollum, or five fantastic friends. They each have a personality which the author draws from one or more real-life people.

We would laugh about it in my room, my new 'friends' and me. And they would quite often suggest new books to read.

It was about this time that I began to see my new friends. And although I never asked them any questions (I was a child, remember, without the capacity or understanding to know what questions to ask), I began to 'know' their personal stories, their lives, their loves and their deaths.

Yes. I knew they were dead. I wasn't afraid. From a very young age, I understood that death was not the end. I had seen what was on the other side and I knew I would find out more about it. Death was not a bad thing, not a thing to be feared. And their companionship proved this to me further. There were similarities in their deaths to mine. My earlier deaths, I mean. Acts of violence and drownings. Looking back, I think there was some life lesson for me there, but I didn't know what to ask or even if I should.

Terrence, a grown-up who was quite old in the opinion of a small girl, wore a collarless shirt tucked into rough textured trousers, the waist of which gaped at the front as though he'd borrowed them from someone much fatter. They were held up with braces – buttoned onto the trousers with one button on each side. There should have been two buttons on each side, but they were missing, and one of the remaining buttons was a bit too big. He had a wonderful smile that started at his mouth, reached up to his eyes and melted all the way across his face in little crinkly lines; it made you feel all warm and as though he really cared about you. He smelled of sweat and coal and beer and the toilet, but that didn't matter at all. He'd been hit around the head several times shortly after leaving the pub on pay day. They had stolen his coat, his boots and his pay packet and left him for dead behind a wall. He lay alive, unable to move or speak for two days before death finally came for him. Alone and in pain.

He used to tell me stories about the horses on his farm. As he spoke, I felt like I had been transported to the places with him. I could see what he saw. Smell what he smelled. Hear what he heard. Feel what he felt. I was him, but a viewer – an observer of his life from his side. He came from a large family – bigger than mine, he said – and because the farm couldn't sustain all of them, he and two of his elder brothers went to work in the mines. It was a long way from their farm, but they would walk there every day, grab a pint on their way home to keep the chill out, he said, and then walk all the way back. He loved that walk, he said. He thought that heaven would look like the countryside of his beloved home. I loved the stories he would tell, but I wouldn't tell him about my death. I didn't think he would like where I went because there weren't any ponies and there weren't any trees.

Lady Catherine was a bit older than me. She liked playing with dolls but didn't like mine. She didn't like the feel of the plastic and couldn't understand why one was so dark. She also liked horses and would talk about them all the time. Not like Terrence, though. Her horses were quite a bit different. Cleaner, for a start, with smooth coats and fine leather tack, the smell of which reminded me of the shoemaker's shop next to the corner shop. She was allowed to ride every day and had a private tutor to teach her about the world, but she wasn't allowed in the big house while her daddy's wife was there. But when she went away, Lady Catherine and her mother would go up to the big house. Lady Catherine would stay in the nursery but didn't like it because it was babyish. She preferred the room that belonged to Daddy's first wife because it was very pretty and smelled nice. Her daddy's wife wanted to have a baby of her own and was always annoyed when she saw Lady Catherine or her mother. She said that Catherine wasn't a real Lady and she'd be damned if she didn't stop this nonsense. Lady Catherine didn't know why she was in my room at first. She wondered if she had accidentally walked into the servant's quarters of the big house. But even they wouldn't be this bad, she said. When she first realised that she was dead, she hid inside the wardrobe and cried for three days. She was so loud that she kept me awake at night. Other children in the house could hear her but thought there were mice or bats in the walls! When she eventually came out, her face tear-stained and sad, she said that Daddy's wife had come home early and found her in the big house. She began to beat her with a riding crop and chased her through the house. Lady Catherine tried to run home to the cottage she shared with her mum but had to go through the stable yard, where she tripped and fell. Daddy's wife picked her up and threw her in the water trough, then put a large saddle on top of her before walking away. The next thing she knew was that she was with me. Like with

Terrence, I felt as though I was there with her when she died. She kicked her legs for several minutes, the water drenching the fabric of her thick, long skirts, so she was unable to get up. I tried to lift the saddle from her upper body, but I wasn't in her physical world, so I could only watch as her body convulsed and her Soul escaped.

Shortly after telling me of their deaths, my friends would go away. Some of them only visited me once; others, like Terrence and Catherine, were my friends for a long time. I missed them when they left. But there was always a steady stream of new friends to keep me content.

I wondered, once, if the telling of your death story would send you to the other place. I still had vague memories of the other place – the peace that I felt there, which was the total opposite of my everyday life, although I didn't remember it. I hope that doesn't sound too confusing.

I decided that I would find someone I liked and trusted and would tell them my death story. I didn't remember about the baby death at this point, but very clearly remembered the reservoir episode, so I decided I would recount that story.

I had recently started a new primary school and one of the teachers was a bubbly old woman called Mrs Taker. I liked her. She had a lovely, warm personality and smelled of soap and baking. She had a bubble of softness all around her and always had a kind word for me. She would sit me on her knee, with her arms around me in a warm cocoon, let me hold the book, and we would read together. The other teachers mainly ignored her, as did many of the children. But a few of us would sit in the reading corner and close our eyes while she told us amazing stories of foreign countries, being on the stage, and meeting kings.

After a couple of weeks, I decided that this was the time and I plucked up the courage to speak to her. Now I have to just add in a little side story here. As you may have gathered my home life was not that of a happy child; there were things happening in our household that no child should ever be witness to, but there was an unspoken rule that you didn't speak of family matters when you were out of the house. You didn't discuss the happenings, the arguments, the beatings, the lack of money, food and love with any other human being. This meant that trying to talk to an adult about something that had happened whilst I was with my family was something I feared. I feared it more than standing face-to-face with Beastman when he was in a bad mood!

But ...

I really wanted to go 'Home' to The Light House. And if this was the way to do it, I was going to be brave.

Mrs Taker was sat at the shared teacher station, writing notes. I walked up to her, reached out my arm and gently tugged on her yellow cardigan sleeve. She turned to look at me with the biggest smile I had ever seen. This woman was pleased to see me – I had never seen anyone smile like this at home, not even Terrence! She reached down and lifted me up onto her lap and looked expectantly at me.

"Miss, I think I died in the water," I said.

"What on earth are you doing sitting in my chair?" uttered a voice much younger and harsher than Mrs Taker's. "Go and sit on the carpet. It's milk time." The shorter, slimmer, younger teacher, whose name I don't think I ever knew, grabbed my arm and pulled me off the chair, then, with her hand on my back, began to steer me toward the other children already gathered on the carpet.

I looked back for Mrs Taker, but she wasn't there.

"Where's Mrs Taker gone?" I asked.

The chatter in the room seemed to stop the instant I opened my mouth. I think I heard a pin drop in Mexico. Then there was one of those awkward silences that seemed to last an eternity, but it was, in reality, a moment or two. The adults exchanged glances. One sniffled, another looked like she'd been slapped in the face.

Do you already know what I'm going to say? Do you really need me to say it?

Okay. At pickup time, the adult who was collecting me from

school that day was called into the school office – a poky little room where I'd had the pleasure of spending the previous three hours, fortunately with a book, with the school secretary who kept looking at me, shaking her head and tutting. I think she was tutting because the whole class had erupted in wailing and keening the likes of which had only ever been heard before at the funeral of a well-loved local celebrity – said local celebrity, a Mrs Taker, had keeled over in the school, the week before I started and had died in hospital of a massive stroke later the same day. So. As well as sounding like their voice is both inside and outside my body at the same time, newly dead people also, it would appear, have a soft glow around them resembling a bubble - unlike the glow of living people.

I learned that all by myself and without a book. I also learned that telling someone wouldn't get me 'Home', that adults became deeply upset and believed that I should not 'tell lies', AND the whole school believed I had a very active imagination and I wasn't allowed to sit with the other children for a week in case I upset them further.

Lessons can sometimes be quite difficult to learn. Rule one: Don't talk about fight club. Well, it's very nearly the right rule!

5

A Change of Friends

It was around this time that I noticed a difference in the people who came to see me. I still had a small core of 'friends' with whom I regularly played and spoke. They were also my educators and would occasionally visit me in school. I enjoyed those playtimes more than most others; instead of being forced to play games like 'kiss chase' (bleurgh!) and 'what time is it, Mr Wolf?' which both involved lots of children wanting to put their bodies in the space near your body (which always made me itch!) I got to sit in the corner of the playground and talk with my 'other friends'. Most of them were older than my peers and our conversations were more intellectual. Of course, I didn't know that at the time, I just thought that kids my own age were boring. We discussed characters in books I'd not yet read, countries I'd never visit, places that made my eyes widen in wonder, and sometimes a wee bit of fear when the man told me about the bore wore! And animals – oh! I looooved animals! Furry ones, flying ones, swimmy ones, they would sit with me and share images of their lives and masters.

Most of my friends had kind eyes – my non-living friends, I need to add here. But the new ones seemed to always want me to talk to people. To tell them things.

"Tell our Mark his sister hid his toys under my bed," one lovely lady asked me one day. Mark was sat next to me in class.

"Your sister hid your toys under the lady's bed," I told him.

"Which lady?" he asked.

I looked at the lady and asked, "Which lady?"

"I'm his Granny Margo. I passed last week, but they haven't found me yet," she replied, smiling at the boy with such love it made me hurt inside. I don't think anyone had ever looked at me like that and I was pretty sure I didn't have a granny, but I decided that I'd ask my mum next time I saw her.

"Your Granny Margo. She passed last week, but nobody found 'er yet." I repeated what Granny Margo had said.

Just then the teacher came to our table and took my paper from me, absentmindedly ticking in a red pen at the scrawl on my page.

"Miss?" Mark asked. "What does that mean?" He looked perplexed. "She said me Granny Margo passed last week, and nobody's found 'er yet."

"Corner," she said irritably, pointing me in the direction of the place where only the naughty children sat.

"Why?" I asked. I wasn't being naughty. I was doing as I'd been told by an adult, so surely they couldn't tell me I'm naughty? But asking "why" was naughty apparently and into the corner I went and I stayed there through playtime and lunchtime (I refused to leave and go for lunch) and all afternoon too. I don't think any child had spent that long in the naughty corner, EVER!

Anyway, at pick-up time, my adult was upset and angry with me. She didn't like having to speak with the headteacher; reminded her of her own time at school, apparently. She kept telling me that I had to stop making things up and scaring the other children. But I don't know who was scared, it wasn't Mark, I'm sure. However, a week later, he didn't arrive at school on Monday morning. Mark always came to school, even when he was poorly, because his mum had a job and she'd leave him at the gates at 8:15am every morning whether it was sunny, rainy or snowy. He would usually open the gates for Mrs Morris' car to drive through, and, as the headteacher, she would open the building, let him in and turn the heating on early in winter.

That same evening, there was something in the paper about an old lady who had died in her bed and had been found by her grandson! Her doors were unlocked and there was rotting food on the kitchen table and a strange smell throughout the house. He didn't come back to the school, or at least not whilst I was there – we moved again not long afterwards, so he might have come back after I'd left. But I know that seeing a body without its Soul inside is a bit strange and can actually be quietly scary. And I think Mark would have been upset.

Around the same time, one of the girls in school – she was scary and most people were frightened of her – came to sit with me. She told me that we were friends now and I had to do what she said or we wouldn't be friends anymore. I wasn't bothered, if I'm honest. I wasn't overly fond of living people – they were really complex and emotional, unlike dead people who would mostly tell the truth and be quite blunt.

I'd also started to get a few 'different' shiny people visiting me. They had a different kind of glow about them than the usual ones. It was a flat glow, dull, more grey in colour than the shiny white I was used to, but it wasn't grey, either. It is so difficult for me to describe these things from the point of view of a child who doesn't have the vocabulary, the knowledge or the understanding of these things. But I have to describe it as best I can from the point in which it was first observed.

Anyway, these new people were very much like the girl – the alive girl – in that they would say things almost without thinking. They would be quite rude and downright horrible sometimes. They left me feeling sad and tearful so I didn't like to be around them if I could help it. But they always seemed to appear when this girl, my new friend, whether I liked it or not, was nearby.

I tried to ignore them most of the time; they would say things about the teachers: "She's having it off with her dentist." Or, "What a fucking ugly bitch she is."

Sometimes, they would say things about the other kids – I didn't understand some of the words they used, but I knew they were horrible. Then they would laugh – there was always a group of them. They were never alone. They were like a pack of hyenas, predators looking for weakness. The smallest hint of fear and they were all over the object exuding the fear. Some of the other kids could feel them too. One particular boy would start to scream when one of the greys went too close. I kept away from him in case the teachers thought it was my doing!

Obviously, after the incident with Mark, I wasn't going to start sharing again, especially not using some of their vocabulary. I knew swear words and that I wasn't supposed to use them until I was a grown-up, but I really didn't understand some of the words they used. I had just discovered a dictionary in school and looked up some of the words in there. I still didn't understand them, though.

My new best friend, Karen, had taken to sitting very close to me and holding my hand everywhere we went. It wasn't too bad – she had a real sadness about her and smelled of fear, although we never talked about it. I didn't talk much at the best of times and had learned that if I concentrated very hard, I could block out the bad, shiny people's voices. She felt a bit angry, a bit sad, a bit lost and I think she saw me as something safe. I was the thing that stopped her from crashing into the rocks, I was told by one of my good, shiny friends, but I didn't know what it meant.

After a couple of weeks, her behaviour in class started to become erratic. One moment, she would be happy and jolly and smiling, and the next, she would become angry and volatile, screaming at someone, child or adult, for no apparent reason. Her mother was called into school on a regular basis and would take her home. Both of them were in tears as they reached the school gate.

One day, Karen asked if I wanted to go to her birthday party. The other girls and boys would have birthday parties and sleepovers – there would be the excited chatter as one child or another came into school clutching a stack of envelopes and would eagerly and assuredly hand them out telling each child individually, "You can come to my birthday party", to which the individual child would squeal and reply with a, "I'm going to wear my blue princess dress" or, "My mum said I can buy you a car from Thompsons Toy shop for your present". They would always run out of envelopes before they got to me. Even when I was standing next to them as they came into class, they seemed to empty before they reached me – or my name, mysteriously, wouldn't be on an envelope. "Sorry, I can only have ten at my party." "Oh, I've got none left. I'll bring another for you tomorrow." They never did, though.

Parents can be really cruel. They don't necessarily mean to be unkind to their own children, but children, in general, are quite nice human beings – they notice unfairness and injustice more than most adults. And they feel it more acutely. When a parent singles out one child from the class as being unusual, odd, strange, poor or different, they encourage their child to feel the same. They ostracise the odd child and talk about it with other parents in front of their children. So, although the children may like the essence, core or soul of the ostracised one – they KNOW that child is good and honest and true – they feel guilty for not disliking the child as their parent would want. Guilt and rejection are such a horrible thing to teach your children when they are so young. Why not teach acceptance and tolerance, I think, but then it's easy to want something that you are not given.

So, I got my first birthday party invitation. I was told I couldn't go, but Karen's mum seemed to know we couldn't afford to buy a present and told me that presents weren't needed, she just wanted to give Karen a wonderful birthday because she hadn't been herself for a while and she really wanted me to be there because I was the best friend she'd ever had.

That made my mum tearful. She told me how proud she was and how lovely of me to be a good friend to such a poor girl. I didn't understand what she meant. I wasn't really being a friend but being dragged around the school and playground by someone who I didn't have any particular feelings for if I was to be totally honest.

But anyway ... before I make myself out to be someone who is totally uncaring and unfeeling, I'd better tell you about the party!

It was an unusually hot spring day. Rain had been forecast, so I was put into trousers and a jumper. The jumper had sparkles and snowflakes dotted around the yoke. We didn't have any party dresses, so I just had to make do with what we had. My other siblings felt both excited for me and a bit envious – none of us had ever been to a birthday party before, so I was expected to return afterwards and tell all about it!

By the time I arrived, all the other children were there – many in pretty dresses or dapper little shirt and tie ensembles (the ties were on thin elastic – the boys excitedly grabbed at each other's ties to pull and have them snap back slightly out of place; the boys erupting in laughter each time they did it), many of them clutched fabulously coloured boxes, some tied neatly with ribbon, others with a white, pink or yellow envelope stuck atop. There were many more presents piled up on the table at the side of the entrance door. I wondered why the other children were squealing and realised that this must be excitement. But I didn't feel it.

You see, I was feeling a sense of dread. The grey glowers had been around me almost constantly, day and night, since the moment I'd got my invitation. They seemed really excited by my presence and made lots of really quiet comments, followed by sniggers that I didn't understand. My usual glowy, non-living friends had not been near me for almost as much time, so I was feeling a bit strange and out of sorts.

For the most part, I stood alone in the kitchen of Karen's home. I didn't know what you were supposed to do at a party, so I waited for someone to tell me. The other adults flitted in and out, ignoring me, and the other children were shout-talking and playing games.

I hadn't yet seen Karen, but the man who lived with her mum was standing at the bottom of the stairs, staring at me through the kitchen door. He had mousey hair and a sharp nose. His small lips pursed into a tight line, hardly passing the edges of his nose and dipping at a sharp angle; perfectly following the line of his mouth was his sparse-haired moustache. His eyes, though quite large, were heavily hooded, causing him to look as though he had narrow slits roughly downturned at the outer edge like his mouth. Surrounding his whole body existed a thin layer of soot grey smoke, tendrils of which crept outwards and were drawn up by the spirits that had been with me since my friendship with Karen had started but were now surrounding this man. Their laughter and sinister sneers matched the feeling I got from the living man.

A sudden dread began to creep over me. Within me. Around me. It began to smother me. I abruptly knew without knowing, sensed without understanding that I was here for a reason. Every hair on my body stood to attention, every pore painfully forcing out icy water – I could feel the sweat trickling down my neck and onto my back – the heavy woollen jumper holding it against my skin in an unpleasant puddle. I needed to leave, but I couldn't move.

Out of nowhere, Karen's mum appeared. She looked at me and then out into the hallway. "No!" she said quietly as if to herself. The man nodded, half smiled, walked through his spiritual companions and turned up the stairs.

"Karen!" she called out towards the living room. Karen came in, an excited smile on her face – I don't think I'd ever seen her so happy.

"Your friend can't be comfortable in this heat," her mum said, looking far more uncomfortable than me and a little tearful. "Take her upstairs and let her put one of your dresses on."

Karen's eyes widened. She opened her mouth. Then shut it. She looked at me. She looked at her mum. She looked through the door to the empty space where the man had recently stood. She opened her mouth. Took a deep, ragged breath, a tear in her eye. She wiped it away with the back of her hand and smiled a big, false smile that I recognised as the one she wore to school every day.

"Come on," she said to me, shaking slightly, as she grabbed my hand, "you can wear my other new dress that I told you about."

We headed to the hallway and made our way up the stairs and down a short corridor. Happy family photos in frames leading the way.

Her room was above the garage, away from the kitchen and the living room where the party was being held. I'm telling you this now so you'll understand, hopefully, the events that follow. But you probably won't understand. I can't really make sense of it myself.

Karen pushed open the door to her bedroom. It was beautiful. I remember looking and thinking, in my living head, how lucky she was to have such a pretty room. There was a shade over the lightbulb – pink and lacy. The walls had pale pink wallpaper with fairies, butterflies, and princesses, and toadstool houses interspersed and lots of unreal-looking but very pretty pink and yellow flowers. The curtains and bedding matched the wallpaper. She had pretty pale pink furniture – a bed with a heart cut out of the headboard, a wardrobe with a heart engraved in the door, a dressing table with drawers, a big mirror and a stool with a pink velvet upholstered cushion. I thought this must be what a princess's room looked like. In my other head, the one where my Soul is in charge, I thought *this poor girl*. And I don't really know why I thought that especially when I saw the dress laid out on the bed. Pink. I don't know why I liked pink so much. We didn't have much 'colour' at The Home – everything seemed to be shades of greige there – pink looked like a happy colour. A colour that happy people would wear.

"Oh! No, no, no, no, child," said a voice from everywhere and nowhere all at once. "These are very sad people."

It was then that I noticed the man standing by the window,

smiling. There was a smell coming from him that I couldn't place, but it made me feel really sad, made my stomach churn and made me think of darkness. I felt my face and neck flush uncomfortably hot. I suddenly realised why the greys were with him. They weren't nice. He wasn't nice. I realised that I'd always thought of the greys as harmful creatures but had tried to push it away. But now that feeling was stronger.

I realised that Karen was telling the man about the dress ...

"It's okay, Karen," he smiled. "I'll help her get changed. It's your special day. You go and enjoy your party."

The door slammed shut so quickly I didn't have time to follow. A dread began to build in my belly as the man stepped forward and I felt as though I was pinned in place, unable to move. Unable to speak.

"Take your clothes off," he said and my bladder released its hot liquid contents. "Now then, don't ruin it or I'll fucking slap you and no one will hear you scream."

Downstairs the volume of the music had increased along with the excited screeches of happy children.

Okay, let's just take a breath.

I know what you're thinking and we need a moment to process everything before we go on. Imagine, if you will – if you can – that you are standing here in my shoes right now. What would you say about this man's behaviour? Guilty! Guilty! Guilty! Right? Hmm. Yup. Life is never so easy, though, is it? Do you think Karen or her mum would stand up in a court of law and describe the events of the early part of the party with truth, the whole truth and nothing but the truth? Do you think that the man would tell the truth? Well, we honest people know that he wouldn't tell the truth, don't we? Except ...

After the fact (or after I'd left Karen's bedroom, to be more precise), he came downstairs and told the truth, the whole truth and nothing but the truth to the WHOLE party; adults, children and the local party clown who had just turned up at the house –

but he didn't tell the bit that made me piss myself, I might add.

So, back to what happened. And then I'll tell you how I contributed to the death of my mother.

6

What Happens in Vegas Stays in Vegas

So, I stood, stock still and in my child head, I was thinking, *this must be what it's like for Mum when Beastman is in the room.* The fear is physical. You can feel it in every muscle, every bone, every fibre of your body. You can't fight and you can't flight!

You can smell it – it makes you want to retch, but your body is locked so tight you can feel the vomit rising up your gullet and start to choke you. You can taste it – it's like rusty metal steeped in vinegar and mould and piss all dried out on a hot sunny day, then plunged into the rotting flesh of a decomposing cadaver before being brushed onto your tongue with a dirty floor mop.

Fear. I wouldn't wish it on my worst enemy. I wouldn't even wish it on Beastman or Karen's mum's boyfriend.

The thing is, wherever there is fear, there is also hope.

Hope is actually much stronger than fear and this is something that bullies, abusers, tormentors and tyrants throughout the history of history have always disregarded. They have this concept in their heads that because they cause you fear, you will rely on them, depend on them, need them, respect them – well, not respect perhaps, but you get the gist, the sense of what I'm saying, I think.

You may wonder how I – a small child – can know this. Well, the truth is I only found out at that particular moment. The moment the man reached for me with one hand whilst unbuckling his belt with the other.

I had an ongoing relationship with 'the other side' if you recall.

There were many 'on the other side' whom I called friends, and they called me friend, too. Spirit never forgets. I'm going to say that again, just so you are clear ... SPIRIT NEVER FORGETS.

And so, at that precise moment, the room began to fill with my non-living friends. Those I had helped and who had helped me. There must have been thirty that I could see and count, but I knew there were more. Many more. And I smiled. The man saw my smile and was taken aback. You see, people like him feel more in control when you show fear. The more fear you show, the stronger they feel. They don't become stronger – they are basically very weak people. Only the weakest people would ever consider hurting or abusing another individual, especially a child. Power, as I mentioned earlier, comes not from fear but from love. From kindness. From empathy. And all of this came to me in that moment. But there was more!

If you have been concentrating (and if you haven't, you might want to stop here and go back to the beginning of this story!), you will know that I spent some time in the waiting void ... sorry, waiting room! I forget that description may be frightening to some of you (but keep reading because I'll tell you what happens after the waiting room a little bit later!), and in the waiting room was the 'being' that was me but wasn't me.

This particular being is the 'guardian' if you like, of the void room and he/she/it could sense that I was about to make another visit. Unfortunately, I don't have nine lives, like a cat, so there are only so many times I could go there before 'goodnight Vienna', 'adios muchachos', 'the final countdown' – (and we all do visit, although we don't always remember) before we are moved onto the next part of ... let's call it heaven, because you will understand that slightly more than any words I could use at the moment without going into a week-long diatribe of explanation.

As the man's hand touched my hair and the room filled with 'friends', I felt something warm, happy and homely melting into the top of my head. Tiny prickles trickled across the crown of my head, swirling like the bath water as it left through a tiny plug hole. His grey comrades began to 'pop' – an audible sound that even the man could hear – I'm so pleased the room was above the garage and the music downstairs was so loud because it sounded like the house was breaking apart, so audible were those noises. The man turned his head but saw nothing; he sensed something but without understanding. The warm, happy, homely feeling spread throughout my body, and I felt my form expand and grow. I sensed the glow of brighter-than-white light moments before I saw it emanate from my body. The man lifted his head to look at me as I was now taller, by at least a metre, than him. I looked downward and saw my child's body still standing with his hand on my hair. My light body had merged with the body from the void room – The Light House – heaven – and expanded to fill the room, consuming, enveloping and taking in all my friends until we became one unit. One entity. One body. We were the room. We were the space. We were space. We were everything. Everything was silent but for the rapid beating of the man's heart. We could hear the blood pulsating through his veins. WE could feel his ragged breath within his tiny personal atmosphere, which was reducing moment by moment until only a tiny sliver of his aura remained. We could see his eyes widen – not with fear because we don't use fear. We use love and empathy and we showed him his options: where he could go, physically, mentally and metaphorically, if he changed now, or where he was going if he didn't – when his time on this earth was over. We didn't tell him what to do. We didn't ask him to stop this behaviour. It wasn't within our power or our will to ask anything of him. He had freewill. It was his choice. And he had the information he needed to make that choice wisely. Or not. It was at that point that he opened his mouth and sound came out. Not a sound I have ever heard before. Or since. And neither do I want to.

And then I was in The Light House. The White Room. The Void. I was at peace. The silence was soothing. I was alone and not alone. Completely surrounded by love and silence.

"You are getting too fond of this place," a warm, loving voice, connected to everything and nothing, spoke.

I thought *I'm going to look around and try to remember everything about this place so I can remember it when I go back. If I go back.*

"You can remember it," said the voice, "we will allow that." The white light smiled at me.

I know that sounds odd, but I imagine if you were a blind person, you wouldn't be able to see another person's expressions, but you can feel their emotions in the sound of their voice. The pitch. The tone. The timbre. The texture. You can feel or sense anger, sorrow, fear, and wonderment without seeing it on a person's face. That is sort of how it felt to 'see' the smile.

We began to converse – the Light and I. I won't bore you with the details of the discourse yet because I guess you want to know what happened at the party. And I have something else to tell you, too. Something I don't really want to revisit, but you need to know before I can tell you anything else.

7

When the Party's Over

As quickly as the light appears, it disappears again. At least on the living plane. What felt like hours of time in the other place was less than a moment in the bedroom with the man.

He gasped and pushed me away. My long hair caught in his fingers and he pushed and pulled to free his hand. Strange sounds continued to come out of his mouth, his face contorted with something akin to fear, or maybe surprise, or possibly shock.

"You fucking evil bitch," he spluttered. "You fucking evil bitch," he repeated. His eyes were wide and wild. His previously grey outline had softened and became slightly lighter with a dull, dark greenish hue to it. I knew he wasn't going to hurt me now. I knew that I was going to be alright. But I also knew I had to leave here as quickly as possible, so I lunged for the door, pulled it open and, taking two steps at a time landed heavily on the ground floor.

There were a group of mothers in the kitchen. They stopped talking when they heard my arrival at the bottom of the steps. One of them wrinkled her nose and commented on the smell. A second parent made a compassionate sound and began to move toward me.

"Leave her, she's odd, and she's pissed herself."

Another mother grabbed her arm and stopped her from coming toward me. I felt sad – I needed the warmth of a human hug, a human touch.

"YOU FUCKING EVIL BITCH!" The man was shouting from

the bedroom. He walked to the top of the steps. The music in the party room stopped abruptly. "YOU FUCKING EVIL BITCH!" he repeated as he began the descent. The mothers in the kitchen and more parents from the living room swarmed to the foot of the stairs.

"YOU FUCKING EVIL BITCH!" he shouted again as the children also flocked to the hallway.

I thought the parents might have said something – anything – he was using foul language in the presence of very young children. But they just stood staring at him as he made his way down the steps toward them.

Another child noticed me.

"Eww. You've wee'd yourself." He screwed up his nose and whilst the adults concentrated on the mad wide-eyed, ashen-faced man trembling his way down the stairs, the children, losing interest in the repetitiveness, changed their focus to the girl who smelled of wee. And if you think that adults can be nasty, I can confirm that nasty adults generate nasty children. And I won't repeat any of the names that were shouted down the street after me as I fled the 'nice' house on a 'nice' estate full of 'nice' people.

The man's name was Tony. Antony Marcus Davenport, to give him his court name. That's what it said in the newspaper, anyway. He had been arrested at the party for punching two of the mothers (I don't know which two, but I kind of hope it was two particular ones!) then screaming at the children about hell and demons and how they were all going to die – that bit wasn't in the newspaper, by the way, that is what all the ladies in the supermarket were talking about for the next month or so.

The children, apparently, were traumatised by what he came out with. The parents also – he was obviously sick in the head to even think about that kind of horror, they said.

Initially, Tony was remanded in custody until psychiatric assessments could be carried out. The newspaper said he would be held in a secure unit for his own safety while undergoing therapy.

The lady at the corner shop said he was having electric shock treatment. I didn't know what that was, but it made me feel sad for him for a moment before I remembered what his intentions were. I think he used to hurt Karen and her mum. I still felt sad for him, though.

I remember reading a proverb that said, 'You can lead a horse to water, but you can't make it drink.' I used to think it meant an actual horse and actual water, but I realised at that moment that not everything is as straightforward as we would like it to be. Tony was shown the water but chose not to drink it. You can't force people to change. You can't force people to choose the correct path. You can try to enable them with kindness or with the full might of the 'other side' at your back, but the choice, ultimately, is theirs.

8

Where There is Death There is Life

So, I promised to tell you about my mum's death. What I didn't tell you, but might have hinted at earlier, is that I killed her.

Do you remember the night Beastman came home and 'hell hath no fury like a man who thinks his terrified wife is being unfaithful, so shall beat her to a pulp just as a warning'?

Well … after the other kids had come upstairs, we had all huddled together on the bed, not talking, just whimpering our pain and discomfort. No blaming. No bravery. Just the exhaustion that comes from fear and shock. We slowly, one at a time, began to nod off and sat upright until an older sibling suggested we lie down and go to bed properly, with the promise that he would stay awake and wake us if Beastman came upstairs. Shortly afterwards, though, he too fell asleep exhausted. As the only child awake, I heard the external door creaking – do you remember?

Despite my fear of what or who might be downstairs, I slowly descended, clutching Myaa whilst listening carefully for any signs of anger or movement. I had heard what sounded like thuds against something soft – booted foot against a body – moments before the door had creaked, but no sound since.

Holding my breath, I gently pushed open the door and saw my mother's bloodied body. A pool of sticky red blood pooled around her remains and splashed up the wall behind her, making pretty patterns on the grey plaster wall. There appeared to be what I can only describe as a snow globe surrounding her. Johnny Pattinson

– I don't know why I remember his name so well after all these years when I can't remember the names of people I knew well – had brought a snow globe into class to show the teacher at school. His aunt had visited The Big Apple – New York in America – and brought him a plastic toy with water and white bits that, when shaken and placed on a surface, would fall and look like snow. That was the image I saw that evening.

Looking closer, I saw that actually, there were four white bodies emanating a white light from the centre of each one, which merged with the other three – from the sides and top so that mother was totally enclosed in this dome of light. The light flowing from and between them held flecks of brighter light. 'Energy' was the word that I felt inside my head.

I stepped closer and noticed the energy flowing from these beings was also flowing into the prone, still body between them.

"Is she dead?" I asked out loud. I didn't think there was any point in being silent.

Without moving, turning or interrupting the flow of the current, the four beings spoke as one, "Almost. The Soul doesn't want to be in this world any longer but is in shock and can't get out."

I appreciated their honesty and moved closer still, wondering if I might be able to help.

"Yes, child, of course you can." They said individually and together in a beautiful harmony.

You are healing Angels, I thought. Then I realised that if Mum died, we would be left alone with Beastman and, for probably the first time in my life, I felt panic. Real panic. My heart began to beat fast and irregularly – it felt as though it had been cut loose from its moorings and was running haphazardly and blindly around inside the cavity of my torso. My eyes began to sting and my thoughts – usually so calm and together – suddenly began to tumble one over the other and a thousand disconnected, dislocated voices began to speak all at once in a thousand different languages, some earthly, some quite alien.

Then Terrence appeared and wrapped his arms around me. He was the same and yet different, familiar and a stranger. He was far more glowy than he had been before, and his face and voice showed the most serene calmness and understanding that my whole body, mind and being relaxed. I couldn't help thinking that this must be how other people view death. They aren't happy that their loved one has passed onto a better place. Instead, they fear the consequences of them no longer being in their life.

"You forget your purpose, little one." A light with the face of a beautiful woman appeared beside me. She began to take on the form of a living person. A loving person. Mary. I knew her. From before. And after. I don't know how, or when or why. But I knew her.

Her hair was long and dark and parted in the middle – like my mum's hair. She looked, I realised, like my mum and my dad, and Terrence and … actually … everyone I had ever met, living or dead. *She is the archetype of human*, I thought. But didn't know what that meant.

Mary and Terrence surrounded me with their light, their energy, and a discussion was had right there that lasted hours and yet moments.

Mother's body was severely damaged but could survive with human medical attention, I was told. The problem was that the Soul had been damaged whilst trying to escape. Apparently, when the physical body is going through trauma, it has what I can only describe as an escape hatch. Imagine, if you will, the ejector seat of a military fighter plane. If the plane has been hit by enemy fire and is going to crash, the pilot pulls a lever, the transparent dome above his head pops out and his seat, with the pilot strapped inside, is launched out of the plane, at which time a parachute opens and the pilot floats safely to the ground. The same can be said for the human body. When trauma hits the body, the Soul can be jettisoned from the body until the trauma recedes and the Soul can then resume its place.

Occasionally, though, the Soul doesn't make it out in time. In human terms, this can result in the Soul being trapped until the physical body dies. This can be days, like with Terrence, weeks, years or a whole lifetime.

The Soul is what makes us human. Without a Soul there is no smiling, no eating, no love, no communication – just an empty shell. Like a snail in the garden. Have you ever come across a shell? Empty? In the garden? You know it belonged to a snail, but you know it isn't a snail now. It's just a shell. The human body and Soul are just like that. Without a Soul, the body is an empty shell. Without a Soul, the person ceases to be alive.

If the Soul has been damaged or has not fully returned to the body, it ceases to function. So, the body lives on, with the Soul inside, until the body is no longer able to function – its organs deteriorating, weakening and failing, just as it does with the normal ageing process. But the 'person' you used to know isn't there any longer. Their eyes are unseeing. Their minds unthinking. Their bodies unable to move or feed or toilet themselves without the aid of another 'living' being.

This is the situation we were in now with my mother. Her Soul had begun its escape when a blow from a foot had ruptured its form, confusing it and forcing it to stop still. The Soul doesn't generally feel fear. It is normally a being of love and as we know, love is so much stronger than fear. But when you have been inside a human shell for almost thirty years, it isn't very easy to just throw off the human-ness.

Emotions like fear, anger and hatred are still attached until the Soul reaches the waiting room – if it reaches the waiting room.

The four beings standing above my mother were not trying to save her human life but the life of her Soul. It is two completely different things!

I had a choice, they said. Because we all have freewill, they said. I could leave her as is or I could help her Soul to escape. If I released her Soul, it would be saved, but I would lose my mother.

I have to be honest. It didn't take me long to make the decision. I knew where the Soul would go and I knew what would continue to lie in wait for my mother if she stayed here – the choice was simple, wasn't it?

Wasn't it?

I won't tell you what I had to do to free the Soul from the human shell because I've done it again a few times since. It is not pretty. It's not nice to watch. It is absolutely dreadful to perform. And if another human were to witness it, they would call it murder. Some humans would use it as a form of murder, so I can't share it with you yet. If ever. I'm not sure I will ever be able to release the trauma it caused me.

Her Soul, once freed, was very weak but ever so beautiful. I met her once again afterwards, many years afterwards and have to say her Soul was one of the most beautiful I had ever seen (and they are all stunningly beautiful beyond the ability or vocabulary of a human to describe).

When the deed was done, I sat down and cried. Proper tears that had never left my eyes before. I cried for all the sadness in my life that had come before the now. I cried for my siblings. I cried for my mother and I cried for her Soul. I cried for the deed I'd had to perform. I cried for every human woman who had ever been treated the way she had been treated. I cried for every child that had ever witnessed his mother suffer. And then I cried some more, just for good measure, because I knew it would be a very long time before I cried again and I wanted to make sure I used up all of my current tears.

"There has been a change of plan," Mary spoke quietly and so full of love I could have burst with happiness and I didn't even know what the plan was. But I hoped it meant I was going to live in the void room.

"We fear the safety of the Souls of you and your siblings," she said. "You all have so many wonderful things to achieve in your lifetimes. So many lessons that your Souls need to learn in order for them to move on to the next level. Without a mother, you may all come to harm."

I had to look down at my body at that moment. I wasn't sure if she was talking to the me in my tiny human body or the me that was made of light and love and power and forever. But it was just the little me of meat and bone that she was speaking to. Again, I felt gratitude for her honesty and for not treating me like the child that I was.

They were afraid of what Beastman might do or what we might become without the guiding hand of a mother. You see, even a mother who seems ineffectual serves a purpose that we might never understand while we are alive. My mother's purpose was to protect. You might think she did a really bad job considering the harm we came to on occasion, but for the most part, Beastman took out his anger, fear, frustration and weaknesses on her. She was the shield that protected us. I later learned that there were at least a dozen occasions where she had stood up to him to protect one child or other – the wrong noise, a snatched toy, crying, speaking back – these were things that would send Beastman into a rage and the children fleeing – literally – for their lives. But she stood and took beating after beating. For them. Her children. Her dependents. Her proteges. Although none of us knew at the time, she taught us so much about caring for others. We may not have had hugs and kind words, but we learned. Human beings have a great ability to learn not only from what they are taught but also from what they are not!

"What's a walk-in?" I asked Mary as the four beings continued their stance above the now Soul-less body of my mother.

Apparently, and I have to tell you in my words rather than Mary's because it's actually really complicated and not as easy as I'm about to make it sound, a walk-in is when a different Soul offers to take on the body that one Soul has left.

You see, a Soul usually has lessons to learn. Each lifetime it lives, it learns a new lesson and when its lesson is learned, it either goes home (to the Light Room) or chooses a new lesson. We, the human shell, are never aware of this as most of the conversation happens before it becomes human before we are born. Sometimes, when the human body is sleeping, the Soul pops out to visit The Light House, where it will speak to its Soul Family and alter the lesson or add a bit more if it thinks it can help it move along further within this one life.

Sometimes, when we are awake we meet members of our Soul Family who are in another body and we feel like we know them. We feel a pull toward them that is stronger than any other relationship we have. But we don't understand why. We are attracted to them, but they might not be our 'type' of person. They may not be from the same social, economic or cultural background. It can be quite scary and a bit frustrating sometimes.

This evening, though, I wouldn't know this Soul. The new Soul that would be taking over my mother's body. This new Soul was hoping to learn about parenting. I think it might be in for a shock – most parents learn by having one child at a time, learning each child's talents, vulnerabilities, humour, and sharing their own to shape this tiny human being before taking on the next child. This Soul was getting five fully formed humans with diverse talents, personalities and behaviours, with the added burden of abuse thrown into the mix just to add a little flavour! I may be a child, but I thought this was a big ask for any being, never mind one who had no experience with the little buggers!

"When the Soul normally enters a body," I was told, "the stress causes the Soul to forget who it is and where it is from. Over a matter of days and weeks, it begins to take on the body's own memories, its feelings, its uniqueness. So, to anyone who knew the person before, they will be exactly the same person."

Mary looked at me with love and empathy as she continued. "You will know that she is different. You will know that she is not the mother you grew up with. Your siblings won't. She is the mother who gave birth to you here on earth. And that is what she will know. That is what memories she will hold. You must not love her any differently to the mother you knew."

I nodded. Unsure of what else I could do or say. She told me to go and fetch help as the healer beings had done as much as they could for the body, and I wouldn't want to see the new Soul entering.

I did want to see the new Soul entering. I wanted to see what it looked like before it went in. I felt a pang of sadness, and I admit, anger, that someone else was taking her body. HER body. I was also curious to see how it got in. And if it was the same place it came out.

But I said goodbye to them all and left the room. I managed to squeeze through the outside door, which was still slightly ajar and stuck because the crack in the door had warped and misaligned it.

I walked outside into the dark, cold night, across the road and round the corner to where there was a red telephone box with a light above it showing where the door was. The door was really heavy and it took me three tries to open it. I realised I was still carrying my doll; it would be so much easier if I put her down. But she was my comfort blanket and I was not letting her loose for anything!

Once inside I lifted the receiver, dialled three nines and when the lady answered I told her that my mum had been killed. I tried to tell her where I lived, but I couldn't remember the address so I just told her I was in a phone box. Twenty minutes later, I was still speaking to her – she was very kind and asked me all kinds of questions about the street I lived on, the school I went to, whether there was a park or a church or a shop. She asked me about myself, my daddy, my brothers and sisters, and, of course, my mum. When a police car stopped at the roadside, two uniformed policemen climbed out.

One policeman came to the door and asked if I was okay. I nodded. The lady asked if the policeman was there and if I would pass him the phone. He took my hand – he felt safe and smelled like new babies and Yorkshire puddings. We walked to my house and into the room where my mum was still laying. Alone now. No healers. No Terrence. No Mary. Just the dull glow from a bare lightbulb overhead.

The body was breathing. Shallow, rangy breaths. The younger policeman retched and threw up in the hallway. I sighed. I would need to clean that up before the ambulance arrived.

9

Hello, Mother

We weren't allowed to see her for the first month. And when we did, she looked like a different person. Her face was still heavily swollen and bruised. Her eyes were puffy, purple and hardly open. Every visible part of her body was covered in white bandages or hard pots. Tubes and cables were attached to several areas of her upper body and arms. She was very groggy, we were told by the police lady who took us to the hospital. She was, and she didn't recognise us. That's because of the medication for the pain, we were told. I knew differently. I knew the Soul hadn't fully integrated into the body, so hadn't fully assimilated the memories. It's a bit like when a person has a heart transplant or a liver transplant … the new organ doesn't take instantly and the body has to have drugs to stop it from rejecting the new body part. Unfortunately, there is no drug available to stop a body from rejecting a new Soul – I'm pleased the doctors and medical professionals hadn't known or they may have tried injecting all types of poison into her system!

The rather short first visit was with the doctor, a rather rotund man with sagging skin and not too long for this world (according to his mother-in-law, who stood behind him throughout and had apparently been following him around since her own death six months ago. She was haunting him, she said, because he hadn't treated her daughter as well as he should.) He informed all five of us that our mother had received some very severe, life-threatening injuries, but due to the hard work and brilliant care of the surgeons and staff at this hospital, she would be well enough to return home in about two to three months. She would still need a lot of care and we would have to be very good children, apparently. I think this was more for the reporter who had been 'monitoring' the family since the incident. His initial story about the 'Little lass that found and saved her dying mum' made headlines around the country and made him a sought-after journalist. But to his credit, he stuck with us when he was offered a top-flight job in America and continued to tell our story.

We were returned to the children's home we had been taken to on the first night. Because of the media attention, we were initially treated better than some of the other children, but my elder sister – a rebellious girl with a humour that could cut a grown man into pieces while making him laugh – began to mention certain 'differences' to the journalist, in front of the manager. The manager would cringe and tut and give her a look, while she would smile patiently and innocently and the other children would get the same 'privileges' as us.

It was the journalist who told us, in such a lovely manner, what he thought had happened to Beastman. The thinking was, but it couldn't be proved, that he had snuck out of the house thinking Mother was dead and the children asleep. He'd gone to the building where he ran his business and had dug a deep hole in the back. He had telephoned his friend and told him that his wife, in a mad rage, had attacked him and the children and then thrown him out of the house whilst she packed her bags. Her lover was coming to pick her up and poor Beastman was going to be left with five kids to bring up on his own.

Most of this was published in the newspapers with varying levels of dramatic writing. One account suggested he was a drug dealer who had been stealing from his 'employer' and had been 'taken care of', which is why there had been no sightings of him. Another account suggested he had been whisked away to Cuba by the cult that he was a senior member of.

And I'm the one with the active imagination, right?

Mother was released from hospital several months later. She was very fragile but could walk, feed and dress herself, so she was allowed home and so were we. We had spent lots of time at the hospital with her, and some intelligent medical person had suggested that the children each spend time alone with her so we could get used to her and she to us prior to us all being dropped into the pot together. I thought that had to be Angelic intervention, to be honest because although it is quite the thing to be child-centric nowadays, it certainly wasn't back then. But we each had ten minutes of alone time with her once a week, allowing her to build up her strength and her memories.

On my first scheduled visit, I'd had my first-ever dental appointment, so I couldn't go. They had wanted us to go in age order, eldest to youngest, but I ended up being the last to visit.

I'd been sitting next to her bed for a few minutes before she woke. My siblings, each excited at their visit, had shared that she was awake when they had arrived, so I had been slightly disappointed when she wasn't for me.

She looked at me for a long time before saying, "Are you one of mine?"

I nodded but said nothing.

"You are different to the others," she said, slightly confused. "I don't know them, but I know you. Why do you seem so much smaller than before?"

The house seemed different. A local charity had been set up to help us and families like ours and lots of donations of money, clothing and household items had been offered over the previous couple of months. They had provided all new furniture and carpets downstairs, along with a shiny new red telephone, in case of emergencies. Upstairs, there were individual beds for all the children and we each had our own sheets and blankets. There were new clothes and shoes as well. It was a bit like a dream come true.

Except we didn't have any lampshades.

And there was a policeman in the house because they wanted to speak to Beastman. And not just because of Mother! Apparently, some of the things in the newspaper had been true. About the drugs, I think. It would certainly explain why he was frightened so often.

The last time Beastman had been seen was actually by the policeman who had thrown up in the hallway that night. He was getting out of the police car to follow us into the house when a man stopped him and asked what was happening.

"Oh! Poor kids," the policeman told him. "It appears that their dad has just killed their mother. Some bastards around, isn't there?"

Beastman walked away, shrugging his shoulders, and was never seen again! The television wanted a photo of him, but he hadn't allowed a camera in the house. When anyone tried taking his picture, he would turn away or put a hand over his face. There are certain tribes around the world who believe that a photograph captures your Soul and it is then stuck there for all eternity. That isn't true, by the way. But I feel that Beastman knew this day would come. He knew that he had to rid the world of any sign of his existence before it became evidence.

He emptied the safe at work. We don't know how much money was actually in there, but he hadn't paid any bills for the business or the mortgage on the house for over six months, although there was evidence of large sums of money coming into the business.

The bank was wonderful to the family, letting us stay in the house for a full twelve months whilst the police investigation and newspaper coverage were still high. I can't say that life went back to normal because it never had been normal. How do you know what is? I would have loved the life that Lady Catherine had – that sounded normal, but there was a catch. I would have loved the perfect pink bedroom of Karen, who everyone in the school was envious of before the party, but of course, that was far from normal. But there was no money and no home at the end of the day. And so we had to move again.

10
Life is Like a Great Big Onion

The new house was on a council estate. It was bigger than any house we'd ever lived in before and had three bedrooms and a large bathroom upstairs. Downstairs, there were two rooms – one for dining in! A big kitchen separate from the living rooms and a little toilet under the stairs. It was very posh. I thought this must be about the same size as Lady Catherine's dad's house, but then I realised that was a bit silly because we didn't have stables!

There was a large garden at the front and the back garden had a little gate leading out into a wooded area. We'd brought all our new furniture from the other house and we were given some curtains to cover the many windows by our old neighbours. The curtains were a bit short, sitting just above the windowsill, but we all felt so happy and thought this must be our happy ending.

Our new neighbours, Meryl and Roger on the left and Sherry and Jim on the right, both had children of similar ages to my siblings and me, so we would spend lots of time outside with them – usually in the woods that jointly backed all our houses.

Newmum spent most of her time cleaning and tidying her home. She was happier than I'd ever seen her and she even gave us hugs at bedtime. She'd changed her hair to a short style that hugged her head. She'd had to have it shaved off in hospital so the doctors could mend her cracked skull, and she'd kept it short afterwards. She cooked nicer meals than the old mum and would sing along to the radio and jiggle her bottom to the rhythm of the music whilst preparing the food, which would make her children giggle and jiggle along.

We all went to bed really early as Newmum was still weak and on lots of different medications for all the different issues she had. When she went to bed, the children would sneak into one bedroom and talk about 'the past', 'Beastman' and of course 'Newmum'. They were so happy that she was well again, and a renewed joy and bliss had settled on us. The children looked out for each other more than before, and we would sit and talk together in a way we would never have done in our old lives. We would have been too afraid!

Happy ever after? Hmm! Well, we can call it that – but you do know that those Disney Princess movies stop at that point for a reason, don't you? I hope I haven't disappointed you. But you must know that life is full of ups and downs, right? The rollercoaster euphemism isn't just there for effect, you know. Sorry! I don't mean to be rude. Let me explain …

After a couple of months of our new life, Newmum began to have moments when she would burst into tears for no reason. She would be wiggling along to some rhythmic tune on the radio. Happy. Smiling. Then a sudden change in her face and body and tears would come. Sometimes, she would be silent, but tears would flood down her cheeks. Other times, her whole body would be wracked with sobs and a quiet wailing. It was difficult for us all, but the younger children were really affected by it. We had been warned by the doctor that this might occur, but as children, you forget. We each felt individually guilty of some personal behaviour that may have caused her tears.

The thing is, and you have no idea about this when you are a child (or as an adult, sometimes!) when a person has gone through a trauma, no matter what that trauma is, you can't heal it with plasters, bandages and operations. Even medication can only do so much. The best healer is time. That goes without saying, but it also means facing those horrors head-on, which is easy to say but not so easy to put into practice. Most people who have suffered deeply are not able to verbalise their trauma. They don't know what caused the trauma. Yes. Of course, they know they've had an accident, scare or incident, but not the exact moment the trauma occurred. That moment when the psyche was no longer able to cope with what was happening to them. That moment is when the trauma occurs. And everybody's psyche has different breaking points. If you consider a rollercoaster ride, for a moment. Two people of identical height, weight and background can take a trip on Kingda Ka. One can leave the ride traumatised, while the other can be smiling and whooping, full of joy and adrenaline. You can't see the trauma you don't know it's there … yet!

Trauma tends to manifest in the simplest ways, yet also the strangest ways … now, I'm not a medical expert, so please do not be offended by my naivety!

I think of trauma as being a bit like an onion. On the outside, you have a shell-like skin, but as you peel that away, there is a layer of white skin. Taking off that layer you come to a white flesh and there may be a touch of liquid that makes your eyes water. The next few layers are similar and then you have a very thin layer, a sliver, right in the centre. To me, this is where the trauma centres. Something happens that your psyche can't quite handle, but it manages and you go about your daily life and wrap that little trauma in a skin of onion. The liquid that makes your eyes leak is there to stop you poking in and getting any deeper where you might touch that traumatic memory. As you grow and live your life, other life events occur, which may also affect your psyche, but you just wrap another layer of onion around it until the traumas are wrapped so tightly that not only can nobody else see them, but you have forgotten that anything happened in the first place.

True healing can only begin when you have removed all those layers and got to the heart of the matter – or the onion if you like this connection!

So, you can imagine that trying to peel back those layers isn't going to happen overnight. Each layer will take as much time as each individual onion needs. And each onion has its own amount of layers. And its own amount of eye-stinging liquid!

11

Newmum Visits a Spiritualist Church

Doctors, back then, couldn't really deal with women of a certain age coming to them in tears. Hysteria, the doctors liked to call it. They didn't think about the abuse that may lie behind it. They didn't think of the hormonal reasons that may have caused it.
Hysteria.
Full stop.
Here you are, missus. Here's a prescription for some recently designed drug that'll make you a bit docile and calm but won't stop you from cleaning the house, taking care of the kids and ensuring your husband is well cared for, if you know what I mean, wink, wink.

Newmum was fortunate. She had recently spent a considerable amount of, very well publicised, time in the hospital, so her doctors were slightly more sympathetic, if sympathetic means they wanted to look like they were amazing at their job in case the journalist showed up again. She was offered psychiatric support as well as happy pills.

The problem with the happy pills was that they put her in such a state of relaxation that she was able to 'see'. I haven't mentioned my 'friends' in a while, but they still came to see me in the new house. They were particularly prolific in the woods, so I would spend time outdoors with my siblings, our neighbours and my 'friends', but a few of them had taken to sitting in the house when I wasn't there. This was something new to me, as they usually spent time with me, or they weren't there.

But they knew that Newmum was different and so they would sit with her sometimes. Although she didn't know it, she was connected to them in a way she wasn't connected to the living, breathing people.

One day, as the other children were going upstairs to brush their teeth and prepare for bed, she quietly called me back.

"Who are you?" she asked me. "Really. Who are you really?"

I didn't know what to say. I was her daughter, but not really HER daughter. I couldn't tell her that.

"Do you see them?" she pointed to Terrence, who was standing at the window looking out at cars passing in the street. He liked the cars. He particularly liked it when a car honked its horn. He would giggle like there was a private joke that no one else was privy to.

"Are they ghosts?" she asked. Terrence looked at me, then toward Newmum.

I shrugged my shoulders. Not daring to open my mouth. Afraid of what might come out.

"But you can see them?" she asked. "Am I going mad? I just need to know that I'm not going mad … that he didn't do more damage to my head than ..." Her voice cracked and stalled.

I looked at my feet as I felt a prickle in the corner of my eye. I blinked fast, trying to push the lick of water back inside.

Terrence spoke first. "You should tell her," he said. "She'll only worry otherwise."

I looked to Newmum. She was looking at me expectantly, eager for me to answer in a way that would make her feel better. But she hadn't heard Terrance. She could see, but she couldn't hear.

"Yes. Ghosts," I said.

Two streets away from our new home – and I use that word in the sense of a place where I lived as opposed to the place where I felt at peace and at one with the world and the universe – there was a spiritualist church. Meryl and Sherry used to go once a month because they quite fancied one of the blokes who did the 'freaky stuff', as they called it. When Newmum mentioned that our house had ghosts, they got really excited and suggested we go with them to the next service.

Like Beastman, I wasn't overly fond of churches. I loved the buildings. The architecture. The peace. But on the few occasions when we had been to a church service, I found the ritual and liturgy to be dull and dirgy. I believed in God – not quite the God we were taught about in school – but a being of 'beyond'. It's difficult to put into words because it is more like a feeling. But this God that I believed in, that was as real in my mind as bread and butter, would not have enjoyed or appreciated this mournful, monotone dirge. So, the thought of being dragged along to a church with Cinderella and the Ugly Sisters made me grumpy for the three days leading up to it. And on the day itself, I was in the worst mood I'd ever felt. Actually, it was the first bad mood I'd ever been in, insofar as I can remember, so it was obviously the worst!

The night approached and Newmum put on a slick of lipstick. It was a gift from the charity when we first moved, and this was the first time she had worn it. There was a whole bag of brand-new makeup donated by the local chemist shop. Apparently, you are not a real woman without this makeup brand I recall the advert in the newspaper saying! I remember thinking that a real woman wouldn't actually believe that, but it might have been one of my 'friends' who said it!

I think it was meant to give her courage like a mask. If people see the lipstick, they'll not see the person behind it. The person who was still fragile and frightened and trying so hard to fit into a world that she no longer felt she belonged in. A person who secretly wished she had died that night all those months ago. But of course, she couldn't say that to her children. She couldn't say that to her new friends and neighbours. And she certainly couldn't tell the psychiatrist; she had been judged constantly from the moment her story was front page news, and she was trying to stop the judgement, but that wasn't under her control. It still amazes me, all these years later, how little control any of us have over our lives. We live in a world of judgement where it only takes one sad person to damn another with neither care nor evidence. All you need to do is comment with confidence that another person is too fat, too thin, too loud, too quiet, too confident, too shy, on the booze, sleeping around, a bit strange, not normal. Well! I know all about that, as you may recall! But I have never really cared about the judgement of the living. Because they don't know what the cost of making judgements against another brings to them afterwards, they only really care about the now!

The spiritualist church was not quite what I had expected. The building itself was rather bland on the outside, not grandiose like many religious buildings, but plain white stone, darkened with age and dirt. There was a beautiful arched door with large, black gothic hinges and turned metal handle. Not quite in keeping with the building itself, but I liked it. It felt strong and protective and had been touched by thousands of loving hands throughout the years.

Inside was one large room with a toilet and kitchen area added sometime after initial construction, giving the room a slightly odd shape. The kitchen had a little window where two older ladies were preparing and offering tea for a small donation to church funds. The windows were high up. *It must have been built in Victorian times*, I thought, *as they didn't like you to look outside when you were praising the lord.* If only they had known then that the best way to praise the Lord was to be outside and enjoy the beautiful world that He had made.

Newmum chose not to have a drink. We'd just finished one before we came out, she had said to the lady who seemed to be in charge. It always surprised me when I saw people in charge. They were what some people called 'natural leaders', but mostly, they were bossy people who wanted to be in control of everyone and everything – you could see it in their auras. They didn't always want the best for others, or the organisation or the community, but what was best for them. Sometimes, you can smell it, too. This lady didn't smell of wanting to be in control, but I think she would soon. Her name was Melinda, a very modern name for a woman who wore very old-fashioned clothing. It was part of her dominating nature, I think. She wanted to look mature and in control but hadn't got the memo that said, 'true confidence and control comes from being your true self'. She was also the chief medium. That was what they called those who gave out messages from the dead and departed, and they all sat on a low stage at the front of the church. There was already a man and woman sitting there when Melinda 'harrumphed' loudly, made her way dramatically to the wooden chair in the centre of the stage, and sat down with a small flourish.

The congregation, about thirty middle-aged and older people, quickly took their used teacups to the kitchen hatch and took their seats. For some reason, I was expecting lights to come on above the heads of the trio on stage and for a brass-sounding fanfare to erupt. It didn't. The man to the left of Melinda stood and began to explain the evening ahead for those who were new to this evening's service in a voice that sounded devoid of all interest. I felt like he needed a hug or a touch of something exciting in his life. As he continued with a prayer, my attention was drawn to the lady on Melinda's right. She was what the newspaper journalists and story writers would describe as 'non-descript'. She was someone who could walk naked through a room bashing together giant shiny cymbals whilst squawking like a demented chicken and she would not garner any attention. But ooooh, if you could see how she lit up from the inside as the spirits began to gather around her. She shone like a beacon to the sailors lost at sea.

It suddenly hit me – The Light House – My Light House – it was a beacon for lost Souls! My eyes began to prickle; the warm liquid rested on my lower eyelid and I felt it glisten. My body smiled from the very depth of my being, a warmness. A feeling of

'Home' enveloped me. Every muscle in my body released its tension. Every nerve freed of its pressure. I felt reborn in that very spot at that very moment. I also felt love for the first time in my human life.

This is not the love of a man and a woman, by the way. Or the love of a mother for her child. I often feel perplexed when living people talk of love as a 'thing' that you can only feel toward certain other 'things'. In the English language, there is one word for 'love'. The Italians have about a million! Well, I may be exaggerating a bit, but they have words that describe the love you feel for a parent, friend, spouse, sexual lover, pet, Mama's spaghetti Bolognese, and probably many, many more. There are probably more words in Italian for 'love' than there are words for 'snow' in Inuit and words for 'rain' in English!

Love is such a huge and complex subject that it surprises me that there hasn't been scientific research done on it. Perhaps there has been, and I missed it! But I know that in the English language we use the same word to describe how much we enjoy eating chocolate, that we use to tell our spouse or lover how we feel about them. We even use the same intonation!

But love – real love – is not fleeting, like the bite of a bar of chocolate. It fills you up from the inside and spills outward, cascading throughout your life like a waterfall of crystal clear, warm water. It flows into your work, your home and your relationships – every one of them. Until no part of your world is untouched by it. It is warmth and satisfaction and peace and understanding and care. Not just for one human being but for every living thing. Animal, mineral, vegetable, spiritual.

I remember once overhearing an adult telling another adult (parents at school) how much love she had in her heart. She closed her eyes, tilted back her head and smiled a 'loving' smile as though those actions proved her love for the world. But then the two adults began talking about one of the teachers and how she shouldn't be teaching children. They debated as to whether she could actually speak the English language because she was an immigrant. They called her names related to her place of birth, which made me sad. Neither parent had love in their glow. One of them, my spirit friend told me, didn't even love her own child, so she would never be able to understand real love.

The love I felt in that moment was the love of 'Home'. You see, the spiritualist church was a place where the Souls of those whose bodies were no longer here, living, on earth, would gather to speak to those of us who were still here in living flesh bodies. It felt as though a gateway to the other side had opened up and the love and light had flooded through like a swollen river having broken its banks after torrential rain. Suddenly, I loved everything and everyone, everywhere, past, present and future and I thought I might burst.

Newmum's voice broke through my rapture …

"Are you okay, lovey?" her nervousness swiftly brought me back to the here and now. "You're not scared, are you?" she asked.

I reached out for her hand, shook my head and smiled. She told me how warm my hands were, and a smile broke out across her face.

"It's exciting, isn't it?" She would never understand how exciting this was for me. I had learned the purpose of The Light House and realised there was something more there that I hadn't yet seen. I had felt pure, pure love. The love of the world, of nature, of the universe, of God. And I'd found people who were like me. And I knew that life was going to get better.

12

Meeting Mrs Marton

The evening was fun for me. Melinda was the person most of the congregation had come to see. Apparently, she was a famous medium and spiritualist. She had travelled the world and been on the television. She could see your loved ones in spirit and bring messages from them.

Apparently.

For most of the evening, she stood on the stage – it was very low and not a proper stage, probably no higher than the length of a ruler – teetering toward the edge every so often and calling out names of the deceased she was in contact with. I was a little confused, though, that she didn't actually speak to any of the dead people who were surrounding her.

There was a gentleman called Tom, who had died in a car accident two months earlier, who wanted to tell his wife, Carol, who was sitting in the front row, that he loved her and he knew she was pregnant. He wanted her to know that he was there with her when she found out. He wanted to tell her that it was going to be a boy and he would be taller than her before he left school. He wanted to apologise for not being there and to thank her for the poem she placed in the pocket of his suit as his body lay in the coffin, the poem he read to her on the day of their wedding. He wanted to tell her that there was another man coming into her life soon and he would make her happy and that she should go for it and he was so proud of her and loved her so much.

But Carol didn't hear any of that.

Melinda told her that someone was with her, and it could be a man or a woman. This person died when they were five or it could be fifty. They passed quickly and have no regrets about their life, but they would like to tell her one day about their death. Tom didn't tell Melinda this because she wasn't listening. He didn't want to tell Carol about his death – he hadn't come to terms with it himself yet.

There was a dog, too. I loved dogs. Well, I loved most animals, but I particularly loved those who showed you they liked you back. Usually dogs. The dog was sat at the feet of an old lady. She was very old. She had the glow of someone who would not be here very much longer. The dog's name was Lucky. He loved the old lady so much you could see the light shining around him. He wanted to tell her that he was waiting for her and that it was going to be okay. He looked at me and asked me if I would tell her, but I was too shy to say anything. Strangely, when you pass over, it doesn't matter what language you speak or how you communicated when you were alive; you could still be understood by those who took the time to listen. Melinda was asking the old lady about a friend from childhood who wanted to remind her of a joint holiday they'd taken. I think Melinda was seeing different 'people' to me.

The lady to the right of Melinda stood up after about twenty minutes. Her neighbour had flounced down with another flourish, throwing her hand across her face and sighing deeply, which meant she had exhausted her spirit connection!

"Good evening," The lady to the right said as she stood. "It's wonderful to see so many new faces here tonight," she looked directly at me. "I hope we can bring messages of love to you all tonight."

I giggled. Newmum poked me with her elbow and shushed me. The lady at the front had spoken directly to me, though. She knew what had happened to me earlier. And she knew what I was. It made my heart soar higher.

Her first message was from a young lady standing almost hidden behind her. She wanted to speak with her mums. I knew that, biologically, we only had one mum, but it made sense when she said mums in the plural. I don't know why. The lady looked around the room and settled on three women who were sat very closely together, holding hands.

"I have a young lady here who passed over very recently," she said in a clear, calm and empathetic voice that reminded me very much of The Light House.

"She was taken before her time with an illness that nobody could have anticipated," she continued. *What a lovely way of saying her heart gave out when she was running in the park,* I thought. Three women, as one, whimpered and tears slid down their faces.

"Ah!" said the lady on the stage with a giant smile on her face as the girl whispered something in her ear. "I wondered why there were three of you. She loves you all so much. She wishes she had taken the advice of ..." she frowned a little, "... is it Maureen?"

The three women all made soft sounds of both sorrow and joy rolled together – it is one of those sounds you hear so rarely, but it is such a lovely sound. "That's me," the central woman spoke clearly, "I'm Maureen. I told her not to run so much cos she'd end up hurting herself. She had a weak heart, see."

There were a few more kind words to the three and a few messages to others, but I had suddenly become very aware of Newmum beside me. She seemed to have bristled and sat rigidly upright, and her breathing rate had increased. Her body began to tremor ever so slightly and a small sob escaped her throat. I held her hand firmer and whispered calmly to her, asking if she was okay. There were no spirits near us; they were all on the stage. They were all good spirits – their glow clear and bright and white, with a few lesser glowing but still not 'bad' spirits. The man on the stage had said prayers at the beginning and asked that only "those of the highest vibration, from and of the light" be present in the church as a prayer of protection, so there weren't any greys that I could see.

"I'm shiny," Newmum whispered to me. "Why am I shiny?"

I didn't have the words to explain that her Soul was happy. That she recognised the beings in this place as having come from a place she knew. That she, too, was feeling happy.

As the service came to a close, the kitchen was reopened for cups of tea and people began gathering their coats. Newmum grabbed for her coat and bag but couldn't quite keep hold of it. Once, twice, three times, it slipped from her grip. Except it didn't. A glowing woman – one without a physical body – kept pulling it out of her hands. I was bemused, as I'd never seen anything like this before. *She has a lot of power,* I thought.

"Let me help you with that," said a lady on the right as she picked up Newmum's handbag and smiled, firstly at the glowing lady and then at Newmum.

"Please let me get you a drink. My treat," she said quickly before Newmum could refuse, and appearing as if from nowhere, one of the women from the kitchen placed cups of tea into each of their hands.

She ushered us to a couple of chairs at the side of the church and introduced herself as Mrs Marton, Church Warden and Former Lady of the Manor. Her voice smiled when she spoke. Her tone was kind yet speckled with pain. She told Newmum that she knew what she was going through and to not feel embarrassed or frightened. That she would like to help if she could. And no, it wasn't charity. She just knew that if she helped Newmum, she would pass on the favour to someone in need later.

"It's called paying it forward," she said, matter-of-factly, as though it was the most common thing in the world. "Someone does something for you, such as buying you a cup of tea when you are thirsty and feeling a little off-kilter. Then, maybe next week, or next year, or in twenty years, when you see someone who needs something that you can give, you give it freely with no expectation of repayment."

Newmum's eyes filled with tears and she struggled to contain them as they spilt down her cheeks and splashed onto the sleeve of the hand holding her cup of tea. She croaked out a whispered "thank you" and delved into her pocket for a tissue.

Mrs Marton, Church Warden and Former Lady of the Manor turned her attention to me and asked how old I was. She told me my gifts were very powerful for my age and asked if I would like help in understanding them more. I didn't understand what she meant, but I nodded anyway. She asked Newmum if we would both like to visit her for tea on Thursday that week. Mum agreed, and then we had to go home.

"We can't go, lovey. We've got no one to look after the littles," Newmum told me as we made the short walk home.

13

If It's Meant to Be, It Will Be

That was Tuesday evening. I won't lie. I was miserable for the rest of the evening and the following day. I had finally found someone like me. Someone who understood what was happening to me and understood that I had friends who were 'real' people even if they didn't have bodies and were invisible to everyone else, but Newmum wouldn't let me see her.

Newmum wanted to see her, but I think she was a bit scared of what Mrs Marton might say. Perhaps Newmum thought she was going crazy and didn't want anyone else to know. But Mrs Marton knew what was going on with Newmum and me, so it was surely winner, winner not a sinner?

Now I want to tell you about the web, the reason Mrs Marton knew about me, but I think I need to explain a few more things first in case you don't know what I mean. So, I'm going to tell you about coincidence.

I'm sure you are aware of coincidences happening in your life. Things like, you think of your mother and then the telephone rings and it is your mother telling you that she was thinking about you. Or you decide you want to change your job because not only is your current role no longer challenging you, but you want to save up for a car and you just don't earn enough money at the moment. The following day, you bump into an old friend who you haven't seen for five years. Whilst chatting, he tells you he has just set up his own business and is looking for someone he can trust to be his right-hand person. When you tell him you are looking for a new challenge, he not only offers you the job on the spot but also offers you a fantastic financial package, which includes a company car. Tell me that's not a coincidence. Perhaps it's luck? What would you call it?

Because of Newmum's ongoing health issues, along with the disappearance of Beastman, our family had been put on the at-risk register of the local council's social services. They didn't bother us much – in fact, we had forgotten we were even on their radar until Wednesday afternoon that week when there was a knock on the door just as the kids were arriving home from school. The big kids would take the little kids to school in the morning before walking on to their own school and would collect them again on the way home. We children decided this together when we first arrived at this house and spent time together after Newmum had gone to sleep. It was actually Arrien's idea. She was my new 'friend', and she had told me what to say to my siblings so it would sound like their idea.

Anyway, my elder sister would usually make us jam and bread in the kitchen when we got home. Today, though, we didn't get jam and bread because Newmum was making a cup of tea for the bearded gentleman with the wonky glasses who had knocked on the door. He had a piece of card with his photo and name attached to his jumper. The top corner of the label had poked through a hole in his green bobbly jumper, so it sat at a jaunty angle and obscured the bit that told us who he worked for. But he was a nice man. He smelled of fried food and old people and wet dog, but it wasn't a horrible smell, and he had the right type of shine to him.

Whilst looking at Newmum, he told the children there were some activities that had been set up in the local village hall and school for children like us that would take place on Thursday evenings during the school terms. He couldn't understand why we hadn't received invitations to participate, but in order to keep the funding in place, he needed to make sure the activities were well attended so we would be attending tomorrow.

He excitedly told us what the activities were. There was one for the older children, which involved acting, sports, music, cooking and arts and one for the younger children, which involved music, dancing, arts and stories. We could choose which activities we wanted to do and even if we were the only ones wanting to do cooking, for example, we would still be able to do it. He filled in the names and ages of my youngest siblings on one form. Then, he started with the second form for the older children. When it was my turn, and I told him my age, he stopped writing and flicked through his folder. He looked at me, then Newmum, and then looked in his file again, looking a little bit flustered. He asked Newmum for my age. She gave him the same number.

"Oh, dear, we seem to have made a mistake with the ages," he said, looking, quite rightly, embarrassed. "You don't fit into either activity centre."

Coincidence? Well, Newmum, bless her, giggled like a little girl. The children all looked at her and giggled too. She guffawed a great big snot-laden laugh, which sent the children into full-blown laughter as she covered her nose and dived into the downstairs loo for some toilet roll to blow her nose.

The poor man looked ever so confused. He had no idea what had just happened or how he was supposed to rectify this mistake – he couldn't possibly leave out one child, could he?

Newmum suggested that the other kids would go to the activities, and I would stay at home with her in case she needed help. The man was ecstatic, and so were my siblings. And me? Well, I was dead chuffed as Newmum and I could visit Mrs Marton.

14

The Big House

Mrs Marton lived in what was once called 'The Manor House'. It had been built in the fourteenth century by a family closely connected to the King of England and was surrounded by acres and acres of farm land, a large church, several large houses scattered around and two small villages which would have been built to house the farm workers and servants of the big houses. Over the years, as happened with a lot of such families, bits of land had been sold off here and there. Some of the houses had also been sold off, and finally, most of the village properties had been sold to individual new owners. The land had mostly been sold off to private construction companies or the local council, who shoehorned as many small dwellings as possible onto each parcel of land, resulting in one of the villages being renamed a town and the second village beginning to be swallowed up by that very same town. Some of the larger houses had the only remaining countryside in their own backyards!

'The Country House', as it had been renamed several generations previously by a snobby incomer to the family, had been in Mrs Marton's family for over 200 years. She had been born in her parents' bedroom at the top of the grand stairway and, apart from a brief stint at an all-girls boarding school and two years in India with her late husband, had lived here all her life. The house retained all its original features and furniture, and many of the curtains were over a hundred years old. The pictures on the walls were of the previous owners, their thoroughbred horses, cows and dogs and some were of Mrs Marton's family, along with a few landscapes by Victorian artists.

Mrs Marton didn't tell me this, I have to add. It was the scullery maid from before Mrs Marton was born. She started talking to me as Newmum and I walked up the drive to the big house and I don't think she stopped until I fell asleep, exhausted, that night! It wasn't the scullery maid who exhausted me, though. It was the information that Mrs Marton shared with me. But let me go back a little bit …

Newmum and I arrived at the bottom of The Country House drive at 4:15pm. My siblings had been picked up by the social worker and a care worker, who would be their guardians for the journey to and from their activities, at 4pm sharp, and we waited a good five minutes before leaving the house (just in case one of the children should return!).

Mrs Marton was standing at her open door as we rounded the bend in the drive. The driveway was impressive but looked slightly shabby, as though it had not been properly cared for in recent years. The house, as it came into view, was magnificent with bay windows, turrets, crenelations and chimneys. Loads and loads of chimneys. You hear people say, 'It took my breath away,' and I suddenly understood what they meant. The age-darkened white stone seemed to shine as the afternoon sun placed her rays across the glorious frontage.

The windows contained early glass panes, possibly original to the building. Each one was small and rectangular. I remember thinking how much work had gone into every single pane of glass, then each panel of window. The placement of each stone felt so personal to me as I mentally built the house from the ground up and crowned the building with impressively constructed chimneys.

Mrs Marton giggled. "I feel exactly the same every time I walk up this drive," she said. "I used to think this house was full of magic!" she winked, then stood aside and gestured us inside.

The hallway was as big as the whole of our house. The walls, floors, stairs, doors, everything was made of a beautiful honey-coloured wood that immediately made your breath light and your head calm. *This must be what it feels like to be rich,* I thought.

"The house is beautiful, but we are no longer rich," she answered my thoughts. She told us how there used to be servants and another wing to the house, but when her ancestors were strapped for cash, as well as selling parcels of land, they sold part of the house and it was taken away stone by stone, floorboard by floorboard to a new life in America where they couldn't get enough of the English gentry and proper English houses! There was a photo, somewhere, she said, of the house in its new home and there were real American Indians in the photo, too.

We were taken through a large wooden door to the left of the staircase, which smelt of beeswax, coal, lavender, and faded cigar smoke. I loved that smell. It smelt like I belonged there.

Mrs Marton had prepared a tray with a teapot, cups and saucers, sugar bowl and milk jug, all matching and very old and dainty, with a plate of small, crustless bread squares with something I hoped wasn't meat paste sandwiching two pieces together. We could have stepped back in time in that room with that tea tray, except there was also a plate containing chocolate digestives, bourbon biscuits and custard creams. I'm not sure, but I don't think they were around in the previous century!

Mrs Marton put Newmum at ease almost instantly. They began chatting like old friends and I realised that this was because Mrs Marton was also conversing with a lady who stood very close to Newmum! I hadn't noticed her before; she was so close to Newmum that she could have been attached! She looked at me and spoke without sound – *I'm her spirit guide.*

A spirit guide, Mrs Marton told me later, is different to a ghost. A ghost is the spirit of a person who once had a living body, like ours, but it had died and their Soul came out but didn't realise, or didn't believe, that it was dead. Because the people they knew when they were alive tend to not be able to see or hear their ghostly bodies, they tend to attach themselves to young children or people with 'the gift'. Young children are more able to see, hear and feel the spirit world, she said, because they haven't learned hate, fear, cynicism and prejudice. They don't judge others but take everything from their surroundings without thinking too much about it. Not every living person will be able to sense ghosts. Not every living person who can sense them will accept that there is something there. Not every living person will become a ghost, so there aren't actually that many ghosts floating around!

A spirit guide, on the other hand, is like an extension of your body. Every living person has one. A spirit guide is sent with the Soul when it first enters the world at birth. It is sent by God or the Universe, or whatever belief you have in a higher power to watch over you, care for you, and help you.

Do you remember that feeling you got just before a fight broke out right next to you in the pub? That feeling made you get up and go to the toilet even though you didn't need to? And when you returned, and the fight had calmed down, you noticed a smashed-to-pieces pint glass with pieces of glass embedded in the very seat you had sat in.

That feeling was a warning from your spirit guide. If you stop and think for a moment, you can probably bring to mind hundreds of such examples – not as extreme as this one, but we sometimes like to call it coincidence. We are walking along the street on a really hot day, desperate for a drink of water but without enough money to buy one; you feel the urge to tighten your already tight shoelace and as you bend down, you spy a coin of just the right amount to purchase your drink.

Maybe you recall that time when you were first pregnant, and fearing that you couldn't afford to clothe your baby, you felt compelled to go to the church hall. As you arrived, they were putting full bin liners in the bin out the back. One of the church wardens spotted you and asked if you wanted any baby clothes and a pram as they hadn't been sold at the jumble sale. There were also milk bottles and an unused, new, still-in-the-box bottle sanitiser and blankets. It felt like a lottery win and you sobbed with joy all the way home. That was your spirit guide guiding you to that which you most needed at that time. And occasionally, you get a bit extra like a brand-new bottle sanitiser.

Your spirit guide is sent to help you with the lessons you are here on earth to learn. I'll tell you more about that later, but for now, you just need to understand that they are here to help and guide you, and no matter whether you believe it or not, every living human being has one.

They once had human form and lessons to learn, and they have lived on earth. So, they know what we living humans go through mentally, physically and emotionally, every day. They are here to help guide you through this maze called life – helping you to learn your lessons and move onto the next level in 'heaven'. Part of their job is to complete the lessons they didn't achieve whilst they were here, too. So once that lesson has been learned, or they have learned as much as they can with you, they leave and are replaced by a new spirit guide.

If you look back at your life, you can sometimes see evidence of one guide or another. There may have been a time when you were desperate to learn how to cook good food cheaply so you could feed your family well and still pay the bills. And then your cousin opened a cafe and asked you to do the cooking. Perhaps you felt the need to communicate, so you learned three different languages and travelled the world trying out your new skill, only to find the love of your life living on a distant shore. But if you find your own, you may be able to find out not only the lessons you came to earth to learn but also what your spirit guide at the time was trying to teach you.

Mrs Marton broke off the conversation to show us around the house.

"It's a bit like a museum," she said, "except everything in this house was collated by a single family line. You can see every interest, every journey that any member of this family ever had by looking at the objects they gathered." Mrs Marton's ancestor had been a bastard descendent of the original owner, the scullery maid informed me. Mrs Marton raised an eyebrow, shook her head and showed Newmum, who couldn't hear the scullery maid, a tapestry that was sewn in France a long time ago by a group of nuns.

The original part of the house was built on ley lines, Mrs Marton told us, which is why the energy in some rooms is much higher than others. Newmum smiled and nodded but didn't really understand what she was saying. I realised that it was connected to the big web, but wasn't sure. I thought I might ask Mrs Marton later.

It was suddenly time to go. We should come again next week, Mrs Marton suggested. She got lonely, she told Newmum, who felt we shouldn't impose upon her kindness. We would be helping her if we visited occasionally. Newmum smiled and said we would visit again next week if it would help Mrs Marton and the other children were on their activities.

"Oh! I almost forgot to ask," Mrs Marton said as she showed us to the door, "I don't suppose you know someone who could do a bit of cleaning a few days a week, do you? I pay well and in cash. My cleaner left this morning, you see, and as much as I'd like to do it myself, the house is far too big."

She smiled and looked expectantly at Newmum.

"Well, I have a bit of time while the kids are at school if that might help," Newmum replied, her throat tight, her voice strained.

I smiled a big smile. Mrs Marton leant forward, gave her a hug, and winked at me. You see, while she was walking around the big house, her spirit guide told Mrs Marton and me that Newmum was worried about how she would feed us after the last of the charity money ran out. Although she was on benefits and had the housing rent paid by the local council, she would still have a shortfall of a few pounds a week just to make ends meet. She was beginning to feel anxious and thought she would have to get a job, but she knew she wasn't strong enough to take on a proper job where she would have to keep to certain hours and days.

Was it a coincidence that Mrs Marton's cleaner had left that very morning?

15

An Education

As Newmum and I were leaving, Mrs Marton bobbed back into the library and brought out a couple of books, which she handed to me, saying I was welcome to visit her library anytime and could come through the back gate, which connected to the same woods as our back gate.

It wasn't until I got home that I looked at either book. I was just really happy to have books that came from the big house and weren't children's books. I held them tightly to my chest all the way home. The school I had started attending since turning eleven insisted on making me read 'age-appropriate' books. Many of which I had already read, and the local library – built from the same stone as The Manor House, by Mrs Marton's ancestor, to allow local people to have access to learning – was very small and their selection of books tended to be mostly modern adult fiction about a woman who fell in love with a man and the angst and longing she felt whilst falling in love with him. They were really boring and not a very accurate portrayal of women, I thought, and some parts were enough to put you off love altogether. The factual section of the library was mostly recipes, fresh water fishing or books about religion. So, you can imagine my delight at receiving the old books from Mrs Marton.

For the first few days, I just held them. I could feel the energy from the hands that had held them before. They practically vibrated with the energy of long-dead readers. I wanted to feel what they were like and I kept getting flashes of another life, swishes of expensive colourful silks, a puff of crushed, smoked tobacco leaf. An echo of voices in laughter and argument. The laboured breath of consumption. Just holding a book can tell you so much history before you even crack the cover for the first time.

Mrs Marton's books were fantastic. They were spiritual books that talked of ectoplasm and seances and man's place in the universe. I consumed every page like a starving, long-bearded homeless man ravages his long-awaited meal. I enjoyed reading every word of each book, but I didn't learn anything new. I already knew it, if I can say that without sounding big-headed or know-it-all-ish. It was old information that was already within my memory banks, probably not from this lifetime. But I'm not sure what I mean by that.

So, it wasn't long before I took a journey through the woods to collect another book. The back door, which was directly opposite the gate at the bottom of her garden, was open when I arrived. Anybody would think she was expecting me.

An old tin kettle was whistling on the stove top as I stood at the door, knocking politely before walking in. I felt I could walk in without invitation. I felt like this was home. Not the place I lived with my family or The Light House kind of home. Just a place I felt safe and comfortable. A place where I was accepted for who I was.

Mrs Marton took the kettle and began to pour the boiling water into two large brown mugs that had strings with little labels hanging over the edge.

"I take it you drink tea?" she asked warmly, looking at the books in my hand and tilting her head toward the table as a suggestion that I should place them there. I did, lining them up carefully so they sat together neatly. It was the least I could do. To be respectful of the books. And respectful to their owner.

After she had removed the teabags and poured in a splash of milk, we took our hot tea in the large mugs out of the kitchen, across the hallway and into the library. The last time I had been in here was with Newmum, and I had been so in awe of Mrs Marton and her ghost and spirit companions that I hadn't taken notice of the room itself.

"There are originals of almost every bible printed before the 1800s," she said matter-of-factly. I stared at the bookshelves covering every wall and rising to the very top of the room, seamlessly flowing around every straight and curve of the walls, apart from the window and the door, and lined beautifully with old books, without a single space. *I hope this is what heaven looks like,* I thought, *books as far as the eye can see.*

"Do you know why I'm telling you this?" she asked, bringing my attention swiftly back to my host.

I shook my head and waited for her to tell me.

"What did you think of the books you've just read?" she asked, sitting in one of the large, faded armchairs that sat either side of the table from which she had served sandwiches on my previous visit with Newmum. I answered her in my head, as I would with my spirit friends – I had realised that Terrence and Lady Catherine were what we would call ghosts who had recently passed over, but they hadn't had time to organise that information. Arrien, on the other hand, was my spirit guide. She helped me in a way the ghosts didn't. The ghosts wanted me to help them, although they didn't know it at the time. Sometimes they didn't know that they were dead or what they were supposed to do now that they were.

Arrien had been around for quite a while, in the background at first, then chipping in with answers to questions or reminding me to be nice to children in school who were getting on my nerves. "You don't know why they behave that way," she would tell me. "Not everybody has a good life just because they have expensive things." It reminded me of Karen and I would feel a pang of guilt and I knew she was right. So, I listened to what she said.

Mrs Marton was looking at me and I realised she wanted me to answer with my voice.

"Do you get in trouble at school for not answering the teachers?" she asked before I could answer her earlier question.

"Yes," I smirked. I was always being told off for not answering a question, not participating in discussions, staring into space or saying "Uh-hu" and nodding at the window. I guess that's why the other children and most of the adults thought I was a bit weird. I was answering. Just not the questions the living teachers were asking. They were too boring.

"You have to wake up now," she said softly but sternly. "You must start to speak out with your voice!" She stressed the word 'must' with such expression that I was taken aback. My heart began to beat louder inside the cavity of my body. Pinpricks pushed warm liquid onto my eyelashes. But it didn't fall. It never fell!

She took the cup out of my hand and placed it on the table beside her, then bent down and enveloped me in a warm hug – the kind of hug I had longed for my whole life and not been granted.

"I'm so sorry," she said sadly. "There is so much to teach you and I have so little time." Her eyes began to fill as mine had moments earlier. She allowed two large drops to escape and run down her cheeks before she wiped them away with the back of her hand.

She stood and beckoned me to sit in the second chair at the round table. The table was draped in a beautiful, white, square tablecloth made of linen and hand-embroidered beautifully by Mrs Marton's mother. I don't know how I knew that. The scullery maid didn't tell me; she wasn't here today. Nonetheless, I knew it to be true. Beneath it was a faded, deep red cloth which perfectly skimmed the floor – the very edges slightly tattered from years of feet and sweeping brushes touching and caressing it.

Mrs Marton began to speak – I will have to tell you what she said in my words rather than Mrs Marton's because I think you might get confused and lose interest. But it is as important for you to know this as it is for me. Well, some stuff you really don't need to know, but I will share only that which you need to know at the moment.

The bible, she started to tell me, was a book of stories written many hundreds of years ago by lots of different people. Their stories were passed down to them, generation by generation. You see, we didn't always have books or paper to deposit our stories, so the elders of the tribes or villages in countries throughout the world would share firelight stories with their tribes and families. The same stories would be told again and again and again. People would discuss and share these stories as they went about their daily chores. And they would sing them too.

When the elder of the tribe died, a new elder would take his or her place and continue telling the stories. A new elder might alter one of the stories occasionally so it would fit with their way of leading. Only a little bit. Initially, people would notice, but after a while, they would forget and the new stories became the truth.

When the first writing was invented in western Asia on clay tablets and later in Egypt on a type of paper they made from a river plant called papyrus, they began to put down their version of the stories. The version of the story that was the truth at that moment.

Now, these aren't the stories of baby Jesus in a cradle in a cowshed that are told at Christmas to every schoolchild who has ever lived! These are the stories of how we came to be – the stories of creation. The story of why the world is here and why it is inhabited by living, breathing human beings. This is why Mrs Marton's ancestor had collected so many early bibles from around the world. He had wanted to see if every country had the same creation stories. Because he wasn't sure that he believed in God the creator, so he started to search for a truth he could believe in.

To cut an extremely long story short, there were similarities.

"You might be particularly interested in the Hopi version of how man was made." She smiled a knowing smile and I filed that away for later. I wasn't at all sure what a hoppy was, but I would find out because the look she had given was one of such deep knowing and understanding I felt there was some secret about me she was not revealing!

A lot of the stories spoke of light and dark; they talk of giants and eggs and how man was created by gods; they talk of planets being made from spit and blood. All the stories are fascinating, and I wish I could retell them all to you right now. But there are far too many.

Her ancestor had found enough similarities that he thought there might be something to this 'God' thing, but he was deeply troubled by the behaviours of his own countrymen, including his king. If this God was real, then why did he allow man, his creation, to behave so appallingly toward another human being? And having witnessed so much death, her ancestor wondered if there was such a thing, even, as heaven!

I liked this ancestor, I decided. I was still very young at this point but had already read the bible all the way through (apart from a few boring, dirgy parts!) several years earlier. I thought the same as him. But I had had the fortune of having visited the Light void, so I knew there was more than we currently knew on earth.

"Do you know why I'm telling you this?" Mrs Marton spoke suddenly. I had been lost in her story-telling voice. It is difficult to express the nuances of a story to another human being when you have been inside it and felt it and lived it. You see, that is what happened when Mrs Marton began talking. Her voice sucked you inside a new world, an old world, and I saw this man – her ancestor. I felt his internal struggle at a time when religion was important, when everyone would attend a church service on Sunday and venerate the leader of their church. The priest, father, vicar, pastor, whatever title he had, because it was always a man, would be the conduit between God and man. The king was supposed to derive his authority from God. And yet, here was this ancestor, struggling to piece together the truth of two men – his local minister and his king – whose sins were extensive and common knowledge throughout not only his country but the countries on the neighbouring continent.

If that was God's work, he wanted none of it.

"Because God is not what they write about in the bible," I replied with my voice.

Her mouth formed a tight line, but with a smile inside, she blinked and nodded her head once, firmly.

"Good." She rose from her seat. "Well, I hope you will come and see me again," she smiled.

"Your mother is doing a fantastic job, by the way." She swept her arm around the room. "The old one was ever so slow and missed all the cobwebs in the corners." She chuckled and then nodded toward the door, indicating I should leave. I stood up and took one step before turning. There were two more books on the table, which I hadn't noticed before. She silently picked them up, handed them to me, smiled, and then sat back down. Time to go!

16

Healing

I thought I had been with Mrs Marton for hours and expected the sky to be dark when I emerged from her kitchen, but it had been less than an hour and the sun still shone high in the sky. I giggled to myself as I skipped along the worn grass path to the back gate. Her house really was magic!

As I closed the gate behind me, I thought I heard a sob coming from the woodland ahead. Then I heard the sound of a man talking through his sobs, the sound getting louder as I walked forward. I wasn't scared. I felt very sad, though.

I saw his spirit guide first. A male of about thirty, wearing a uniform. It was blue in colour and had an arm missing. He had an arm missing, although I could see it clearly. It is quite difficult to explain unless you can see it yourself. It might sound odd. But that is what I saw and I want to tell the truth. The whole truth, so help me God – if God exists.

He was looking around a rather wide tree and had a slightly worried expression on his face. He looked directly at me, realised that I could see him, blew out an exasperated breath and beckoned me over.

"Please can you talk to him?" He asked, pointing to someone on his side of the tree. "He doesn't hear me." I walked around and said hello to the person sitting there. He jumped sideways and let out a strange noise. He was quite a round man, a living being, I have to add, not a ghost or a guide. He was wearing a white shirt that smelt like new cotton and plastic, with a black tie loosened and slightly skewiff over two undone buttons. In his hands, he had a rope that he was trying to tie a knot into, but it kept slipping out of his grip. If you had eyes like mine, you would have seen there was a small child sitting next to him, slowly undoing the knot as he was trying to fasten it. The child was a ghost. A boy with a cheeky grin and belly as round as his father's. Sometimes you know these things without anyone telling you.

"Your son loves you," I said. The man made a mewling sound filled with sorrow.

"I can't go on," he said with fat tears running down his ruddy face and merging into the snot that was escaping like a wayward moustache down the side of his plump-lipped mouth.

"I buried him this morning. I can't go on without him. I have nothing to live for." He began to wail again.

"He's untying that knot quicker than you can tie it," I told him.

His head turned toward me in a flash. A bone in his neck cracked; he flinched with the pain and grabbed at his collar, rubbing with his chubby hand.

I chuckled. "He's saying that you'll never cope with the rope if you can't cope with cricking your neck."

The man laughed through his tears. "He's got a right funny sense of humour, my lad." He smiled, then realised he'd used present tense, screwed up his face and began to bawl again.

I sat down beside him, placed my books against the root of the tree and held his hand. Reaching into my cardigan pocket with my other hand, I brought out a cotton handkerchief I'd taken to putting in there. My sister said they were dirty and that you should never use cotton hankies but paper ones that came in a box. But I realised now why I had taken to carrying it. Some might say it was coincidence!

The man took it from me, wiped his eyes, and then smeared the snot around his face a little, gathering some of it into the hankie. He took a deep, ragged breath and turned his face toward me.

"Thank you," he said. "I don't know why, but I feel so much better for talking to you. I felt like I couldn't go on. I love … loved … my boy so much. And I thought I couldn't go on. But I think I can. I really think that I can."

He squeezed my hand gently. "Is he here? With me? Now?" he asked.

"He was," I replied. "He's gone now, 'cos he knows you'll be alright. But he will come back to see you."

The man grabbed hold of me so fast I didn't know what was happening. He wrapped his arms so tightly around my body that for a moment I could hardly breathe. Then he was sobbing again. It was different this time. When I first heard him, he was sobbing tears of despair. Fear. Pain. And sadness so deep only a parent who has lost a child will ever feel, ever know, ever understand.

Now his sobs were lighter. Still full of pain. Still full of fear. Still full of the sadness only a parent who has lost their child will ever know. But now the despair was ebbing away and being replaced by hope. He knew it was not the end. He knew the love he had shared would never end.

Although my eyes were dry, I could feel something dripping from the end of my nose. A tickle. I took a sharp breath in through my nose and sucked back the offending dribble as the man released me from his arms. He thanked me again, then began to gather up the rope he no longer needed. I stood up and began walking away – the snot attempting to escape once again. I should never have given him my hankie. Instead, I used the sleeve of my cardigan to wipe across my face, then retched as some of it went on my hand and across my cheek. I saw the line of slime that I would have to wear until I got home and decided that next time, I would take several paper hankies.

17

Healing (Part Two)

The new old books from Mrs Marton were about energy. They started off all sciencey, saying that the world was made up of only a few elements that were in every living thing, and these elements were made up of atoms – teeny, tiny things that couldn't be seen with the naked eye. Even scientists needed giant telescopes or microscopes or something more scientific in order to see these things. Science isn't my favourite subject, though, so I didn't take too much notice of it.

Anyway. These atoms vibrate. Very fast. I did skip quite a bit of this because it didn't seem relevant. I hope Mrs Marton doesn't give me a test!

This was the interesting thing, though. Everything in the universe has its own vibration. Our bodies, living bodies, vibrate. The chair you are sitting on is vibrating right now. The clothes you are wearing are all vibrating. The blade of grass in your garden? Vibrating. The food that you eat? Vibrating.

Now you might think I'm crazy. You wouldn't be the first to think that, so I won't hold it against you, but it's true.

Not that I'm crazy!

Things vibrate! The level of the vibration is what keeps it together and makes it look like a solid object. Everything vibrates at a different frequency. Or, to make it simpler, every 'thing' vibrates at a different speed. You can't see it and you can't feel it. Except you can if you try!

This is where it starts to get a bit complicated and I'll completely understand if you nod off or decide to skip a few pages. But please, try to bear with me. I'm going to talk just about living bodies because you can investigate this for yourself.

What causes the vibration? Energy. Where is energy? It's all around you! Everything in the world is made up of energy. It's in the earth, the plants, the sky, the sun, your body. Everywhere. Are you still with me? Okay … Let's step back a little bit. I'm not a teacher, and I don't fully understand all this myself yet. I'm still a child, remember. I already know this stuff inside of me, but trying to explain it to people who can't see the energy is a completely different kettle of fish.

Do you remember when I found the man in the woods who was trying to hang himself because he'd just returned from his young son's funeral and was feeling really sad? Do you remember that I held his hand? Well, as I touched his hand with mine, I felt a great heat surging through my body, through my arm, through my hand and into his. At the same time, it felt as though a million microscopic ballbearings, freshly removed from the freezer, were doing an infinitesimal spiral dance in the palm of my hand. Can you picture that? It was all happening at atomic level. Tiny, tiny atoms were beginning to vibrate faster throughout my body – that was causing the heat – and the tiny vibrations were flooding from me through into the sobbing man. As these atoms arrived at his palm, from my palm, he would have felt the heat and the sensation from the billions of tiny ballbearings – but he may not have felt it physically because he was in such emotional pain right then. But that energy will have travelled from his palm up his arm and into his body. This vibrating energy causes the atoms and particles that make up his body to all vibrate faster, too. As each atom begins to vibrate faster, it forces its neighbouring atoms to begin vibrating faster and so on and so forth until the whole interior of the body is vibrating really fast.

Now, under normal circumstances you wouldn't feel this

happening – apart, possibly, from feeling a rush of heat through your body, a swirly feeling where the energy is entering your body or maybe feeling extra relaxed and calm. But what generally happens is that when those vibrating atoms reach a part of your body that isn't working properly, it forces those non-working atoms to pick up the pace and work more efficiently. Does that make sense? So, for our friend in the woods, the high vibrating energy went to his emotional centre and calmed his fear, his desperation and his pain. Because those feelings and emotions had taken over his whole being and he couldn't see further than those feelings.

He won't ever forget the pain of losing his son, but he was able to find acceptance and calmness in the moment, at that particular point in time, when he thought there was no other way to live. Can you understand that?

It also can work on illnesses, according to my books. If a person, like me, who can see the energies in the body and throughout the universe, knows where in the body an illness is sitting, they can boost the flow of energy – the vibrating of tiny atoms – to that particular spot and encourage the poorly part to work harder to get well. The body is a hugely complicated machine of muscle, flesh, bone, blood and all sorts of other stuff, but it is made to fix itself. In the olden days, when we lived in caves and hunted for food, we didn't have illnesses like we do now. We might cut ourselves and after bleeding for a while, which is the body's way of cleaning the wound, a scab would form. This is the body's way of keeping out any nasty bugs or poisons while the body remakes the skin to go over the bit you cut. Can you remember that feeling when you removed a scab and saw the new skin beneath? A little bit pink but bloody perfect!

If you broke your leg back in those days, you would probably die because you wouldn't be able to catch and kill food, and a bone break takes weeks to mend – even today, with all the medical advances we have made since our cave-dwelling ancestors started building their houses, you still have to have a pot on a broken bone for several weeks.

The book had lots of examples of how people got better from having their energy jiggled about a bit. And I wondered if I could heal Newmum so that she would be physically and mentally better.

It was time for a visit to Mrs Marton. It was Wednesday afternoon. I'd been thinking about it all day at school and had been told off twice for daydreaming. I had asked Arrien not to be around in school because I was trying to do what Mrs Marton had asked and wake up whilst I was in lessons. I couldn't do that when I was surrounded by ghosts and spirits who constantly wanted to talk to me or for me to talk to their living family. When I got home, Newmum wasn't there so the other children went straight to the kitchen for their jam sandwiches. I told them I was going to Mrs Marton's. There were a couple of eye rolls and a tut, but they were happy for me to go. They all thoroughly enjoyed their Thursday evening activities and knew that if I decided it wasn't fair, they would all have to stop going. I really loved my siblings. Although we would fight, like most children, we always knew what was right and what was fair. Not just in our homes but in other families, on other streets, in other towns, and in other countries. We were all really lovely humans.

When I arrived at Mrs Marton's, the back door was slightly ajar, but I could see her, so I knocked and walked in. Newmum was sat at the large pine kitchen table. I loved to touch that table because it brought through a hundred former servants and workers from the Manor House. I wouldn't always be able to hear them, but I could see aspects of their life, their loves and their deaths. It's amazing how much you can learn about human nature just by touching a piece of wood that was cut from a living tree hundreds of years ago!

There was a woman sitting opposite my mum. I recognised her as my English teacher, Miss Dougal, from school, but I was momentarily confused.

They all turned at the same time to greet me, warm smiles across all their faces. Newmum looked a little sheepish, though, so I took a step nearer to see what had made her feel embarrassed. Miss Dougal was a very stern teacher who had high expectations of everybody's behaviour and academic progress. I always thought she didn't like me, but here she was looking happy and relaxed and talking in a non-teacher way. Between Newmum and the English teacher was what looked like an oversized pack of playing cards with pictures, some in a pile and some spread out in a pattern on the table.

She was telling Newmum that the future looked really rosy, so she should relax and not worry about anything. She asked Newmum if she was happy with that. Newmum nodded, her face a little flushed. I thought I would ask Arrien later what had been going on. But Mrs Marton looked at me sternly and asked me if I knew what the cards were. I shook my head and pouted, feeling as though I had been told off. Mrs Marton seemed to always know what I was thinking, and she had previously told me I should rely less on my spirit guide for a while. I didn't like that. It made me very sullen, and I would frown, pout my lips and push my chin into my chest. I did this now.

Newmum laughed and pulled me close to her side in a sort of hug, telling me I wasn't a teenager yet, so I should put away my attitude.

"These are tarot cards." Miss Dougal picked them up, split them into two piles in her hands, then pushed the two piles together on their sides so most of the cards slid neatly together to make a single pack again. She repeated this action a couple of times, the cards shuffling into a different space and getting mixed up whilst telling me what they were for. Apparently, they each had an image that had a specific individual meaning or, when matched with another image from another card, could have a totally different meaning and were imbued with universal energy. If you asked a clear question, they could tell you the best outcome of that question if you did nothing to change what you were doing. But they could also give you an idea of what to do to change that outcome if you didn't like it. This was all done in a reading, where a person who understood the images on the cards could read the meanings to the sitter, who was the person asking a question. You needed a good reader to be able to translate the different cards and their meanings.

"Pick one." Miss Dougal was holding the pack out toward me. She had fanned the cards outward from her hand so the edge of each card was visible.

"We can see what's going to happen to you over the next few months," she smiled. "Maybe you will finish that essay that was due in yesterday," She winked at me. I turned my head so Newmum couldn't see me blush. I'd told her I was doing better at school than I actually was. I didn't want her to worry about me when she had so many issues to contend with, so I was embarrassed to be caught out in a lie! I reached out to the outstretched cards, picked the first one I touched, and turned it around so we could all see the image on the card.

Newmum gasped and put her hand across her mouth. Mrs Marton's brow furrowed momentarily, but her smile stayed in place.

"Ooh! Now that's not as bad as it looks," giggled Miss Dougal like a teenage girl, so I wasn't quite sure that she meant it.

You see, the card had a very plain white background, but there was a black skeleton wearing a black top hat and a red bow tie and holding a silver-topped walking cane. Its skeletal skull was wearing a grimace that would frighten Satan himself. Beneath the image in black capital letters and splashed with red was the word DEATH.

18

Death (Another)

The tarot card with the title 'Death' did not, according to Miss Dougal, signify an actual death, so we shouldn't worry. I think she was telling Newmum this so she wouldn't have something else to worry about. Personally, I thought the card was meant to frighten rather than ease. The image felt quite aggressive but indicated, according to Miss Dougal, an ending of something.

"Like a life?" I asked seriously.

Flustered, she returned the card to the pack, saying it could be an actual death or it could, more likely, be the end of something that is happening in your life. If you were struggling with something in your day-to-day life, that would come to an end, and things would be easier, she told the room. It could also mean the end of an essay and the handing in of said essay being the end of someone constantly requesting it. She giggled again and Mrs Marton winked before gathering up the mugs of the now-cold tea her two guests had been drinking.

I walked through to the library and placed my returned books on the table where we had previously sat.

"Your mum is ready to go," Mrs Marton had followed and was reaching for a book on the shelf beside the door, which she handed to me. I waited for another, but instead of offering me a second book she asked, "Do you actually read these books?" She said 'actually' with a harsh intonation, making her sound a little stern and she placed her hands on her hips. I felt a little confused and as though I had disrespected her, but I didn't know how. I tried to reply but didn't have the understanding to respond.

"You only took those books yesterday," she pointed to the books I had placed on the table. "Do you read really fast? Or do you feel the information?" she asked softly. I smiled a gigantic smile and my insides felt like they had lit up.

"I haven't read a word. But I know what is in them when I hold them," I said in a conspiratorial whisper, so pleased that she understood. I think she understood. She stood to the side of the door and ushered me out with her hand, saying this book would be enough for now and she would see me again soon.

When we got back to the kitchen, Newmum mentioned how many books I was getting through and thanked Mrs Marton for her kindness and Miss Dougal for the reading. We left out of the front door and walked down the path and onto the road. Turning into the avenue at the end of the road, we saw a man with a long, scruffy, greying beard just ahead. He sat against one of the large, old oak trees that lined the street just beyond our house. The hairs on my head bristled. The hairs on my back stood up tall like soldiers. I could feel them touching the fabric of my school dress, which was one size too big and hung from me like sails at half-mast. I felt my underarms become hot and damp and my breath raced in and out. In and out. In and out.

I knew him.

I knew him.

I feared him.

Newmum was fishing in her handbag, paying him no attention. I wanted to scream at her, "RUN, RUN, it's Beastman," but I couldn't speak. She passed me some coins and I had to wrap my fingers around them as I couldn't grip them. My body had decided not to work. Why does your body do that? When you need it most, it just shuts down!

"Give this to the poor man to get himself a warm drink," she said and continued walking past him, confident in her ignorance.

I stopped right in front of him and he was looking at me through clouded eyes.

He saw me.

He knew me. But he didn't recognise me. He didn't move. He blinked his eyes. Once. Twice.

It was then that his stench hit me and I took a step back to take him in fully. I had stopped looking at people's auras a while ago. Most people were very similar in their auras. You could see their happiness, their sadness, their illnesses, their problems. And it became boring after a while. It wasn't as if I could tell anyone else what I saw or what I knew about other people. That would make me like one of the greys. And I wasn't ever going to be one of them.

This man, though. Beastman. My earthly physical father. I suddenly saw what I had sensed but never seen, never truly known before. He was soaked in fear, self-loathing and self-pity. Anger flicked around him like the flame of a candle. He had been living rough all these years to avoid his crimes but had returned to take back his family. The wife and children he felt were his. His belongings. His to own and to do with as he pleased. They had done so well without him and that angered him more than anything else. To know that you are neither loved nor wanted is the most painful of human emotions; even when you do not have the capacity to understand or feel love. I could see in his aura that he had spent most of his last years drinking – an addiction he had when Realmum was alive – but in his attempt to stay out of view he had turned to other substances, other ways to survive. I could see his Soul inside his shell screaming to get out. It had had enough of this life and wanted to go home. Not to The Light Room. There was a different place for Souls like this.

I wanted to help this weak, useless bag of maggots who caused our family so much hurt, pain and torment. But I wanted him to suffer too.

Newmum had reached the gate to our house and called back to

me to give him the money and come away. I threw it at him, then bent down until my face was very close to his…

"You are going to die tonight. It will be painful. But it won't be as painful as what you did to her, and I hope the devil feeds your Soul to his demons."

He let out a breath into my face, bringing a bit of spittle with it. The smell was worse than anything I could ever imagine. He reached up to wipe away his spit, but I got there first, slapping his hand away. He would never touch any one of my family again. Then I walked briskly away.

I smiled to myself as I entered the warm house and closed the door behind me. I thought about the tarot card – death – it had come true. Not me, though, so that was okay. Or not, depending on your view. I still yearned to return to The Light House but settled for knowing that it would be a while before I returned. Except, I wasn't prepared for what happened next.

19

A Dead Man in the Street

Shortly after, the family sat down to eat tea, a large homemade steak and kidney pie with hand-cut and deep-fried potato chips made by Newmum. While she smiled and shimmied her slim hips to the radio, we saw blue flashing lights through the front window. It was late summer so it was still light and warm outside. The youngest child ran to the window, lifted the white, nylon, lace curtain and shouted,

"It's an ambulance!" and dashed outside, swiftly followed by three more excited children. Newmum and I sat at the table. Silence. She asked if I thought it was the tramp down the street. I nodded and pushed a piece of the kidney around my plate. I wasn't a big fan of meat at the best of times, but I always found the steak in steak pie to be stringy and hated how it stuck in between your teeth. The kidney was rubbery and had a slight squeak when you chewed it. I was trying very hard not to think about the tramp down the street.

There was a knock on the door and the children came back in, quieter now, with a policewoman in tow. She smiled at Newmum and asked if she could have a word in private. Newmum stood up, wiped some imaginary crumbs from her skirt and invited the uniformed woman through to the lounge, telling us to "eat up before it goes cold" as she closed the door.

There was excited chatter as the kids started talking about a dead tramp in the street. This was their first dead body and they could only see the shell. They wouldn't have recognised the shell as being anyone they knew. They could smell him, though. Not the same smell that I could smell, but it was bad enough to the living nose. There were mouthfuls of pie being eaten in between pretend retching. They made up a story about who he was and why he was here, each child chiming in with an extra gruesome or humorous detail, sending laughter whirlpooling around the kitchen. I didn't have the heart to tell them to stop. I didn't have the heart to tell them who it was. I knew if I mentioned him, they would feel that fear.

It never leaves you. Fear. It's like a claw at your back waiting to nip and grip you when you hear a word, a sound, a song, or smell an odour – it grabs you and pulls you back to where you were and your insides are ripped apart time and time again and moment by moment. Over and over again in one tiny millisecond. How could I do that? To people I loved?

But then there was a sound that silenced them. Guttural, low, like an animal. Then a low keening. A sound of sorrow so deep I'll never get used to it. But this is the thing I mentioned before about death. People feel it. Newmum was feeling it now. That sense of loss. Knowing that you will never see this human being again. But in this case, it was also relief. Release.

For so many years, she had not known where he was or what he was doing. She knew he would keep his distance for the first few years. His description, his actions had been in every newspaper across the country. He was ... had been ... an intelligent man. He wouldn't put himself in danger by coming anywhere near us until the attention had died down. But he had been near us. Only two doors down. He was obviously on his way to our house; the newspapers would report in the coming weeks. Obviously on his way to see his children. And the wife he had left for dead.

We were kept off school for a few days to mourn the death of our father. We weren't mourning his death; we were feeling a sense of relief and you can't tell people that you are gladdened by another person's death. People would judge you as heartless. But the truth is, we were relieved. All of us. We knew we were free.

But also, Newmum was in shock. Deep, dark, touching the root of your being shock. She had walked past him. She hadn't known him. She hadn't recognised him. The man who hurt her. Hurt her babies. The man who beat her violently and the man who killed her. Because she had died that night. She had been declared a miraculous survivor afterwards because every one of her vital organs had sustained life-threatening injuries. EVERY ONE. Just one of those injuries would have been enough to kill a man twice her size. But she was a fighter and she came back for her children. But … she had asked her child to go close to this killer of women and harmer of children. Forced her, in fact, when she sensed the child was afraid. What kind of mother was she to put her child in such danger? What kind of danger had she put all her children in? What kind of danger had she placed herself in? Allowing him to find her and her children? So, she was suffering now from guilt, anger both at him and herself and a self-loathing that she should never have had to feel.

We were all very quiet for the first few days. We mainly stayed indoors and read books or coloured pictures. I completed my English assignment for Miss Dougal. We talked very little to one another. When we did, it was always the same thing. Where has he been? Why is he back? How did he find us? I tended not to take part in the conversations. My chest hurt a lot and I had started with a cough. I thought maybe it was grief, but I knew it wasn't. Maybe it was my heart hurting and not my chest. But I ached all over. Every muscle seemed to be screaming at me and I came down with a fever. I was sent to bed with a hot water bottle and told to rest.

Two days later, I coughed so hard there was blood on the blankets and I was shaking uncontrollably. Sweat leaked out of every pore of my body. A body I began to feel no longer belonged to me. I saw a light at the end of my bed – this wasn't the light of a being. This was the chink of light from the crack in a barely open door. If a door wasn't door-shaped but like a curtain being gently pulled aside. If a door was invisible. And didn't belong to this world. I reached out toward it and a plume of smoke-like matter, shaped like a hand, drifted out and reached for mine. I felt immediately better. No aches, no pains, no coughs, no blood. No body. I was in The Light House.

"We brought you here this time," said a single voice or a million – it was difficult to tell. Calm, warm, loving. Everywhere and nowhere. Inside of me and outside of everything. Beautiful. The voice of home.

"Am I dead?" I asked in the same voice that had spoken to me. It was my voice. My earth voice, but multiplied by a thousand 'me's and a trillion other 'not me' voices. Harmonious, like a beautiful choir. But I knew the answer as soon as I asked it. Because I could see attached to my fluid light form in The Light House, was a silver string that went through the door that I had never felt, seen or noticed on my previous visits here. It was attached to my physical body laid in the real-world bed.

"Darling. You are death!" she/he/it/me said so beautifully it made me ache for this love. A smile so warm spreading throughout everything.

Behind me, the real door, the door to my bedroom, banged open and Newmum arrived, flustered, with a very young-looking doctor. Even though I was mesmerised by the here, I felt myself moving back toward the body in the bed.

"Could she have it?" Newmum had a terror in her voice that I hadn't heard for a long time. It was different this time – a deeper terror – because it was me causing this terror. One of her babies. Not Beastman, whose terror-making days were over.

"We need to get her to the hospital," the young doctor told her, "and check the rest of you, too."

Then the white light grew bigger and brighter and swallowed me up.

20

Inside The Light House

I was standing – but you already know I don't have a body with legs and arms and everything – in The Light House. I could see much clearer now. It wasn't a single room at all. It was a bit like a Rubik's Cube, but without the colour – lots of boxes of light all stacked together as high and as wide as the eye could see – except I didn't have eyes here. Everything here was sensed without senses.

I know you may struggle to understand this, and I apologise, but if it is easier, just imagine a square room with a doorway on each wall, one on the ceiling and one on the floor. All the walls, the floor and the ceiling are clear, as though made of glass. Not super clear glass, though. I would say slightly misted. You could see everything in every room for as far as the eye could see in any direction. There were beings in these other rooms moving around. Working. Undertaking tasks. They were also clear but visible. They were shaped like living people but with slightly less form. Their edges were hazy and glowing. They were mesmerising to look at. The way they moved was also fascinating, hypnotic. I moved toward the doorway directly ahead of me, but before I could go through, I heard Arrien's voice.

"There you are. I've been looking for you." She smiled and her form looked almost human. Real. "We thought it would be easier for you if I came dressed like this." She swept out her arms as she chuckled and did a three-hundred-and-sixty-degree turn, spinning on feet I had never noticed before. I giggled. I'd never seen her human form before. I could feel her presence in the living world and knew what she looked like in my head, but I had never actually seen her as she always stood beside and behind me when I was alive. I was struck by her beauty and her resemblance to a drawing I'd seen of Boudicca, a historical queen from Celtic times. She was physically a very strong-looking young woman, yet not large. Her hair, fiery red and long enough to reach almost to her knees, was frizzy and knotted and twisted and held from her face with what looked like twigs. She was enthralling with a look of long-held intelligence. *She would have made a great queen,* I thought. She giggled a fresh, grown-up sort of sound as she read my thoughts.

"You are still alive," she told me, taking my arm and walking toward the open doorway. "We've just been wanting to show you this for ages, but you haven't been to visit." I stopped abruptly and she pulled back slightly.

"I can come when I want?" I asked, slightly annoyed.

"Yes. I thought you knew," she responded, looking slightly puzzled.

"How would I know?" I asked, feeling a sense of mild anger that began to flow away before the feeling took hold. I wanted to be angry. But all I felt was love and compassion and caring.

"You know everything. You just don't know that you know everything." She giggled again, turned to mist and swirled through the doorway, turning once again into her 'living' form when she reached the other room.

I followed her through and found that we were in a room which, although identical to the one we'd just come from, reminded me very much of Mrs Marton's library. Except – and this is going to blow your mind – although I could still see all the other rooms exactly as I could before, the library seemed to stretch on for an eternity in every direction. There were shelves a hundred double-decker buses high, crammed with books all beautifully bound in what looked like antique leather. But each book looked almost new, as though it had never been touched before.

"This is one of your rooms," Arrien said intentionally, looking directly at me. I felt as though I should also be in my body and looking down, I realised that I was. My body was dressed in jeans and a jumper, but it was made of light and energy and glowing with hazy edges. I had so many questions and had no idea where to begin.

"Mrs Marton," I began – *this looks like her room, so I may as well start there,* I thought, "she was sent to you to help you," Arrien responded before I could even finish my question.

She went on to explain that throughout our lives, our living, breathing, in-a-body lives, we were meant to learn lessons. These lessons were not for the living, breathing, in-a-body part of us but for the Soul. Our Souls had lived for many hundreds and sometimes thousands of years. Sometimes on earth, in a body; sometimes on earth, as a guide, like Arrien, and sometimes, here, in this place. Not just the library, but other parts of here too.

This library was part of my domain when I was here. My job, if you like. But they didn't use the term 'job' here. Everyone – every Soul – had a task to do that would help it to grow and vibrate higher. By growing and vibrating at a higher frequency it enabled other Souls to grow and become higher, better Souls. As part of a convergence of millions of Souls, each one had a task that assisted the 'whole' community here whilst also supporting the world we knew as earth.

"What did I do here?" I asked. "What am I going to do now I'm back?"

"Oh, you won't be here for long. You're just on a fact-finding mission today." She smiled and continued to tell me about the library.

This library holds the records of every Soul. Because of my memories of libraries and books holding information in my earth life, that is what I would see here. When I was here before, in previous lives, I would have seen scrolls or clay tablets or heard the voices of storytellers. In the future, she told me, the earth will no longer use books and paper to hold information, as it will all be held in mind banks. She told me this as if the future was already in the past, but it kind of made sense.

She told me that I was one of the keepers of the books before my current incarnation – that means before my current life on earth. Apparently, each Soul reincarnates several times in order to learn their lessons. If you don't learn your lessons whilst you are incarnated in a flesh body, you come back home for a while – maybe an hour, maybe a day, maybe a thousand years – to learn how to help yourself learn the lesson. Sometimes, a lesson was as simple as teaching another Soul about love. It could be to change the world with an invention or an idea. It could be to show someone loss, fear or aggression. I thought it was horrible to teach people about fear and anger. But then I realised it wasn't. You see, every human being who comes into your life has a reason. It may be to teach you, or it may be to teach them. As much as we are here to learn, we are also here to teach. How can we understand what love is? Or peace? Or happiness? If we don't know life without these emotions?

In the world now, Arrien explained, the vibe is all about selfishness. People don't want to help each other. They want to take, take, take and have everything. This has caused a problem here. At home. At The Light House. And more souls have to be brought down in order to help put things right. But as soon as they are born, they are brought into a world, a city, a family that needs 'more'. And so that is what they are learning as children, she told me. And so we are struggling here – Home – to keep everything in balance.

It's about maintaining equilibrium, you see. There has to be an even balance of good and bad, both here and there. When people became too selfish, too self-absorbed, too focused on getting more, they resorted to ways of being that tainted their Souls. A tainted Soul could not enter The Light House.

She reached her hand out and a beautifully bound book appeared in it. She placed it down on to nothing ... except there was a lectern. Except there wasn't. But she lay the book onto the invisible lectern and moved aside, beckoning me to the book.

This is the Soul record of the man you know as Antony Marcus Davenport, she said. His name and picture appeared on the page. The picture was of a younger man. Happy. Smiling. Shining. This was a good man. This is not the man I remembered.

"That is because his circumstances altered," Arrien responded to my thoughts. "His father required more and so would hurt and punish his family; not much different to Beastman." I smiled as she said that. I was glad she didn't say 'father'. Flipping through the pages I saw what he had been in previous incarnations. He had been a sailor who rescued half the crew of a boat that sank. He died, but one of the crew went on to be an inspiration to the man who invented steam power. In another life, he taught love to a tyrant – he was a woman in this life. In each of his lives I could see what a beautiful human being he was. What a beautiful example of a Soul. And I could see his Soul inside – shining beautifully and full of love, goodness and hope.

Then I turned a page and saw the day of the party. I was standing in front of him. His hand was in my hair. My Soul rose up from my body and mixed with the Souls of all the non-living beings in the room, along with that of another bigger, brighter energy (I'll tell you about that one later!). We showed this version of his Soul – the dark, angry, aggressive version – what his choices would be if he were to carry on causing hurt and harm to those who were smaller and physically weaker than him. Then we showed him the alternative, a life (and death) of peace, love, harmony and bliss. Unbeknownst to the living beings, myself and him, his Soul had risen from his body and refused to accept the way of love. He would choose his own way and no one would choose it for him, his Soul said. There was a long discussion – that happened within seconds of living time – and he threatened all kinds of hurt and pain to so many people.

My Soul reached out to the living man and placed its 'hand' on his head. His Soul looked frightened. Asked what I was doing. I did not respond but pushed my Soul 'hand' inside his skull and swirled my hand like I was stirring sugar into coffee with a teaspoon.

I looked up from the book in a panic, searching for Arrien. She was standing beside me. Looking at me. Waiting. "I did that?" I asked, certainty pouring over me like sickeningly sweet syrup. "I made him go mad?" I continued, not giving Arrien time to respond. "I made him go mad," I repeated with the conviction that it was true.

"He would have done what he said," she sighed. "We consulted this book and the change was inevitable. It started to show in his pages as he spoke. We can't have any more unplanned dis-ease. The world would be ruined. We did the right thing." She closed the book abruptly.

"Was it me?" I asked her, afraid of the response while quietly hoping it was me that had ended his sickness.

She smiled one of those smiles which seem to stretch throughout the universe and nodded. "Of course. That's your purpose."

I felt nauseous, disoriented. I started to think of Oldmum and Beastman. But before I could grasp the thought, the room began to swim …

21

A New Beginning

I felt my physical body begin to stir and I opened my eyes. The room was blindingly bright, but a nurse stood by my bed, her hand on my forehead. She was very small, I noticed. Smaller than Newmum, and she was small. But a little rounder and wearing a dark green silk dress with a bustle and a white apron. I had to look again. A bustle? She reminded me of images in a book of Florence Nightingale and Queen Victora but merged together and without a crown or any other jewellery apart from a watch pinned to her breast that she kept touching and looking at. Her hair was tied tightly to her head in a low bun and she had a stern but caring look on her face. She nodded and harrumphed, then told me I was going to be okay.

"I'm thirsty," I said. She pointed to a small table beside the bed that I hadn't previously seen and told me there was plenty of water. I reached toward the glass of water and my hand seemed to go straight through it. I reached again and opened my physical eyes.

The room was pitch black.

I didn't know where I was.

There were strange sounds I couldn't quite place. I felt something pressing against my face and around the back of my head. My head ached. My body ached. My heart began to beat faster. It, too, ached. I tried to take a deep breath in but was racked with pain – a beeping sound began and a strangled sound came out of nowhere. Out of me!

There was a scuttling sound from the dark corner of the room, a rattle of metal on lino, a catch of a breath from someone else's throat. A dim light came on and there in front of me was Newmum. A whimper escaped her lips and tears sprang from her eyes. She took my hand in hers and stroked the side of my face. She let out a howl. *A release of tension*, I thought. And then I drifted back into a deep sleep.

Two days later, I woke up fully. I had been in and out of consciousness since the first awakening and had been 'very poorly' according to doctors and medical staff.

It was several months later before I learned what had happened.

Beastman, when taken from our street in the ambulance, arrived in the mortuary, and after a couple of days, his body was forensically examined to ascertain the reason for death. This happens all the time. If the doctors and coroner don't know why a person has died, they will do a postmortem. Most often, it is something like a heart attack where the heart just stops beating. With Beastman, they discovered that he had cirrhosis of the liver (from his drinking), several other illnesses that I can't quite remember and a very nasty form of pneumonia. When his spittle and lungful of air was breathed into my face, I would have breathed in that disease and caught the pneumonia.

I had died, too, for a short while – so Newmum and my siblings kept telling me. They thought I was an absolute goner according to my youngest sibling, who had never been good at keeping secrets or being subtle.

My hospital room was full of flowers. I love flowers. I love the colours, the shapes, the smells. There are almost three hundred and seventy thousand different species of flowering plants in the world. And I'm pretty sure I had a sample of every single one right there in my hospital room. The smell was glorious. So much better than all those 'people' smells that I would usually smell. There were also lots of presents piled up in the corner and bags full of envelopes from well-wishers.

Once again, our story had gone nationwide in the newspapers and the media. Stories were coming in daily now of 'sightings' of Beastman before he found us. Some people were saying it was the fault of the newspapers for printing so much about our family, making it easy for him to track us down. There had been such an outcry that several of the newspapers' journalists had been physically attacked or had their cars scratched. Right outside the hospital!

It reminded me of a conversation I'd had with someone about the human race becoming less than nice. But I couldn't remember the whole conversation or with whom I'd had it. I felt a bit strange and a bit 'unattached' to everything. But I guessed that was something to do with the medication I was on to help strengthen my lungs and fight the infection.

I had lots of visitors in the hospital whilst I was recovering. Family, neighbours, friends from school who I hadn't realised were friends. The mayor came to visit and promised to give money to a homeless shelter and a substance abuse shelter. A television reporter came to interview me about my bravery. I just nodded to most of his questions and smiled weakly because I didn't know what he was talking about. Mrs Marton came to visit me and brought me books from her library. But they looked really old and a bit musty and a bit boring.

But mostly, I was visited by Meryl's eldest son. His name, weirdly, was Marcus, but everyone called him Marc. He came after school every day. Even though his school, a Catholic school for boys, was on the opposite side of town and he would have to go past the end of our street to come to the hospital.

The first time he visited, he brought flowers from the hospital shop. They were white, daisy-like flowers with a clear plastic cone-shaped wrapper. I thought they were beautiful. He looked a bit embarrassed, though, when he saw the expensive and diverse collection of flowers already filling the hospital room.

"I'll bring you something else tomorrow," he said.

"You could pick me some flowers," I replied and pointed to the bouquets surrounding my bed. "You could draw them for your art class."

Marc was a talented artist. Whatever he drew looked like a photograph. When Meryl came around to the house to visit with Mum, she was always complaining that he would never get a proper job if he spent all his time drawing. But she would bring pieces of his artwork and show them off with pride. When Mum asked if it was really a drawing and not a photo, Meryl's chest would puff up, her face would flush and she could barely hide her pride. It was one of the things I really liked about Meryl. She was a nosey old gossip and would describe in detail the personal business of everyone she knew – along with everyone she didn't. But she was a woman who loved her children. With every part of her being, she loved them and I admired that about her.

One evening, shortly before I was released from hospital, Meryl came to see me instead of Marc. He'd had to stay late at school for something.

"He insisted that I come," Meryl told me. "He didn't want you to be on your own and didn't want you to think he had forgotten about you. He's got a right soft spot for you," she smiled and my face went a little pink. Because if I was honest, I'd got a bit of a soft spot for him too.

22

Homecoming

I left the hospital on Tuesday morning. Roger and Meryl had brought Mum in their car – a white Audi that looked like a racing car. The front passenger seat had to be folded forward to access the back, and I had to fold just as much to get in. I was placed as gently as possible, given the circumstances, into the backseat with a warm, fluffy blanket wrapped around my legs and under my arms. Mum climbed gracelessly in through the driver's side to sit beside me and held my hand all the way home. Her eyes were filled to brimming the whole journey and how she managed not to spill a drop, especially with the way Roger drove into every pothole, dip and crevice that it was possible to have on one stretch of road in a civilised country, was beyond my comprehension!

We arrived home and were released from the vehicle with equal composure. Mum, holding on a little too tightly to my elbow, led the way up the path into the house where all my siblings were waiting.

"Surprise!" they all shouted at once and produced a homemade birthday cake for a birthday I had missed, which had been cooked that morning. I could smell the chocolatey warmth of freshly baked loveliness and wondered who had licked the spoon of the raw cake dough. I felt a twinge of sadness and envy that it hadn't been me.

There were balloons all tied together with a ribbon and I wondered for a moment whose house I had come into. Whose family was this? It hit me suddenly. The years of my life. The blame. The anger. The fear. The frustration. The sadness. The guilt. For only the second time in my life, the dam of tears I had kept inside broke. The liquid flowed fast and furiously in hot molten rivers down either side of my face. Pooling on my chin, beneath my nose and splashing onto my clothes, the floor, the arms and shoulders and faces of my siblings, who all rushed to hold me and hug me and soothe me. And they did. I felt happy. I felt free. And I felt loved. I also felt a huge surge of love for the people surrounding me. And I thought ... *I am home.*

23

Falling in Love

Until my strength was fully back to normal, I was allowed to stay home during the school day as long as I did some academic work, which was sent home daily with my siblings.

As the weather was still mild, and occasionally, the days would be very warm, I would go out of the gate behind the house and sit in the woods. It was very calm and peaceful, with no road noise. No television or radio. And no people! Don't get me wrong, I liked people, but they would always have something to say about how I could speed my recovery by eating this or drinking that or taking some supplement they'd seen on the computer. Alternatively, they would look at me with mock pity and ask if I was feeling better, making little pouty shapes with their lips when I responded.

Computers were new inventions that could do the work of several people and would soon replace books and newspapers, I had heard. It reminded me of something, but I couldn't quite remember what. I still preferred books, and every evening after school, Marc would come through his gate into the woods or to my house and he would do my schoolwork for me. Well, he would tell me what the answers were and I would write them down. Mostly it was boring stuff and if we got the schoolwork out of the way we could spend time together talking.

Marc wanted to be an artist and told me his dream was to go to Paris and New York to study and show his artwork. I didn't have dreams like that. I recalled how I'd wanted to go somewhere beautiful, but I couldn't remember where. Marc brought holiday brochures that he'd got from a travel agent in the town and we would look at all the beautiful places in foreign lands, trying to jog my memory of the places I'd like to visit, places he'd like us to go together.

There was one picture of the ruins of a colosseum with toppled columns made out of a beautiful white stone shimmering in the sunlight beneath the stunning blue, cloudless sky.

"Oh, I've been there," I said, "before the columns fell, it was beautiful and sooo hot."

Marc laughed and said I must be thinking of somewhere else because those columns had fallen hundreds or thousands of years ago and this was in Greece. Mum said I'd never been to Greece. In fact, our family had never been out of the county we were born in and certainly never abroad. That felt wrong, but I didn't know why. I was sure I had been there. I could even see the people I was there with. But it didn't make sense. Mum said I had an active imagination and that was probably it.

As autumn turned to winter, Marc began spending more time at my house and with my family. We were slowly opening all the presents and envelopes that had been delivered to me at the hospital. It was an emotionally tiring task as every present and every envelope came with a letter. Some were a very simple, 'I hope you get well soon' or 'sending you lots of love'. Some had more information about the reason I had been in hospital or about how awful Beastman had been. How fortunate we were to be rid of him from our lives. They were quite difficult to read, but we read them anyway as a family. There were also letters from people, both young and old and every age in between, who had had similar family backgrounds. Similar upbringings. These were the most difficult to read. Marc struggled to understand how one human being could affect so many people. How one family member could cause so much pain to the others. Why didn't they just leave? He would ask, time and again.

But we knew. My mother. My siblings. And me. It was almost as if there was a chain tied to each and every one of us. If one person tried to 'escape', it would pull tighter around the necks and the hearts of the others. You didn't try to leave because unconsciously you knew how much pain it caused the others. And not one of you was strong enough to form a team. To stand up and deny the 'controller' their power. You didn't know that you could and you didn't know what would happen if you did.

Marc's eyes would fill with tears as he read some of the stories. He would ask, "Is this what it was like for you?" or, "Did your family suffer like this?" and occasionally, he would stand up and, without a word, he would leave the room. Leave the house. And return to his own home, two doors away. Because what we were reading was hard. Even for my family and I. It was people's lives. Their stories. Told to us in confidence. Because only those who had suffered could understand. Only those who sailed in the same boat could steer their ship in the same direction. Or. Quite often. Directionless.

As well as the letters there was an enormous amount of gifts. All received with such joy and gratitude both by myself and my family – we couldn't believe that people with so little themselves would try to bring love and joy to another. It swelled our hearts and our education! Some gifts, like teddy bears and dolls – all beautiful but far too many for one girl and her siblings – we gave away to a local charity in the town that looked after women and children who suffered domestic abuse. That is just a nice way of saying they were beaten and shouted at and put down until they believed they were worthless. Domestic abuse makes it sound less horrific, less hurtful for those who have never suffered it and can't understand why you would ever put up with it in the first place.

There was also money in a lot of the envelopes. Some coins. A little girl had drawn me a picture of her holding my hand and saying, 'Please get better'. That picture made me cry, but the envelope also held a copper coin. That made my heart cry. Others held pound coins. Fifty pence coins. Notes from five through to fifty. We sat 'wowing' over the fifty-pound note for days. We put it on the shelf above the fire – tucked behind the clock – so we could see it and wonder at such a large sum of money. We weren't as poor then as we were when we were with him. But we still had never seen a fifty-pound note.

There were also cheques. Some for as little as one pound and some for eye-watering amounts. I didn't know why people had sent money, but Meryl said that people wanted us to know that we were thought of and that people wanted us to have a good life after the difficulties that we'd been through. She actually said 'horrors', blushed a deep rosy red from her chest to her cheeks, stuttered a bit and changed it to 'difficulties'. But she was right the first time. Horrors.

Roger had a friend who was a solicitor. He came round to the house to see me about the money. As a family we had never had so much money and we weren't sure if we were supposed to give it back or give it away or how we were supposed to use it. Roger's friend explained all the legal stuff to us. I wanted all my family to be there – including Marc who all but lived with us now, going to his parent's house to sleep but coming round to ours for breakfast. I wanted them all to have a say about the money. I felt it had come to us because of 'him' and therefore it was family money and not just for me.

We had to go through all the letters to see if the donors had specified what to do with it. One lady had asked that I put her donation – the legal term for the money was donations so we started to use that term to describe all the money – toward a good education. So, legally I had to use it for 'advancement of my education' as the lawyer put it. I didn't particularly want to advance my education any further than the school gates on my sixteenth birthday, but apparently there were ways around it, according to the lawyer. We set up a fund for my education, to which all donors requesting such in their letters would be deposited.

Some letters suggested the money should be spent on a break, or a holiday, or some time away... so that went into a separate account, which we'd labelled 'family jollies'. The lawyer suggested all the monies should go into bank accounts so that it was 'traceable' especially if the government were to become involved. I didn't really understand why the government would be interested in donated money that had already been taxed, but I wanted everything to be right.

Any monies without a suggestion of purpose were put into a third account, and we'd talk about what to do with that later. But we kept some cash back to buy a meal at the local pub. We had never eaten in a public eatery before and were very nervous about it. Marc booked a table for us, talked us through what we should expect and helped us choose our meals from the menu. We all ate starters and shared a spoon or forkful with our siblings when we found something delicious. We all ate a different main meal, which in itself was exciting as we usually all sat down to one meal at home. If you didn't like it you left it for a sibling to share out and finish up. We kind of did the same thing here. Except this was public. We were all excited. And other diners in the pub kept looking over at us. By the time we had finished our main courses, we were feeling a little deflated by the stares and whispers around us. It reminded me of years ago when some parents at a party made rude comments about me. I think my siblings had similar experiences, as they also began to quiet down at the same time. Mum decided we should have pudding at home, and after paying the bill, Marc and the two elder siblings went to the local supermarket to buy a pudding with the remnants of our meal money whilst Mum and I walked home with the littles.

"Marc is good for you," Mum said as we were walking, bellies full and feeling sated, although our minds were a little deflated.

"You are like a different person these days," she continued. "You used to be so quiet and never talk to anyone. You would sit in your room reading and talking to yourself."

I stopped. Something scratched at the back of my brain. What was it? There was something there that I could remember if only I reached a bit further. But it was gone. Mum was still talking.

She was asking me how I felt about Marc. Did I love him? Did I think I would want to spend the rest of my life with him? We had just turned the corner of our street, and I grabbed the hands of the littles and shouted, "Race you home!". They both screamed, broke free from my grasp and pelted at full pace along the pavement. I ran behind shouting, "I'm coming to get you," in my 'monster' voice and their joyful screams increased in volume and sharpness!

24

Growing Up

Marc's art began to take on a new depth. A new style. There was a darkness to his work that screamed of suffering and love. It was almost four years since my stint in hospital and the death of Beastman. Marc was in his second year of college. I was in my final year of secondary education and my siblings were all in a 'happy place' figuratively and emotionally speaking.

Mum had met another man – it was actually the man from the spiritualist church that our neighbours had fancied. Mum continued to go to the church after our first visit, made many more friends, and, as well as doing a couple of hours cleaning for Mrs Marton, took a job at Summer Meadows, the local care home for the elderly. She was an independent woman for the first time in her life and had a partner she loved (and who loved her) to share it with her. Life was good.

Marc had been offered an exhibition of his work in a swanky London gallery. The owner of the gallery had been visiting his nephew, who studied at the same college as Marc when he spotted a piece of Marc's work, which he had called 'Love in Blue'. It was taken from a drawing he had done of me when I was in the hospital all those years ago. He had sketched me during one of his visits when we had a moment of that silence where you feel comfortable … I had turned to look through the window. The image he had captured showed a beautiful young woman but with haunted eyes – you could see a calmness and yet a terror within them, which magnified the beauty of the whole piece. I think it was William Shakespeare who said that 'the eyes are the window to the Soul' – I'm not a Shakespeare fan, though, so don't quote me on that! But in this painting, you could almost see beyond the now to a different life. It was strange to look at, not because it was an image of me; I didn't see it as an image of me but as a beautiful piece of art, but because it felt like there were living Souls in those eyes. Yes, Souls, plural. Not one, not two, but many. Having each lived a life of his own and shed his shell and become locked within another shell which didn't belong to them. I don't know where that idea came from. It wasn't something that I understood, if I'm honest with you. But the gallery owner had said something about it being a masterpiece to be admired by the many rather than being locked away in a backwater college in the middle of nowhere.

Marc and I laughed about that. How funny to think that we lived in a backwater town in the middle of nowhere when it was the only place either of us had ever known. He had seen more of Marc's artwork – there was a series of me in the hospital, each called 'Love in ...' and a colour with a matching floral study on a separate canvas. The floral studies had been meant for me, as each image had initially been sketched from the posies he'd put together from the bouquets at the hospital. Each image was slightly different, capturing a different element, texture, and shade and highlighting something different in the eyes. 'Love in Pink', for example, was my favourite. Instead of paint, he used inks and watercolours, which gave it a very definite yet translucent feeling. You could almost see through the image in the portrait, but her eyes were also translucent. Striking. But translucent. If you looked too long into the eyes, you could almost see a different world. His paintings were exciting, inspiring, beautiful and, I think, if I say 'articulate', it would not be the wrong word.

About the same time, he won a scholarship to a top London art school. Life was exciting and time moving swiftly. We would spend more and more time together contemplating our future. We had spoken of marriage and children and living together in a home of our own filled with Marc's beautiful artwork.

As I was nearing sixteen, we decided that Marc would go to London for his first year at art school by himself and when he returned home the next summer we would marry and I would return with him to London – man and wife.

In the meantime, I would get a job at the care home where my mother and our other neighbour, Sherry, worked. They were always desperate for care workers to help and support the elderly residents and having helped out in the kitchens for the last two summers alongside my elder sister, they knew I would not let them down.

25

Work

I walked out of the school gates aged fifteen and three quarters, with no real qualifications to my name. Don't get me wrong. I wasn't stupid. I knew most of the answers to most of the questions on all the exam papers, but I just didn't understand the purpose of the qualifications. I asked the teachers. I asked the principal. I asked the careers advisor. They all had qualifications coming out of their ears – not literally, I hasten to add, but they were supposed to be the educated and academic superstars of our town. So, it annoyed me when they couldn't understand simple questions or requests. I wanted to know, for example, why the earth was formed and how and by whom. I wanted to know why Jesus was pictured as a blonde-haired, blue-eyed white man and why he was considered the son of God and not a bastard. Why did politicians never answer the questions they were asked and no one admonished them for it? Of course, they would give me answers when they weren't telling me off for swearing! But their answers were lacking! I can't describe how or why or what, exactly, it was that I wanted to know. But I wanted to know something. There was a repetition to their answer, as though they had all read the same books and were repeating what they had read or heaving out their political parties' specific ideologies rather than giving me their thoughts or their truth. And if they couldn't help me or answer my questions, they couldn't be that smart, could they? And if they weren't that smart and had spent almost half their lives in academic institutions of one sort or another, what was the point of a piece of paper that said you were smart when you weren't?

So ... no qualifications, but I had a job. The hours were good, my mum said. The money was good, my mum said. Better if you did overnighters, but she wouldn't recommend them until I was familiar with the job itself. The old folk were ever so lovely and would be delighted to have such a young person on the team, said the manager. But I think he was delighted to have someone so young on the team as he could pay me less than the other staff. I was actually quite excited to have a job and to be earning money. Not that money was a problem. We hadn't touched any of the donated money yet. I think we were still worried that people would want it back, but no one had asked so far, and it was building quite nicely in the high-interest bank accounts we had.

Marc had left for London the weekend before, and in two days, I was due to start work at Summer Meadows – so-called because it used to be part of The Manor House estate many years ago. Wildflowers grew voraciously there during the old summers, and it was often a place courting couples would visit, the young man picking a posy of wildflowers to demonstrate his love. Young brides would also pick from the fields on their marriage days to provide their wedding spray.

Mum was feeling sick, so she asked my sister and me to go to Mrs Marton's house to do her daily clean. My sister had helped out before—when I was in hospital—so she knew what we needed to do, Mum said, and I just had to do as I was told.

We arrived at the front door at nine-fifteen in the morning, and Mrs Marton let us in. Mum had already warned her that she was sending her two daughters, so there were three cups with teabag strings hanging over the side, sitting on the kitchen table as we were ushered in. The freshly boiled water was poured in as Mrs Marton and my sister made small talk. I looked around the room, racking my brain as to why I had such fond memories of it. But nothing was springing to mind.

Mrs Marton picked up her cup, told us she would leave us to it and walked out of the kitchen. My elder sibling took a long, loud slurp of her tea, declaring that this was the best cuppa she had ever tasted and that she was going to find out which teabags Mrs Marton used so we could get some for home. I took a slightly more gentrified slurp of my tea, which I agreed was delicious, as I was handed a tin bucket and requested to fill it with hot water and soap.

I picked up the tin bucket and began walking toward the large porcelain Belfast sink beneath the kitchen window. My sister laughed out loud, telling me we didn't put the dirty mop bucket near the clean kitchen sink. I looked to the window above the sink, covered in dainty French lace curtains that had cost more than I would ever earn in my whole lifetime, I thought, but shook it away, thinking what a stupid thing to think!

"Haven't you been in the utility before?" she asked me. I flushed a shade of pink – I was supposed to know all about this house because I had been here so often, but I didn't know there was a utility. I didn't even know what a utility was!

To the side of the back door, the door I usually used to enter the house, there was another door set into the adjacent wall. I told myself it would have been hidden by the open external door when I had entered previously. I had never taken notice of it before, but my sister, having grabbed the bucket from me, walked through and I heard the sound of water flowing. Following her in, I found a room about the size of our kitchen at home; it had wall-to-floor cupboards on one side and a sink on the other. A third wall housed a long bench with boots and shoes underneath. Some were covered in dried mud, clumps of which had fallen to the floor.

My sister was pouring a powder into the bucket; swirling steam was beginning to rise, and suds were beginning to form.

"Right." My sister handed the bucket back to me with a mop. "If you start mopping the floors down here, I'll go ahead of you with the brush and vacuum. Start in the kitchen, through into the hall, then the front parlour. The other downstairs rooms have carpets," she continued. I was taken aback by her confidence, her organisation skills and leadership abilities. It is strange to see your siblings outside of your usual cocoon – seeing the person for the first time in a real-world setting and finding out who they really are. My heart swelled with pride at the person she was becoming.

I realised she was still talking. Still instructing. I hadn't heard what she said. She looked at me, shaking her head.

"Just clean the downstairs floors, then empty out the bucket. Swill it round and refill it with soap and hot water. I should be back by then." She flounced out of the utility and started sweeping the kitchen floor with a speed and dexterity I didn't think I would ever be able to match. Then she disappeared out into the hallway and I was left alone with my mop and steaming bucket.

I was still mopping the kitchen floor when she returned. She was upset that I had still got over a third of the floor to mop but laughed when she realised that I had been moving all the furniture out of the way to clean each part of the floor. The chairs were very heavy and I'd had to move the table in six small turns on each side. I would lift the table at one end to shuffle it a bit. Then run round to the other end, lift and shuffle. Run to the other end … each shuffle would move it about an inch. When I explained that I was trying to clean the floor beneath the table legs, she guffawed so loudly and for so long I worried she would rupture something internally! Apparently, jobs like that would be done only once or twice a year. Because the table was too heavy for us to lift, Mrs Marton would employ two men to come into the house and lift heavy furniture out of the way so that the walls behind and the floors beneath could be properly cleaned of dust and dirt. The dust, she explained to me, is what smelled the worst.

We slowly moved the table back into position and stood for a moment, drinking the remnants of our cooling but thoroughly delicious tea. She offered to mop the rest of the downstairs rooms if I would clean the table legs and wipe down all the cupboard doors. She was finished before me again and I was beginning to think I wasn't very good at working. I hoped that Summer Meadows wasn't going to be like this or I'd never finish any task.

We decided … in all fairness, I was told, but in a very nice way … that I would do the polishing and dusting upstairs while she would finish the wet work, as she called it, and then she would join me with the dusting. She showed me how to do it 'properly' – spraying the liquid wax into the cloth (not on the floor!) and then wiping over the wood. Turning the cloth and buffing off the remnants with a clean part – and carrying her newly steaming, soapy bucket directed me to the first room upstairs.

I had just started on the large wooden frame of the bed – a sixteenth-century half-tester made of oak, the most prevalent wood around this part of the country at the time it was made and was wondering if I would have to stand on the bed itself, all beautifully made up with plain but very expensive looking bedding, to polish the ceiling height, beautifully carved wooden headboard – when the door opened and a lady walked in. She was quite tall, with dark hair which curled around her face. She wore trousers and bright red lipstick. That's all that I remember before she disappeared. Poof. One minute here. One minute gone. And I'm ashamed to say I screamed!

26

The Reawakening

The moment the scream left my lips, a thousand memories came flooding back in. I felt as though I had woken from a dream that I wasn't a part of. I saw Arrien. I saw the scullery maid. I saw other spirit people. Ghosts. The woman with the dark hair.

Both my sister and Mrs Marton arrived through the door at the same time. Fear and concern on both their faces. My face an ashen white and my eyes wide. But I had calmed myself. I was back to myself.

"I saw ...." I started but didn't know how to finish.

"Oh! I'm so sorry," the younger of the two living women apologised. "I forgot, I hate this room. I'm sure it's haunted, Mrs Marton. I said that before, didn't I?"

"Yes, I'm sure you're right," Mrs Marton smiled and suggested I have a hot sweet tea and a sit down with her so she could be sure I was alright. My sister refused a second cup of tea as she wanted to get the work finished quickly, knowing she would have to finish off my work too.

Sat in the kitchen with the cup of tea – even more delicious with an extra sugar to calm my shock, Mrs Marton looked closely at me. She looked as though she wanted to say something but didn't know how or even if! A smile broke across my face.

"I haven't read anything for a while," I said as an icebreaker. "I'm not sure I've really been myself for this last couple of years." I was looking at her to check her reaction. I felt like I had suddenly woken up from a dream, but wasn't sure if this was the dream. I felt sort of soft and warm yet strange. It wasn't a feeling I was familiar with. Yet it was very familiar. There were spirits all around the kitchen. Some were here with and for me. Some were with Mrs Marton. They were all smiling. I can't remember why I hadn't seen them this morning. Or for the last couple of years. But I remembered them with a huge surge of love.

"No, I don't believe you have. I think a little healing would be appropriate." She smiled.

When my sister returned to the kitchen to check on me a few minutes later, Mrs Marton suggested she call it a day for today and get herself away. She would keep an eye on me for an hour or so and see if she could get a bit more work out of me, she laughed, winking conspiratorially to my sister. They both grinned and she nodded. As she was putting on her coat, my sister came across the kitchen and gave me a shoulder hug, telling me to behave and take care before leaving through the front door.

Mrs Marton suggested we go through to the library and as I walked through the door I was hit by a thousand memories all at once. I struggled to understand why and how I had forgotten about the books and the spirits and The Light House.

"Sometimes we become rather reliant on other people and their energy," she said, indicating that I should climb up on a massage table that I had never seen before. I was beginning to think that Mrs Marton's house really was magic because everything you needed seemed to appear just when you needed it.

"I give energy healing," she said in the way of explanation. "Usually in the front parlour. Where you were supposed to mop this morning," she smiled with a twinkle in her eye. She explained that sometimes we become so entwined in another person, usually when we are in love, although at other times when a person has a really powerful energy that just 'overtakes' us. When this happens we can be totally oblivious to everything and everyone around us, but also the energy of the other person can dim our light and our talents. We share our energy with that person, and they sometimes share theirs with us. She looked at me when she said the word 'sometimes' and I wondered why.

"How is Marc doing at college?" she asked out of the blue. I hadn't been thinking about him through all of this. He was usually uppermost in my thoughts. And it suddenly hit me like a bullet train at full speed. Marc had always been a good artist. That is something I can't deny. But once he started to spend time with me, with my family, in our home, his pictures began to take on a new life. They breathed. They spoke. They were alive with a beauty that was incomparable. Everyone who saw his recent artworks were taken aback and speechless, finding it difficult to put into words what they were seeing and feeling.

"So ...." I began, and then wasn't sure how to verbalise my thoughts. She smiled and told me to lie down on the table, close my eyes and relax. The table was about as long as her kitchen table and about the same height but wide enough to hold one adult body. The top had been upholstered in a soft plush fabric with firm but comfortable padding, and the lower three quarters were covered in a blanket. It was more comfortable than my bed at home, I thought. She placed another blanket over my feet, a soft pillow beneath my head and asked me to take deep breaths in ... and out. Deep breath in ... and out. I could feel my body relaxing, and I thought I might go to sleep, but I tried to keep myself aware as I wanted to know what this healing entailed.

"Go to sleep if you wish," she told me. "I will explain what I'm doing and you can watch with your spirit guide."

I wasn't sure what she meant, but I felt myself falling gently. Being pulled backwards would be a more precise description, so I reached out a hand to steady myself. I felt another hand take hold of mine and pull me upright. Standing in front of me, as real as I could ever imagine, was Arrien. She looked 'alive' and was wearing the clothing I had last seen her in – when we were in The Light House library several years ago. She was smiling at me, still holding my hand, but she turned her body slightly and I saw that we were standing in Mrs Marton's library. Mrs Marton was standing at the head of the massage table and my body was laid upon it, looking very peaceful with a soft red blanket placed over my feet.

"You are still alive but having an out-of-body experience," Mrs Marton said as she placed her hands either side of my head. I looked down at the body I was standing in – it was mine. Dressed identically to the body laid on the bed. She started to explain that my physical body was still suffering pains and problems from my earlier illnesses and this could be seen in my auric body. My lungs were weak, she said. She asked the 'me' who was standing up to come closer and look at the 'me' on the massage table. It felt a bit weird to see myself as other people saw me. I thought the body on the table looked pretty, my body slim and shapely – when the physical me looked in the mirror, I only saw my slightly upturned nose, my eyes looked too wide apart and small, I could see open pores and the beginnings of spots and blackheads on my teenage face. Chunky thighs, a big bottom and flat-chested was how I imagined I looked. But in the real-life mirror, I couldn't see any of these things. *How strange*, I thought, *that we judge ourselves so harshly when we see ourselves with our hypercritical human eyes.* We would not consider – or at least I would not consider – saying the things I say to myself to another person. The thought made me smile.

"When you have stopped admiring yourself," Mrs Marton smiled but had her eyes closed, "look at your aura, tell me what you see."

In my living body I could only see a thin line around people. Usually, I would observe what appeared to be a white or creamy light around them. Sometimes it would be darker, muddier – that would be the people I would avoid where possible. But, now that I was asked to look, in my out-of-body body I saw what I can only describe as a cloud of rainbow. There appeared to be layer upon layer of coloured film radiating out from my physical body. It encircled the body on the bed, appearing to be going through the table below. It reached out about an arm's length in front, behind, to the sides, above and below the body.

I can only describe it as the body being inside a giant soap bubble. You know the ones you would blow as a child? You would dip a plastic stick with an open circle on one end into a tub of soapy liquid. You would pull out the dripping stick, the excess liquid pouring over your hands, the soap would form a film across the open circle. You would lift it to your lips and blow. Sometimes you blew too hard and sent the soapy liquid flying like spittle. Sometimes you blew too softly and the liquid would just drip. If you blew just right, the film across the circular end would bend into an arc and then detach from the stick, wobbling as it instantly formed into a perfectly misshaped circular bubble which would continue to wobble and shimmer with a multitude of swirling colours catching in the sunlight as it floated away.

The body on the table was like that – surrounded by beautiful, shimmering, glowing colour. I moved a little closer and reached out my ghostly hand. I realised I was not 'physical' but almost clear in contrast to the bodies of Mrs Marton and my other 'self'. I placed my hand onto or into the glow around the body. I could feel a light pulsating vibration. The closer my hand went to the body, the lighter and less noticeable the feeling. *The closer the vibrations are to the body,* I thought, *the further away from the light they are.*

Mrs Marton chuckled. "Nearly," she said. "But we'll talk about that later. What do you notice about your aura?"

I noticed it had a few darker spots around the torso. I bent my knees so I could see through the cloak of coloured lights and noticed the dark spots were in different areas on different levels or colours. I noticed layers of colour rather than the mixed colour of the soap bubble analogy. Closer to the body was a reddish colour, moving toward orange, then yellow, green, blue, indigo, then violet, fading out to a bright white, which seemed to also run through all the different layers.

I could hear, feel and sense the vibrating of the coloured layers. The red was a low hum. I found it annoying. The violet colour sounded more relaxing, a hiss, but comforting with a hint of voices behind it.

"Each colour has a purpose for your body," Mrs Marton continued. Apparently, the state of your physical body and its health could affect the colours in your aura. Although all the colours were always there, sometimes one frequency would be louder or more evident than another. The lower frequency colours, like red and orange, are about very earthly and human traits, like money, love and security. The higher the frequency of the colour, the closer it becomes to the spiritual, the empathic part of oneself, to heaven and the Angels if that helps your understanding. Each colour was able to work independently of the other centres, but the body worked much better when they all worked harmoniously and in alignment.

It was then that I saw, from my prone body, what looked like mini whirlwinds swirling in and out of my body, both through the back of my body and the front – each whirlwind held a different colour. Low down by my body's groin, the whirlwind was a swirling red colour – it moved quite slowly in comparison to the higher colours. It sucked in the red from the aura and pushed it out through the back of the body. The red would then circle the body – it was in constant motion – being sucked back into the front vortex. A little higher up, near my naval, the whirlwind was orange. It moved faster than the red but performed in the same manner – except the orange colour sat atop the red in the aura cloud. Next was the stomach area, where the whirlwind was yellow. This spun faster than the orange and as it moved out of the body, it sat atop the orange layer. At the heart, there was a green whirlwind. At the throat, blue. On the forehead, between the eyes, an indigo colour. At the top of the head, facing away from the scalp and moving extremely fast, was a violet colour. I felt my breath stop – I recognised this one. This frequency. This vibration. This colour. I had touched it. I had felt it. I had reached inside it.

That was the connection to the Light Room, I thought. That is the highest vibration and the closest to the vibration of the beyond. The afterlife. The forever life. The truth. Home. I smiled and stood up. I understood everything. Yet very little. So much understanding of my purpose – the purpose of all humans – was so near and yet just out of reach, like a word on the tip of your tongue. It's almost there, tantalising, yet it darts away like a blue flash in the corner of your vision.

Mrs Marton had moved around the table now and had placed her hands over the Green swirling vortex on my chest – I noticed that it was wobbling slightly – not quite in line with the other vortexes. Whirlwinds. Not quite turning properly. *It is out of sync*, I thought. *Misaligned*. The one between my eyes had also been wonky, I remember thinking, but that had now begun to swirl fast and straight with a beautiful sound emanating from it. Mrs Marton's physical hands were pulsating, but out of her physical hands came her spiritual hands – like mist, clear yet visible. Her spiritual hands were picking at the dark patches in the auras around my chest. The darkness was sticky like tar but came away in pieces like cotton wool. Ripping and leaving fragments. As her spiritual hands removed the dark pieces, she passed them behind her to a spirit being. This was a being of light – there was a vague shape of human about it, an oval shape attached to a long rounded oblong which suggested a head, shoulders and body, but made completely of light, but not physical as in The Light Room, I can only describe this as an echo of a being. Does that make sense to you? Can you understand that? Anyway, this echo of a Being of Light was taking the dark, oily, tarry cotton wool pieces and placing them into what looked like a net bag made of strands of light. After two or three pieces were placed inside the top of the net would tighten, as though a string had been fed through a hem and pulled tight. I heard a prayer inside Mrs Marton's head, *I ask that this dark energy be taken to the light, transform and transmute it to love and redistribute it where it is most needed.* She repeated this with every placement of the dark mass into the bag. When each bag had been filled and sealed, the being holding it would shimmer brighter and slowly rise upwards, becoming brighter and brighter until it disappeared. *It has reached a vibrational frequency too high for me to see,* I thought and felt extremely satisfied with myself for working that out.

Looking back at Mrs Marton – she had moved down to my body's stomach area and held her hands in a higher position. I remembered the solar plexus from one of the books I had read in this library. The vortex was yellow and her hands were above this inside the yellow layer. I began to notice her own layers of energy around her physical body. They had attached to my layers and were vibrating at the perfect frequency – allowing my energy layers to re-learn how to vibrate at the correct frequency. *This is very clever,* I thought. I then noticed that beneath the table, her feet seemed to be covered in tree roots. I looked again to make sure that this was what I was seeing.

"She is grounded." Arrien was stood beside me, still holding my hand. "She envisions roots coming out of her body like the roots of a tree and she pushes them deep into the earth to keep her here. Otherwise she may get too caught up in the spiritual." She pointed above Mrs Marton's head, where I noticed a thick shaft of light of pure love and oneness of all mankind – that is the only way I can describe it – was pulsating down from the ceiling and being funnelled into the violet vortex on top of Mrs Marton's head. The excess spilt, like liquid, over her head, down and over her shoulders, where it floated out slightly before flowing down her form – *like wings,* I thought. It was filling her up from the inside. I was able to see through her skin to her insides. I was able to see the light coming in through her head, entering every organ, bone, muscle, and atom of her body. Then, emanating outwards, through her skin and into her aura and then further into the room in which we all stood. The light went further – through the walls, through the ceiling, through the roof, forming a shield of invisible white light around the whole building and stretching down to the pavement at the front of the building.

I realised I had travelled in my Soul form to the outside of the house to watch this phenomenon. I saw a neighbour, I never knew her name, but she wore a triangular-shaped scarf, tied under her chin with a double knot every day, whatever the weather. She had dropped a bag of her shopping, the contents scattering everywhere. Two apples had rolled beneath a car parked on the street and she had missed them in her rush to pick up her groceries.

Arrien's voice brought me back to the library where Mrs Marton was now standing back at the head of the table. I looked toward my body, where the colours of the aura looked shinier, more vibrant. The dark patches completely gone. Then I felt a pulling sensation in my tummy.

I opened my eyes and felt slightly disorientated. I was lying down. My body felt heavy after the lightness of being so free. Mrs Marton took my hand, helping me down from the table and into the comfortable armchair in which I had previously sat.

"You will need to drink a lot of water," she said, passing me a tall, slim glass full of water.

"I have cleared a lot of low energy from you. More than I would for a normal client in one session, so you will need to be very careful. You might get tired, feel emotional or have memories of things that might upset you." I smiled at her, feeling more relaxed than ever in my life.

"Thank you," I said, then asked, "Why? Why would I feel emotional, actually, what was that stuff you took off me? And where does it go? And what ..."

"Whoa, whoa, whoa!" she began to laugh. She had a lovely way of laughing that made you feel as though you were part of the understanding and not the thing being laughed at – a memory prickled my eye.

She took my hand in hers and looked me in the eye. I tried to stifle back the tear that had formed, but she told me to let it go. When bad things happen to us, she told me, we hold them in the body and in our auric fields – the rainbow of colours I could see around us when she was healing me, but also the glow that I would normally see around people. When something is held in our auras, it can grow quite big and then move into the physical body. The darkness around my heart was apparently to do with the feelings of neglect and abandonment of my father and the feelings of abandonment of the Soul of my mother, along with the mental, emotional and physical pain caused by witnessing my siblings being hurt and the physical 'death' of my mother, and the fear and disappointment of other things she said but didn't mention. Although I had coped immensely well on the physical plane, trying to be strong for my siblings, she continued, I had held onto that pain and fear for a long time and the pneumonia was one way of it transferring to my physical body as an illness. She told me that the dark matter in my aura was what had encouraged other lower-frequency beings to come to me. They feed off the low energy and encourage the darkness and fear within you to grow.

"So!" I suddenly had an epiphany. "When I was in the Light Room, they told me that they were having to send more and more Souls to earth because of the fear that was happening to mankind right now. But as each one is being born, they are coming into contact with people who are already frightened and passing on not only their physical fear but also the fear and darkness within their aura."

"Exactly!" She beamed, along with all the beings in the room.

"So, we don't stand a chance." I felt deflated all of a sudden, my moment of genius hit by the doom of 'No Hope Hotel'. "If we are breeding the fear and darkness, then there is no way out. It will just get thicker and darker and stickier."

"Potentially!" She smiled knowingly. I furrowed my brows and pursed my lips, causing her to laugh again.

"People like you and people like me. We are an exception. We have the ability to lift people out of their darkness and misery. Teach them that there is light and truth and a way of living that doesn't have to be so dark." She stood up and began pacing around the room. "People are like sheep." She had furrowed her brow and was talking as though to herself. "They read their newspapers and listen to their news channels and watch inane programs about people who are either largely suffering or living a life beyond the means and abilities of the majority of the world. They watch these people and say, "Thank God that isn't me", or "Why, God, can't I live in a house like that?". All the while comparing themselves to other people. Whether it is the way somebody dresses or how big their tits are. Whether they have a better car or live in a bigger house. We are constantly judging ourselves against our friends, our neighbours and strangers on the television."

She sucked in a deep breath and sighed out a deeper breath.

"We are not meant to be stuck here on this planet, being miserable every day!" She had a tear in her eye and looked so sad and lost in that moment. She shook her head, took in a deep breath and let out another great sigh, her lips pushing out with the air from her lungs.

"So, what is the purpose of mankind?" I enquired. I knew at the back of my mind but wasn't able to put it into words. I hadn't fully remembered it.

"That." She pointed a finger at me. "That is our purpose." She twirled around on her toes, graceful, like a ballerina, in a fairy tale where the big bad witch hadn't yet entered the story. "We are supposed to remember. We are supposed to remember where we come from. We are supposed to feel the love and beauty of this place that was made specifically for us. To remember. And when we remember we can be, do and have anything we choose. Because we have the power." She started to frown again. "Power. People think power ..." she lifted up the middle and index fingers of both hands and bent them to each syllable of the word power in order to exaggerate it, "is about controlling other people and things. They think power is about owning more things…" She used her hands again to exaggerate things. "More things means you are better," hands again to exaggerate better. "Than people with less."

She started to talk about how we attempt to gain power over other people by taking from them. Either taking actual things, like their homes, their jobs, their land, or their belongings. But also by humiliation, emotional abuse and also by physical hurt. Sometimes, she said we would suck their body's energy – like the greys had done with Karen's mum's boyfriend. All of these things lead to fear and anger in the people who have been taken from. But the takers also fear retribution. That those they have taken from will try to take back what is rightfully theirs, or someone bigger and more 'powerful' than them will take what now 'belongs' to them.

This, she continued, is why armies were formed. The so-called powerful people cannot keep all they have gathered from others by themselves, so they find people who will fight for them. Protect them. Encouraging them to do so with promises of possessions for themselves or promised positions of power. Advising that the enemy will harm and steal from them and their families too. Will kill their families. Making the fear stronger. Pushing out all memories of the love and peace that they once knew.

Initially, she began, the chiefs of the small clans and tribes across the world would share the creation stories as they were told to them, but some began to distort them slowly in order to gain more of something that their tribe held dear. It may have been food, a mate, or a bigger shelter. As time wore on, they began to change the stories to make themselves the centre of the story – the centre of that particular tribe's world. They began to ask for worship, sacrifice or other gifts. The better the gift or sacrifice given, the more likely the giver would be to have more food, more children, more … whatever that giver deemed important. And so, that is how the world began to form. Tribes grew bigger, councils of tribesmen were formed to make rules for the ever-expanding groups. Cities were formed, technologies grew and always a group of men making rules and forming plans to enhance their lives and putting down and making smaller any person or group who spoke up about inequality or suffering.

We think of inhumanity and suffering as being a new phenomenon, Mrs Marton continued. The way we, the white society, have treated black people, for instance. But white man was taught how to enslave people through the black man's own countrymen. When tribes fought on the African continent – long before the Europeans knew of the land – they would capture the warriors from the losing side. Often, they would control them themselves. Sometimes they would exchange them like currency with other tribes. Or gift these men, women and children to other tribes as offerings. Payment to pacify tribes they couldn't fight and win. These are stories that have been passed down, she said. I wanted to feel horrified as we were taught that white people were the bringers of this plague of slavery, but then I remembered the bible. Egypt was built by slaves long before the white man conquered the Americas and planted fields of sugar.

"Yes!" Mrs Marton had heard my thoughts again! "But it doesn't make it better! The whole world, tribes of every colour, have, at some point or another, throughout history, enslaved, murdered, raped and stolen. Not just land and people but ideas. They have ripped apart whole communities because they want to own this idea or want to cull that idea. This land is more acceptable than that land. This belief will take away my power, but that belief will make my power stronger. It is still happening today. War after war and we still fight for the same idiots over the same stupid things."

She collapsed, exhausted by her tirade, into her armchair. Then she sprung up with renewed vigour as a new thought caught hold.

Religion, apparently, was as much to blame. By using the Higher Power of a god with which to threaten and accuse the common man, those entrusted to listen and share the word of this 'god' were able to manipulate everyone and everything. If you don't behave this way or that way, you will go to hell. If you behave this way and revere me as the bringer of your deity's message, I can ensure you a seat in heaven. In fact, if you give me money to build a house for your deity, you can speak to him yourself. He won't answer you, though. He will only answer me. So, build me a house, too, so that I can be comfortable while listening to the message from your god and bring it directly to you in a sermon on Sunday.

She collapsed again. Spent. Breathing heavily and sobbing quietly.

"You see, this is what my forefathers were searching for." Her face was shining, beads of sweat sitting obediently on her damp skin, like dogs waiting to be given the signal before rushing viciously to attack. One bead broke free and rode down her face in a long, swift streak that left a line of her bare skin showing through her mask of foundation. She rushed across to a shelf laden with leather-bound books that reminded me of the spirit library and selected two beautifully bound tomes. Large. Heavy. And deposited them in my lap. I lifted the cover of the topmost book. The smell hit me first, I have to interject. The scent of freshly skinned lamb. The meat coated in exotic spices that I could taste even though I had never seen, smelt or tasted them in my current life. The skin dried, cured, coloured and made into the beautiful leather that bound this book. The meat eaten with friends of all colours. All countries. All searching for the same answers. This was a diary. I read every page in an instant. Seeing, hearing, scenting, tasting every entry; recounting days of travelling, meeting, arguing, agreeing, understanding. Changing some viewpoints or increasing the validity of others. Accusations of heresy, threats of death. But never any fear. You cannot fear the truth.

Only moments had passed since the books landed on my lap, but I was mentally and physically exhausted from the journey. Mrs Marton looked apologetic, abruptly grabbed the books from me and started to say sorry. Twice. Three times. Four times.

"I'm supposed to be helping you, healing you, and here I am, burdening you with this." She hugged the books close to her.

"I'm supposed to be starting my job tomorrow," I said, trying to change the subject. "The lady who woke me upstairs. With the dark hair. She's your mother," I said. Not questioning.

"She was the last one to do any research." She looked sad. "I wasn't interested, you see. When I was younger, this," she waved her hand around the library, "was all any of my family ever talked about. I wanted to be like the other girls, the 'normal' girls, so I insisted on going away to school. Then I married really young. By the time I got back here, Mother was really ill. She taught me about the healing, but there was so much more she could have taught me. So much more I should have asked."

"She taught someone, though?" I asked, but already knew the answer. I picked up the glass of water and swallowed the contents in two huge gulps. I suddenly felt very thirsty and very knowledgeable about what I had to do next.

27

The Calm Before the Storm

It was late when I got home. I'd spent another couple of hours talking with Mrs Marton and making arrangements. I had decided to sit the exams that I had recently refused to take at the earliest opportunity, which would likely be October and November. Not because I wanted to. But because I needed to. I might not think highly of bits of paper saying I was able to answer questions written on other bits of paper, but many people out in the world held those pieces of paper in high regard. So, I would have those certificates. Those qualifications. For them. To prove I was intelligent enough to talk with them. And sit at their tables.

In the meantime, she would contact her mother's original student, who was now living and teaching in Spain, to arrange for me to visit and, hopefully, study with her.

When Marc called from his college digs that evening, as he had promised to do every night, he seemed a little distracted. I could hear voices in the background telling him to hurry up. I told him I'd had a difficult day and was really tired, so he happily took the excuse to hang up after his lengthy 'love you, miss you, can't wait to see you, only 82 days till I'm home again' goodbye. Shortly before he called, I'd had an image of him kissing another girl and heard a voice, not one of my spirits, saying, "he's no longer yours". I felt really sad, but knew it was inevitable that, once in his new world of lights, arts, and stimulating new people, his old world, his old life, would fade into the distance. That pleased me as I had new distractions. Plans that didn't include him. I know you may think I'm cold-hearted again! But in healing my physical body, Mrs Marton and her spirit assembly had unlocked a part of Soul memory. I knew why I was here on earth. And I had to do the best that I could to fulfil that role whilst I had the opportunity to do so. Marc had been a distraction for at least two years and I couldn't allow myself to be distracted any longer.

The following day was the first day at my new job. I was supposed to start at 9am but went in with my mum – Newmum as she had been, but I had decided that I could call her just Mum in my head now, as her Soul had been 'Mum' for as many years as the original Soul 'Mum', so I think she deserved that respect and gratitude.

Mum started her shift at seven-thirty. Part of her morning duties were getting the residents who needed help out of bed, washed, dressed, reminded about medications and getting them into the breakfast room. Sometimes she would help them write letters or help them choose and write messages in birthday cards for loved ones whilst they were waiting for breakfast. Other times she would sit and chat with them, asking about their families or what they had done after she had left the previous day. She was really wonderful with the elderly people. She had a wonderful calmness about her and such a beautiful, empathic personality that I didn't see in my role as her daughter. We often don't see the best parts of our parents when we are children. We are so busy trying to find ourselves and fit into a world we most often don't understand that we are unable to see the love and lessons our parents are trying to teach us. I say parents plural because I learned a lot from Beastman. But the presence of Mum's new boyfriend, Bryn, had taught me lots, too. He had been a stabilising force in the family. He made us all feel safe. He wasn't intrusive and seemed to know intuitively when he should and should not participate in family discussions. I say discussions, but when you have a house full of kids, some of whom are getting hormonal and some of whom are still mentally very young, quite often there would be a tornado of arms and legs flying about, screaming tantrums and toys being broken or used for bribery. But I guess, as an intuitive and medium, he was getting a little support from another realm. Whatever. He would speak with the elder children as adults, enquiring as to their health and whereabouts in the nicest of ways. Giving advice when needed and offering support unconditionally. He was sweet, loving and supportive of the younger ones, too, and not afraid to throw himself into a game of pretend at any given opportunity, even when the older children would tut and roll their eyes. I really admired him for that. For a man thrown headfirst into a damaged family like ours, I have to take off my hat and give him a floor-scraping bow.

As for mum, considering her history of abuse, she was the gentlest of humans and I had so much respect for how she carried herself. I spent my first hour and a half following Mum around and 'helping'. As I was not an official member of staff until I'd had my orientation meeting and induction, I should not have been there, but the manager and staff all knew me and most of the residents were familiar with me from serving lunches during the last two summer holidays.

When I first came to the care home to meet Mum after school for a doctor's appointment, shortly after leaving the hospital two years previously, I had been saddened by the residents. I hadn't realised it at the time, as I was unable to 'see', but they had mostly lost their glow; it was there but dull, not greying like the bad people, but like an unloved diamond allowed to gather dust in a slightly open drawer. They needed a good buff with a clean, lint-free cloth to see if the shine could be brought back. But I realised that they felt weary. Tired of life. Tired of the boredom that comes from not being surrounded by the people and the things that you love or loved you. And tired of a world that had lost its promise. The promise of everything that we still struggle to find. When we are young, we are told to work toward the future. The future is bright. We can do and be anything we want. But as we are working toward that bright future we are told basically that you can be anything you want as long as you fit into this box we've designed for you and don't get above your station.

We are trapped by the very things we aspire to be. Why? Well, it comes back to fear! If those lowly humans learn politics, they may attack the very politicians who have made empty promises. They may take their positions and their votes from the people they want to keep down. I want to tell you about the visit I had to The Light House library, where I looked into the book of future possibilities – I want so much to share that with you. But right now, I need to stay on track!

My first day at work and I was following my mum around, watching what she did and fetching shoes or spectacles, a missing hearing aid, or chatting with the elderly residents when I heard a voice.

"I'm not ready yet, Marguerite." A woman's voice. "No, I won't. Leave me alone." She sounded agitated. Petulant. But she didn't sound as though she was in her body! There is a distinction between the sounds of a living voice and a non-living voice. I'm not sure what it is, so I know I'll struggle to describe it. Perhaps it's a bit 'tinny'. Perhaps more 'distant'. Perhaps it doesn't have the same 'weight' as a living voice. Or maybe it's just that it comes from everywhere and nowhere all at once. Suffice to say, this wasn't a living voice, but it also wasn't quite gone over. It was in that space where the body and the Soul are splitting apart ready for the final departure. I called Arrien to help me find the woman.

Arrien was my spirit guide, and she would only come now when I asked for her. Mrs Marton had taught me how to stop the voices of those in the next world so they wouldn't be with me every second of the day; when I was young, I needed the friendship and reassurance of all my 'friends' and had one foot inside the spirit world. It is difficult to 'live' in both places at once and I needed to be alive. It was the only way I could help the wider world.

Arrien pointed to a door on the right of a long corridor of residential rooms. Each floor of the home was set out in the same way. A long corridor of rooms with an office at one end next to a room full of tables and chairs – the breakfast room – with stairs and a lift at the other end with another room, this time with a large television, comfortable chairs placed in small clusters of twos and threes with side tables, a sofa and bookcase full of modern used paperbacks set against the back wall.

I went first to the office to see if there was a member of staff. I was hoping for a nurse, but the room was empty. I looked into the breakfast room but couldn't see any staff, so I walked two doors back up the corridor and knocked quietly on the door numbered seven.

"Go away!" a whispered spirit voice said abruptly. "Whoever it is will come in and see you!" there was no response from whoever the lady was talking to, so I pressed down the handle and gently pushed open the door.

"Are you both okay?" I asked with my voice, taking in the room and its resident as I entered. On the bed was the prone body with bluish lips, her breathing ragged. She was very close to her end time. Her Soul had started its departure but couldn't seem to leave the body. Sometimes, a Soul will form a deep attachment to the physical body that it inhabits. It can feel a deep sense of loss for the life and the body that it is leaving. This is why you are usually sent a loved one from the other side to guide you into the light where you instantly feel love and compassion for yourself and your former life. Their presence helps you to free yourself from the shell of your body. Looking around I couldn't see anyone or anything else to suggest there had been another being here. Although there was a strange tangy smell that I couldn't place. It wasn't old people smell.

Old people have a smell all of their own; you can smell it in their homes and you can smell it in care homes and hospital wards that deal specifically with older people. It is the smell of decay. But not instant decay. The decay has taken over sixty years to show itself. You see, when we are born we have about ten to fifteen years where our bodies are forming, growing and becoming. After that, our bodies slow down the growth. This is why some people lose their hair, start going grey, or get lines forming on their skin. It's because their bodies have stopped producing what they need to renew all those millions and billions of cells within each body. Think about that time as a kid when you fell and scraped your knee. Your leg bled for a little while, then scabbed over. After a few days or a week, the scab fell off, and your leg felt new again. Fast forward fifty years and your leg bleeds for longer if you fall. It takes longer for the scab to form and longer for the scab to fall off, and the skin beneath stays red and bruise-like, feeling tender to the touch. Then after a while your body stops producing anything that helps growth and renewal. Your bones may start to shrink and become brittle, making them break more easily. The blood vessels around your heart become stiffer, forcing the heart to work harder. The muscles in your bladder weaken, meaning you can't always control when and where you go to the toilet. Your gums begin to shrink back. Your sight and hearing diminish. Your skin becomes paper thin. Your brain stops working the way it once did. Everything starts to slow down. Slowly. It can take a very long time for the body to get to a point where it can no longer continue.

The Soul looked over at me. "What is she looking at?" It was not a question. Not polite. She seemed to think I couldn't hear her. So I asked again,

"Are you both okay?" but this time inside my head. The Soul looked at me and I suddenly realised why I couldn't see this Marguerite person. This Soul was not going to the light. Marguerite, her helper to the other side, was not of the light. Her colour was similar but darker to the greys I'd seen before. A mottled, rough textured dull light. I would add dark, too. The light was dark. I realise that doesn't make sense. It didn't make sense to me either. But as I stood there, I felt icy fingers around my throat. Tightening. Freezing me to my core.

"Get the fuck away from my girlfriend, you dyke whore." A scream whispered into my ear. Into the very centre of my being. A sound like broken glass and chalk screeching down a chalkboard. The sound alone made me feel sick. The frozen fingers dug into the skin on my neck, tightening, keeping my breath inside. I was unable to move.

"Do you like the smell of these fingers," the same rough sixty-a-day voice spat into my face and I could smell the cigarettes, the alcohol, the decay of the dead who aren't aware of it. "I just stuck 'em up 'er cunt and she loved it. Do you want some?" Not a question but a statement of aggression. She was trying to scare me. It was working. I saw a flash of her face. Bitter, like her voice. Desperate, like her tone. Afraid to be alone. Afraid of where she had been and where she was taking her girlfriend. When she could release her from the body.

The fingers released. I felt myself drop and my feet touched the floor. I hadn't realised that I had been elevated.

"Get her out." The voice spoke almost inside my head. I felt the anguish. The pain. The suffering that this woman had felt in her younger life. And the pain, fear and desperation she had passed on to numerous others. For her own pleasure. I saw that she had killed a child. Her lover's child. The vision made me vomit onto the carpet of this resident's room. The torture was beyond anything I could comprehend and my head began to spin. I could feel myself falling.

"GET HER OUT … NOOOOOW," screamed the one I couldn't see. It lifted me from the floor and dragged me through my own vomit across the room. She was terrified. I could sense a terror deeper than anything I had ever known. But I also smelt him. Beastman. Wherever she had come from, he wasn't far away. I could feel the vomit rising in my throat again as her fingers of death pressed into my back, pushing me toward her girlfriend's dying body.

"Ooh, you are a pretty one," said the visible Soul, scrabbling to escape her shell. "We 'ad ones like you, didn't we, Marguerite?" I was torn between letting them suffer the torment of being here, now, and the torment of where they were heading. I took a deep breath and let my Soul arm tentatively leave my body. I wasn't risking letting anything else out. I reached across and cut the cord that tied the Soul to the body. There was a 'whoop' from the visible one and a desperate cry from the invisible. Then silence as they disappeared into their afterlife. I crumpled to the floor. Depleted. Shaking. The scars etched in ice on my back and on my throat. I reached up to the button beside the bed and pressed. Then I let my body fall.

28

Back to The Light House

"I'm so sorry." Arrien was beside me in her spirit form. Pure love and light. I could sense the other beings, too, filling me with a joy and happiness that is so difficult to describe in mere words. I felt my disparate body filling back up with light, and within seconds, or maybe it was hours, I never knew, I was able to stand again. They are completely the wrong words, as I'm sure you realise by now. I am in The Light House in my Soul form. My spirit form. My form of pure love, light and energy. No legs to stand on.

After my Soul family – as this is what I was beginning to understand these energies were – had filled me with their love and their energy and their kind words, or thoughts or feelings. They never used words to communicate up here. It was thoughts and feelings. I felt their sorrow at having observed me go through what had just happened. My Soul family, like yours, are a witness to everything I do on the earth plane whilst in my living body. I felt their joy at how I had handled the situation and their love at how I was able to free a Soul that was dark and not destined to be in this energy. They showed me to a book in the library.

I just have to mention here that when I arrived in The Light House, I was in the usual room. The waiting room. This was my room. Where my Soul family gathered. When you pass over or visit your Soul family when you sleep, you won't come to this particular room. You will have your own space, specifically for you – but more on that later. The moment the thought came about the book, the walls changed – the invisible walls, I have to remind you – into the invisible walls of the library that looked like the room in Mrs Marton's house. Remember, this is my Soul room, so my memories!

The book was beginning to fade, so they wanted to show it to me quickly before it left this particular space. Like the previous book I had seen, the cover was beautifully made of leather, but this one was beginning to decay and mould appeared in the corners. The fetid smell of damp and decay hung around it. I asked if this was because of her age and death but was told it was because she had chosen a different path so her book would go to the place where her Soul would be living for the now. The first page showed a beautiful young woman, educated to a high standard by loving parents who treated her well. I saw the day of her marriage to a handsome man. Educated, intelligent, gentle, caring. Everything you would want from a life partner. I watched her become pregnant with a beautiful act of love. I saw her give birth and feel the love of a mother. There is no love like that of a woman holding her child in her arms for the first time. It is the most splendid image and feeling, with such a glorious light attached to it, that I wish I could describe it in words. Then I saw the day Marguerite entered her life. A woman employed to help clean the house and run errands for his beautiful, loved wife while she tended to the needs of their baby. A woman already tainted by the darkness. A scheming woman who first sought trust from her female employee and then began feeding her titbits of lies and deception. Slowly manipulating mistrust, first in her husband, then her wider family, until she began to depend solely on Marguerite. Within six months, she had driven the wife into a pit of despair, then pulled her out of it with declarations of love. They began an affair and a divorce was imminent.

The husband, seeing the controlling nature of this woman, confronted her and tried to get her to leave his wife and child alone. She manipulated a scene at his work where he threatened her and his wife. There were lots of witnesses when he lost his head in anger.

Two days later, the husband arrived at the house he used to call home to pick up his child for the weekend. The police were called out to a scene that even Beastman would find difficult to witness. Marguerite had drugged and tied both her lover and her husband, then forced them to watch as she brutally tortured the sober baby before placing a knife in her lover's hand to cut off the baby's right foot. She then placed a knife in the husband's hand and cut off both hands. The child was still breathing. It could scream no more. It took only a few minutes for the child to bleed out completely and its heart to stop.

Marguerite then gave drugs to the former couple and told them the story of what had happened. Her version. She showered and changed. Then called the police. She hid one knife, just in case. And told the story of how this evil man had tortured and murdered this innocent baby in order to get his wife back. He would have been convicted to life in prison if he hadn't been murdered – a child killer – whilst on remand. Two deaths, accountable to her.

And now she was free to live and 'love' in her girlfriend's house. Her girlfriend was dragged willingly into a life of debauchery. Marguerite had dark energy that consumed her lover, sucked out all her light and filled it with darkness. There were more pages. More stories not dissimilar to that. Children. Young women. Bodies never found and stories never told.

I shut the book in disgust. As I did so, a wave of love flowed over me. It can be quite confusing when you see something so awful but are immediately filled with love. It wasn't a 'forget it ever happened' kind of thing, but a 'bad people exist all over the world, but we don't have to fear them' kind of thing. I think our society does that. We see something that scares us a little, so we try to get as far away as possible from it. Whereas we should be saying, "Hold on, why are you speaking like that to the child?" or "I know you hit that lady and it is unacceptable," – what is the worst that could happen? The perpetrator may hit us or talk badly to us. But that wouldn't be so bad if it highlighted the bully and everyone knew they were a bully. Would it?

As a couple, they did so much damage to so many people, and they enjoyed it. It was a game to them. They were both going to a different place to here. As I understand it, there are different levels that your Soul can come once it is released from the body. There is a dark place where the Souls of Beastman, Karen's mum's boyfriend and Marguerite would go, for example. Within the dark place, there are lots of different levels. So, you might end up at the lowest level, which I think is where Marguerite had gone. She had come for her girlfriend in order to take her to the same place, but I think she would end up a couple of levels higher than Marguerite but lower than either Beastman or Karen's mum's boyfriend. Above that, there are two further levels of light. Each one is split into hundreds or maybe even thousands of different levels. Each level being lighter and filled with more love.

The majority of human Souls used to start their afterlife in the top third section of the middle layer. But nowadays, they are coming in lower and lower. This is because of fear. I am told. When we live in fear, we do and say things that hurt others, and those people go on to feel fear and then hurt even more people. I was shown an image of dominoes. There was one standing on its end on its own. Then two more were placed in front of the lone domino side by side. In front of those two, an additional three dominoes were placed side by side. The view moved above them as four dominoes were added, then five, then six. As each row of dominoes was added, the image became triangular – the one domino standing alone with a large crowd in front of it. Then, the first domino was touched lightly on its top edge. It fell into the two in front, knocking them down. As they fell, they knocked the three in front of them, which then knocked the four, then the five, then the six, and on and on.

This image was meant to represent how one person's actions

or attitude can affect every person he touches, then every person touched by them. On and on *ad infinitum*. That one person's action or attitude in one day can affect a whole family, a whole town or even a whole country. The living would rather bury their heads in the sand and allow these people to behave improperly than stand up and move apart from the sheep or the dominos.

This was why I was here on the earth at this time, they began to tell me, but before I could hear any more I felt that little knot pulling in my stomach, which meant I was being called back into the world of the living.

29

If You Don't Know the Truth, Just Make it Up

I came to, in the arms of the manager, as he lifted me up from the floor of room seven. There were lots of voices and calls of,
"Keep out!"
"There's too much mess."
"Don't walk in the sick."
"Be respectful of the dead, for fuck's sake."
"Get back to work. I'll deal with this."
I was carried away from the melee and into the nurses' station, where there was a hospital bed in case of emergencies, with Mum fast on my heels. I tried to speak but found my throat was dry and painful. Swollen. The manager told me to relax and try to be calm. They were going to call the police, he said. I wasn't in trouble, it wasn't my fault, everything was going to be okay. But his voice was quivering and his body trembling. Apparently, this had happened to one of the residents last week. Eileen had been a resident for only three days and had been trying to introduce herself to as many of the other residents as possible. She'd heard talking in room seven, so she knocked and popped her head around the door. When she'd been found a few hours later, she had marks around her neck and was laying in a pool of her own sick. The woman in the bed had been unconscious, but the thinking was that she had a moment of lucidity and attacked Eileen before going back into her unconscious state.

This happens quite often, apparently, where the person who is close to dying has a spurt of energy, becomes very active and behaves as though they are in full health. Their families rejoice at the miraculous recovery and are then devastated to find their loved one has passed over. Eileen's family were really angry at her injuries and called the police and reported to the Care Qualities Commission, accusing the care home of abuse and negligence. The accusation that it was a member of staff who had caused her injuries had produced a lot of problems and having a second non-member of staff attacked in the same room was going to cause untold damage to the care home.

Eileen was still in the hospital and refused to speak of the incident, bursting into tears every time she was asked. The manager asked me if it was a member of staff. I shook my head. He asked if it was Mrs Benton, the lady in room seven. She was dead now, and it would be easier to say that it was her. But I couldn't lie. So, I told him, with a gravelly voice, that it was her girlfriend, Marguerite. He laughed.

The police arrived quickly and arranged to take me to the hospital for a check-up, but also to get me away from the care home. They wanted to know if it was a member of staff, too, and thought I would be too scared to tell the truth whilst in the building.

The hospital doctor, a dark-haired slim man with peaceful dark eyes and a mouth that smiled without help, checked out the bruising on my neck and back, looked into my mouth to check for any internal injuries, then took some blood – Arrien said they were checking for poisoning – then announced I was good to go.

The police had taken photographs of my injuries and had found a quiet room in the hospital where they wanted to interview me. As I was still only sixteen years old, I needed an appropriate adult with me. But they suggested it shouldn't be my mum as she was a member of staff at the care home. I asked for Bryn, Mum's boyfriend, and he arrived within fifteen minutes.

Once seated in a small room with a sofa, which Bryn and I were sat upon, against the wall and two office-style armchairs, where the police officers sat, a man and a woman, with a little coffee table between them, I was offered a drink. I chose sweet tea thinking it would be like Mrs Marton's delicious tea, but it was weak and watery and warm and sickly sweet. Undrinkable.

The policeman asked me to talk them through the attack in my own words. But when I started talking, they kept shooting sideways glances at one another. They asked me the same questions over and over. Sometimes the policeman. Sometimes the policewoman. At one point they tried to tell me that I was mistaken, the other victim told them who it was, that I was safe and they couldn't hurt me now. They just needed a name. I felt that any name would do as long as it was living and they could slap on a pair of handcuffs with a "you're nicked, mate" for good measure.

"Have you heard of Marguerite Paxton?" I asked, the surname suddenly coming into my mind. They shot a knowing look toward each other and then looked blankly at me.

"Who is she and how do you know her?" the police lady asked. I reiterated my earlier statement that she had caused my injuries.

"Look, love, I don't know who you are covering for," the male police officer said, "but you shouldn't be blaming an innocent woman who has been dead for five years. I don't even understand how you would know her name."

I was tired. I was in pain. And I was getting really fed up with these two. They weren't looking for answers. They were looking for an easy way out. I felt a huge surge of redness and a low hum surrounding and filling my body, so I had to tell them ...

"I know her name because she was in the room in spirit form. I realise you don't believe me, but it might help if I tell you this." I turned to the policeman, who was in his forties, a bit dishevelled and had an underlying smell of alcohol hidden well by peppermints and garlic.

"Your wife doesn't know that you are having an affair with

your colleague here. But when she finds out, your life is going to change dramatically." They both looked aghast and started to make noises of denial, but I turned to his colleague and carried on. "You know you are pregnant but don't know you are pregnant with twins. This man is the father," I jabbed a finger toward him, but he had gone silent and slightly pink. "You are planning to tell everyone it is your boss's baby because you have slept with him as well, and he is a better prospect. So, you are hoping he will step up for you. Unfortunately, he is about to propose to the mousy fuckwit in your office – you know, the one you keep snarking about to her face when you're making coffee? That isn't going to go down too well with your boss when he finds out, is it?"

I turned back to her colleague and continued, "You! You should be ashamed of yourself and if you think this is coming from me, you can think again. Your mother died last year of a hepatoblastoma associated with her Beckwith-Weidemann syndrome." His jaw dropped open, his face whitened and his eyes filled with tears. "She is standing next to you, shaking her head in shame at what you are doing to your wife, who is ALSO pregnant with your child."

They had both turned a shade of white that one can only describe as grey. Not the grey of dead people's skin but the grey of people who have been caught out in a lie they never thought would surface. And yet, here they both were.

"I have more I can tell you," I said, feeling a little bit smug. But Bryn touched my arm and said in his quiet voice,

"I'm being told by my guide that the dead woman told you who really killed her baby." He looked at me and winked. "Perhaps you could help the police fix another one of their major cock-ups."

I felt guilty when we were allowed to leave the interview in the family room and made our way out of the hospital. But decided I would let the two officers stew for a while before I apologised. They said they would need to speak to me again and I knew it would be the following day. Bryn put his arm around my shoulder and pulled me close, telling me he had always known I had the gift but didn't realise it was that good. Perhaps, he suggested, I could do a stint at the spiritualist church. We both smirked as I had already considered doing just that!

I wanted to tell him that the policewoman wasn't the only woman expecting twins, but I knew that was for him to discover if he didn't already know.

30

Spiritual Detective

Because of the incident at the care home, it was suggested that I didn't return to work for a few weeks until the proper investigations had been carried out. The CQC had contacted the police, who had contacted me to make an appointment for their interview. It was decided by Mum and Bryn, and I wasn't going to disagree, that for the next couple of weeks, I would go to Mrs Marton's and do the cleaning for Mum, and then she could do a few more hours at the care home to cover for the staff shortage they now had. Two members of staff had left after feeling paranoid they would be blamed for everything. The truth was they would manhandle some of the older residents who weren't able to speak for themselves. It wasn't a great loss to the home, but less staff meant more work for those still there.

I arrived at Mrs Marton's back door via the woods at nine-thirty the next morning. There was a man already in the kitchen, a mug of steaming tea in his cupped hands. A freshly poured mug was ready for me. I smiled. I liked it when people expected me and had a cuppa waiting! Well, it was only ever Mrs Marton, but it made me feel warm and welcome.

I sat down in my usual chair at the kitchen table and reached across to the head of the table, where Mrs Marton sat, pulling my steaming hot mug toward me. Mrs Marton mentioned my bruises, so I lifted my head so she could see the full extent of the discolouration. The man sitting opposite me was in his early to mid-fifties, with dark hair speckled with grey and dark grey, striking eyes. Attractive in an old man kind of way. He was clean-shaven but not from this morning – a hint of shadow was just beginning to show. He wore a charcoal grey suit, light grey shirt and mid-toned grey tie. An outfit fit for a funeral. Except this chap wasn't going to a funeral. This chap was the bringer of bad news. Not for me. Not for Mrs Marton either. My guides and other spirits in the room were keeping quiet. This wasn't usual. I was intrigued!

I wanted to ask who he was and what he was doing here at such an early hour. But this wasn't my house and he wasn't my guest. And Mrs Marton would give me the death stare if she thought I was being cheeky. So, I just stared into my mug of delicious tea.

"What tea bags do you use, Mrs Marton?" I asked after a few moments to break the silence. I liked silence, as you know, and this wasn't an awkward silence, but I wanted to encourage dialogue. I wanted to know who and what and why.

"This is Detective Inspector Marion Marton," she said in response. "He's my nephew and has been asked to look into some allegations made yesterday afternoon."

"I bet you got the piss taken out of you at school," I said, looking at Mr Marton. Or DI Marton, to be more precise. "Can I call you John?" I asked, referring to an American film actor called John Wayne, whose real name was Marion. Both he and Mrs Marton sniggered. The ice was broken. And now I knew why he was here. I guessed I wouldn't be getting any cleaning work done. I smiled.

"Before you start with the kitchen," Mrs Marton read my mind and looked directly at me, "would you be so kind as to answer a few questions for my nephew?"

"Off the record?" I asked. "Or do I need a solicitor?" Mrs Marton gave me a not-quite-death stare; she was smiling, so he started talking. He had a lovely voice. Not quite as posh as Mrs Marton, so I guessed he hadn't been brought up in a house like this. I immediately got an image of a council house, not dissimilar to the one I lived in, and a father not dissimilar to mine. He felt like a warm person. I could see him laughing with his children. Three of them. Two boys and a girl. One of the boys died when he was still a baby. It caused the death of his marriage, too, although they'd stayed together for the other children and had only been divorced a few years.

My attention was brought back to the kitchen in the Manor House. DI Marton had mentioned Marguerite.

He told me that originally, she had been a suspect in the murder of the child, but there was so much evidence pointing to the father, along with the testimony of the child's mother, that the investigation swayed toward him as the perpetrator. Jason Benton was his name. His family and friends had argued that he was not the man the newspapers and police were portraying him to be. His colleagues had said how out of character his outburst had been when Marguerite had come to his office, with two colleagues saying they had overheard the conversation and she was goading him. His death in the remand centre had washed away any chance he had of defending himself in court. The case was closed. He was guilty. And dead. And the truth of his son's diabolical death had died with him.

DI Marton looked sad. As though the death of his own child in a freak road traffic accident for which there could be no blame could be put to rights if only he could find peace for this man, his child and the surviving family. What did I know, he asked, that could help him to bring the truth to the fore?

"This," I lifted my head and pulled down the neckline of my jumper so the whole of my blue, brown and black marked throat was exposed. "You know I have gifts," I looked at Mrs Marton as I said this, certain that she had told him, "The dead DO speak, but you already know that."

I recounted my time in room seven, the vision of Marguerite holding the baby and putting the knives into the hands of each parent in turn. The mother – Denise, the DI had told me earlier –

screaming in pain and losing her mind as she witnessed her own part in the murder of her baby but then being pacified by Marguerite with the aid of drugs and false images and her energy filling up every crevice and atom of Denise Benton's body.

I told him that Mrs Benton had intimated that there had been young girls about my age. And I mentioned what I had seen in her book of life, that there were also small children and other babies. They had been assaulted physically and sexually before being tortured and murdered.

"But none of that will be accepted in a court of law." I stared at him, knowing he would need proof. Physical, earth-type proof. Like a knife with fingerprints. Or a body. Or several. They both looked downcast. Saddened. They both thought the same things. First, what a horrible pair these women were. Second, love and compassion for those who had come into their grasp and never left. Third, justice would never be done in this case.

I sighed a loud breath through my nostrils. Mrs Marton's head lifted suddenly, and a bone in her shoulder clicked. The DI looked at me, eyes widened.

"What?" they both said together.

Pushing back the chair, I stood up, lifted my head and spread out my arms. In the most dramatic voice I could muster I said, "Whilst squeezing at the throat of her latest victim, the dying woman confessed to a damning story of love, hatred, betrayal, fear and murder." I punched my fists into my chest, too late, realising I was still struggling with my lungs, collapsing my head to my chest and letting out a deep wheeze. Then I realised I'd had massive healing and actually felt quite numb and had no pain from the energy overload. Raising my head, I smiled again, then brought my left hand to my chin, drumming my index finger against my lips.

"Hmm." I screwed up my eyes. "Where did she say they had buried the bodies?"

Within the hour, PCs Plod and Plodder, not their real names, by the way, were both junior detectives, not PCs, and had arrived at Mrs Marton's house and were ready to take my statement. Having discussed with Mrs Marton and her nephew what I would say to make the statement permissible in court, I would detail all that I had seen in the book along with what had been said in the room, but make it sound as though Mrs Benton was giving her last confession.

As the two PCs sat across from me, I said my apologies for the comments I made the previous day. I told them that I was able to see and hear spirits, which is why I knew Marguerite was in the room yesterday. But the statement I was giving today was what the dying woman had said to me prior to her gripping my neck. She wanted to confess but leave no witness to the confession.

They nodded in agreement. Apart from greeting their boss and Mrs Marton and nodding their heads at me, they had said very little either to each other since arriving. I felt a little guilty. But at least now there would be justice for a baby, his father and their family.

I started talking.

31

Justice Perhaps

Do you believe in coincidences?

As I began talking a gentleman, in spirit, appeared and sat down at the head of the table. He was wearing a pin-stripe blue suit, a crisp white shirt and a red patterned tie. He was freshly shaven and smelt of an aftershave that one of the old teachers at school would wear. A bit musky, a bit spicy, with a floral undertone but very masculine. I quite liked it. He threw a briefcase overflowing with papers onto the tabletop, some pages falling out and floating to the floor, where they immediately disappeared and reappeared in the overflowing briefcase. I tried not to chuckle. He kept pushing hair off his face, too. He had one of those old men's hairstyles where one side of the head had very long hair which was swept across a balding patch in the middle. A poor attempt to hide his premature ageing.

Every so often, he would harrumph at something I was saying, "Won't be admitted", he would say, "Not relevant", he would interject, "Keep to the point," he would suggest. Brusquely.

When I got to the part where I was recounting the burial places of the bodies, he stood up abruptly. "Be careful," he shout-talked at me, making me flinch. "You may be able to see with clarity the exact positions that the bodies are buried. But you weren't TOLD exactly where the bodies were buried, were you? So, try to be a little vague." He had tilted his head as he looked at me, squeezed his lips into a tight line and locked eyes with mine. I wasn't frightened. I think in his time, he would have been a formidable opponent in the courtroom – I was happy that he was on my side.

I acted on all his advice. The PCs were lapping up the information and imagining their promotions after this amazing old case was finally solved.

Several children and young women had disappeared over the past fifty years. It had always been assumed that it was a man who had taken them. One man had been tried in court for the disappearance of one teenage girl. The witness whose statement had implicated him without a doubt?

Denise Benton.

Another case of a child's disappearance, Marguerite Paxton had come forward to say she had seen the girl getting into a car that headed out of town.

As women, their accounts were believed. Because women don't hurt, do they? Women love children. They love everything. Women don't physically, mentally and emotionally damage other human beings. That's what men do. That's what the media says anyway. So, these two women had gotten away with a lot of hurt and misery. And it isn't just the victims themselves, you see. The families of the missing are victims too. The guilt they feel weighs soooo heavy upon their shoulders. It stops them from living their lives. Stops their light from shining and fills them with fear.

Why guilt? Well. If this parent hadn't shouted at her daughter, she wouldn't have stormed out of the house. If that father hadn't ignored his small son's calls to go play football in the park, he wouldn't have gone on his own. If that sister hadn't run away from her sibling to spend time with the bigger girls, he wouldn't have tried to walk home by himself. Do you see? How much guilt would you feel? How much anger would you hold against the person who 'allowed' your child to become lost? How much self-loathing would you hold against yourself for some unfathomable reason that you could never have changed anyway? I could see this in DI Marton as he sat listening to my statement. I could see it in the aura of the spirit lawyer whose story can be told, in part, later.

And I felt it in myself too. Even though, as a small child, I could never have stopped the big bully from hurting my mother, my siblings, myself, it doesn't stop the feelings of guilt. The feeling of pain. The 'if onlys' and 'what ifs'. These forms of torture last for many more years than our loved one endured in their short lives.

After a couple of hours and a few edits I finally signed on the dotted line.

Away they went to share with their bosses, get a little credit, and get warrants for searching the two properties I had mentioned.

Mrs Marton and I were left alone, a fresh cup of delicious hot tea with an extra sugar to give me a touch more energy after the fatiguing session.

It was exhausting. Every time I spoke, I would see – witness if you like – an aspect of the story that I couldn't put down on paper. I would see it vividly. The colours, the smells, the screaming, the emotions. From each individual involved. I knew each person's life story. Every part. From conception to the moments they passed into the afterlife. It was exhausting. And heartbreaking.

"Marriott and Son's," Mrs Marton spoke quietly, purposefully breaking into my thoughts, "English Breakfast Tea." She smiled and lifted her cup.

"Oh!" I smiled and took a sip. I'd visited their little tea shop in town with Marc last year but thought it was just a place to get a cup of tea and a slice of cake.

"The lawyer who was here," she suddenly looked sad, "he was the father of one of the girls. Very intelligent girl. Beautiful. She was questioning her sexuality when she went missing. He'd tried to set her up on dates with young men from his office. Not thinking how hurtful it was to her. Thinking she just needed someone in her life and she'd be happy. Thought she'd run away. The stress of pushing her away, denying her, is what took him in the end. He didn't know, till after he'd passed, any of this." She pulled a face with a frown and downturned lips and flourished her hand across the table as though everything was laid out there. She looked as though she had gone, momentarily, to another place.

"That's why he came," she said unexpectedly. "He wants to make sure they all get justice. All of them. That we don't make mistakes. That those women get named for their atrocities and all the innocent ones are freed from the burden of guilt. That their bodies are found and finally put to rest. But they won't ever be fully free." She sniffed back a clear liquid globule that had gathered on the tip of her nose, then wiped it away with her hand. There was a story here, I felt, about Mrs Marton's past. But I wasn't given permission to view it!

We spoke for a few moments about the British legal system and justice. Then she told me that some justice was far worse than people knowing you were guilty. Far worse than a spell in a prison cell. The place in the afterlife we call hell, she said, was worse than any hell we could actually imagine.

"You will be permitted to visit," she told me, matter-of-factly, as though I was going to visit a family member in jail for shoplifting an apple off a market stall. I felt an icy dread within the core of my body that reached out and began to fill the room.

"You will be protected," she said and sent a wave of warm, loving energy crashing into mine and filling my being. I noticed then that the other beings in the room were also projecting energy and light from their hearts toward me. I felt elevated. Boosted. Lifted by their energy and their love and their caring.

"Your gift will help the world. It will lift the hearts, minds and energies of not only the living but those on the other side." She smiled a smile filled with love and sadness. I wanted to ask what she meant, but I felt an unease. A trepidation. An anxiousness that I didn't want to put into words.

"Spain!" she called out, suddenly, as though she had completely forgotten and only just in that instant remembered. She shot up from her chair with such suddenness that it rocked backwards, almost tipping over, but then righted itself, with the aid of a spirit hand, as she moved away from the table to the dresser that held a mass of papers, letters and files alongside the daily crockery and various decorative pieces of dust-gathering antiques.

Her mother's friend would teach me, she read from the letter she retrieved. She would take me, initially, for three months with a view to six months if I took to her methods. Longer if I needed it, but less if I became burdensome. We laughed as we read the handwritten letter together. There were several 'must-dos' and 'must-nots' included in the letter and a separate list for me, of items I needed to take with me on the journey.

She had also included a price for the education, board and food for the six months, which was non-refundable and would need to be sent by return mail in cheque form immediately. I would need to arrive in her village in Spain by the fifteenth of December that year.

"Synchronistically or coincidentally," I said to Mrs Marton with a wry smile. "That is the very amount in my education money pot!"

"The spirits have spoken!" she retorted with a flourish and we both laughed.

She asked if I would mind missing Christmas with my family. I replied that Mum and Bryn would be getting some good news soon, to which she nodded knowingly so they would be glad of a bit of space at the kitchen table. My elder brother had not long ago joined the army and was about to be deployed – somewhere safe, we both said together – and my elder sister was hoping to spend Christmas with friends in the Scottish Highlands. So, it would be just the two of them with the youngest two – both just reaching their teens and wanting to spend more time in their bedrooms. With the elder three out of the house they would be able to have a room each. Sometimes I wonder if the universe, God, the Angels or spirits arrange things specifically. But there are so many things that need arranging just for one person to get where they need to be at a specific day and time, so there must be a huge amount of sorting out and organising on the other side. It sounded like a lot of hard work, and I was pleased I didn't have to do it.

Just then, there was a sharp rap on the front door. It opened and DI Marton walked in with a big smile on his face.

"Lots of good news," he said. This morning he had looked tired and weary, but now he seemed buoyed up. Light.

"First of all, business, Aunty Em, if I can, then personal stuff that you probably already know, but hey, I need to say it out loud." He was smiling a beautiful smile that made him look really handsome for an older man. His aura was shining much brighter, too. I think this was the shine of love, but I was sure I would find out soon.

They had obtained warrants to search the two properties almost instantly. Neither one was currently occupied, and the person responsible for signing the warrant was Jason Benton's distant cousin. Coincidence?

One property was the house that Denise and Marguerite had lived in together for all those years. The second was a derelict yard with decrepit buildings that Marguerite's family had owned and run as a scrap yard when she was young. The business ended when her father died, falling into disuse and disrepair.

Beneath the sink, behind the kickboard of the ragged kitchen of the ramshackle building at the scrapyard, inside a plastic shopping bag wrapped in a baby's nappy, stained with a dark, dry substance they believed to be blood, was a knife with very clear fingerprints in the blood. Apparently, they looked like two sets of prints and he was sure, but didn't want to get too enthusiastic till they had evidence it would prove that both women had touched the bloodied knife. This would make Marguerite's original statement false. A lie. Proving that she had been there earlier than she had previously stated, had messed with evidence, and possibly witnessed the actual atrocity.

They had also begun searching the garden of the women's home and had found what they believed to be human remains. Again, he didn't want to get excited, but it looked like the evidence was stacking up against the two women.

I put the kettle on and the detective turned to personal matters. He told his aunty that he had proposed to his girlfriend and she had accepted. He wondered if they could hold the reception here at The Manor. She beamed with delight and suggested that he hold the whole wedding here as the house had been approved for use as a wedding venue, as had the spiritualist church when her parents were looking for an additional income stream. Thrilled, he suggested he bring his new fiancée to meet his aunt and to look around the location. *She would love it,* I thought. Then, I felt a stab of disappointment that I would miss it, followed by a chuckle as I had a flash of the nuptials to come.

His second piece of news was that his son had received a late offer to study International Relations and Law in Madrid.

I screwed up my face and said, "But isn't he, like, five years old?" then realised I'd said that out loud and both adults were looking at me.

"Mart lost his first son at five years old," Mrs Marton said sympathetically. "His younger son is eighteen." I apologised and looked down at my feet. I was going to have to remember when to speak in my head and when to use my mouth. I didn't think I would ever get used to it.

Apparently, the term started in January, but his son was going to travel down in November and spend Christmas with his aunt in Teruel, a city near the centre of Spain.

"Who? Carmen?" asked Mrs Marton, surprised.

"Yes," her nephew replied. "Apparently, the two of them have been planning it for months. He wants to drive there in his bloody van!"

32

It's All Go

Mrs Marton had squealed like a little girl and did a little dance on the spot. She twirled around, pumping her arms up and down like a demented tin robot, and then set off around the kitchen. Both Mart and I looked on, perplexed, but before too long, we broke into laughter and began jumping and hopping around the kitchen, waving our arms in pursuit of Mrs Marton like a badly choreographed party conga.

When the laughter began to cease and we all ran out of energy, we flopped back into the kitchen chairs. Mart asked what all that was about and Mrs Marton replied, "Synchronicity," as she jumped back up to refresh the empty cups of tea.

She quickly brought Mart up to speed with my recent plans whilst informing me that 'Aunty Carmen' was a close family friend, a distant cousin of hers, and also a student of her late mother.

"Synchronicity," she repeated as we moved through to the parlour, me carrying the cups of steaming tea on matching saucers, accompanied by a plate of biscuits – posh ones, also from Marriott and Son's on the high street - on an antique wooden tray. Mrs Marton was speed-talking at Mart about passports and me and his son travelling together if everyone would be happy with that, but Carmen had probably already arranged all of that with her spirits, she said, hardly taking a breath.

Having never been into the parlour before, I wasn't sure what to expect. I thought it would be full of honeyed oak or deep mahogany woods like the hallway, library and bedrooms. But, apart from the honey-coloured wooden floor covered in beautiful savonnerie rugs, it was quaint and chintzy. And very French! There were pretty, floral, floor-length curtains at the windows, held back by exquisite silk cords with tassels, allowing the attractive floor-length, antique French lace panels to be viewed. There were antique French sofas and chairs painted in golds and creams with extravagant silk upholstery. The walls were swathed in luxurious deep turquoise antique French silk; golden framed mirrors and pictures took up most of the wall space, with a few golden wall lights glittering with crystal drops capturing the light from the windows and passing the rainbow colours around the walls and ceiling.

Cabinets of gold and glass contained beautiful items collected by generations past from all corners of the world. Large marble busts of serious-looking menfolk sat atop marble columns in between the three windows. I felt my lips forming a silent wow. This was beautiful. I could live in this.

"Still haven't cleared out any of the old tat, then?" Mart was looking around disdainfully. I don't think it would be appropriate to kick a policeman's shins, but I would have liked to.

Mrs Marton used an open palm to point to the 1970s coffee table – rather out of place, I thought – suggesting I place the tray there and she took a seat on the main sofa. It was quite small and would only hold a single person or two very friendly people! Mart and I took seats opposite one another and his aunt poured tea from the same teapot she had used on my first visit to this house with Mum.

The detective was asked if he would mind signing my passport documents when we got them. I realised I didn't have a passport, although I knew what one was. My elder brother had to have one when he went into the army. I didn't think I would ever need one. I didn't think I would ever go beyond the town boundary, let alone over the sea!

A conversation was had between the two elders in the room and I sat listening. Taking in the beauty of the room and enjoying my tea. I took a biscuit from the plate on the tray and dipped it into my cup. As I lifted it to my lips, it broke in two, half splashing back into the cup, causing a large wave to slop over the edge of the cup, the other half starting to sag in my hand. I stuffed the larger half straight into my mouth and closed it quickly. It filled my mouth. It was dry. I didn't want to crunch it in case they could hear me, so instead, I took a wide-mouthed sip from the cup and made a loud slurping sound as I tried to moisten the biscuit. Two sets of eyes alighted upon me.

Mart looked mortified at the wide mouth dripping tea and bits of soggy biscuit. Then, he snorted a laugh, which he tried to hide with a false cough. Mrs Marton's face had creased up slightly, and I knew she was also going to laugh. As I reached across to the table to replace the cup and saucer whilst trying to hold my head up so the tea wouldn't drip out of my mouth, Mrs Marton surreptitiously passed me a cotton napkin that had been on the table before we had come in. *This must happen to a lot of people,* I thought. Or perhaps she knew it would happen to me today! Mrs Marton pursed her smiling lips and shook her head.

Preparations were made for me to meet my prospective travelling partner at the same time that Mart would introduce his new fiancée to Mrs Marton and show off the prospective wedding venue.

A list was drawn up of things that I needed to do: go to the bank to get a cheque for Carmen; post it off quick sharp; fetch and fill in a passport application from the Post Office; have a photograph taken for the passport; purchase the things on Carmen's list; buy a suitcase; buy suitable clothes for Spain.

"Oh, and don't forget to tell your mum," Mrs Marton added. I was grateful for that because I'm sorry to say it had been the last thing on my mind.

I wasn't the type of child to get overexcited about anything, as I'm sure you are aware by now, but I was beginning to feel a flutter of excitement as the plans for me to travel abroad were discussed. One of the things I liked about Mrs Marton was her ability to treat me like an adult – including me in the decisions being made. I found a lot of adults to be condescending to young people, as though our opinions were inconsequential. And as I'm sure you are aware, I'd met a lot of adults trying to make decisions for my family without giving my siblings and me much thought. Some adults seemed to think that because you were under a certain age, you didn't have a brain!

I made my excuses to leave. Excitement aside, I don't think I had ever had the responsibility of so many things to do, and I felt a little overwhelmed. I left through the back door and thought I would sneak into my house without anyone seeing me and go have a lie down to think through my list. Just as I arrived at the Hanging Tree – I had started to call it that; I know it isn't nice, but every time I saw it, I was reminded of the sad dad trying to knot the rope that his dead son was just as quickly untying – I heard a twig crack to my left.

"Hi," said a familiar voice from behind the second biggest tree in the wood. "It's only me!"

"Marc?" I was surprised to see him. "What are you doing here?"

He looked upset. He had only been away for a couple of weeks and wasn't due back until Christmas. I held out my hand, but he took a step back.

"I've missed you," he said, unable to look at me. "We talked about getting married. You mean so much to me. I feel awful." He had started to ramble, but his energy had started to leech out from his body, forming little hooks as they moved toward me. I quickly put myself into an imaginary bubble – like the soap bubble – and as the energy hooks reached out, they bounced back from the invisible protective shield. I let out a sigh of relief and hushed him, reaching to touch his arm, I could instantly feel his pain. He didn't love me as a girlfriend or life partner, I could feel that. But he loved me deeply, all the same. More like a sister. He felt as though he had been unfaithful to me by finding another girl attractive.

I sat him down in the hollow of the roots of the Hanging Tree and told him that it was time for us both to move on. We have strong feelings for one another, I said, but we are living different lives now. He nodded but was still sending out hooks of energy. Trying to unconsciously drag me back into him. I silently asked Arrien for help and for the help of his guide, too.

Yes, we all have guides. You do, too. We don't always see them. We don't always hear them. And we don't always feel them. But they are there. They are doing all sorts of stuff behind the scenes to help you live your life. Remember when you wanted a part-time job so you could earn some money to buy your mum that necklace she wanted, and then there was a vacancy for a paper boy? You weren't going to go in and ask about it, but you tripped on the step and fell in? Yup, your guide was just giving you a little push!!

Marc's guide looked eastern European. Dressed in traditional clothes and with a swarthy complexion. He hadn't been alive for a very lot of years, but this was how he had looked in his last incarnation. So that is how he appeared to me. If you could see him, he might appear differently depending on whether you were part of his Soul family or not. Anyway, Radu – I think that was his name. It sounded like Radu but had a gruffness to the end syllable – said Marc had started seeing another girl, but felt guilty. He didn't want to feel guilty but didn't want to hurt me.

"Listen, Marc," I was formulating the words as I spoke them, so I was worried it came out wrong. "This is the first time you've been away from home. You have lots to think about with college and learning new things and meeting new people and seeing new places. Lots of stuff. I need you to concentrate on that. I need you to be the best that you can be. And if that means we change our plans, then so be it." He looked at me expectantly. I felt let down, if I'm honest. I didn't think he was this much of a coward. He should have just told me he was seeing someone else. Yes. I might have been sad. Or hurt. But life is short and if someone doesn't make you happy – or someone else makes you happier – then you should make a decision and go with it. Instead of this badly orchestrated jig where he wanted to not accept the blame or the responsibility.

"We should split up," I said with a confidence I didn't really feel. "We'll both be sad for a while, but you can get on with your life and studies in London without having to think about me. Maybe you'll meet someone else," he looked shocked, as though I had discovered his secret, "or maybe you won't," I continued, trying to make him feel better.

"When you have completed your studies we can meet up and see how we both feel. How does that sound?"

He grinned from ear to ear. His energy tried hooking me one last time then drew back and began to shine from within. He was happy. He was off the hook. He was free. "You are just the most marvellous thing," he said in a voice I didn't recognise – then I saw the image of his new girlfriend, holding his face and saying those exact same words to him. *What a twat*, I thought. But I smiled.

"We'll catch up at Christmas then, have a beer, yeah?" he said, smiling, forgetting that I was still too young to drink and wouldn't have a beer even if I was old enough. I nodded and smiled and he stood up and began to walk away. He stopped and turned suddenly, as he remembered I was still sitting there.

"I'm good," I smiled. "See you later." *Or not,* I thought as I stood up. Radu stood with me and Arrien for a moment. He looked as though he wanted to say something, but your guides are totally loyal to you – most of the time – and if he'd wanted to say anything, he didn't. As Marc disappeared through the gate to his parents' home, Radu slowly disintegrated from my view. Arrien tucked her arm into mine and smiled. That was one thing to tick off the list, even though it wasn't on the list. Marc would not have been happy for me to go to Spain had he known my plans, so now he didn't need to know. I stood up and walked to my gate, then, rather than go inside, I walked straight to the front of the house, down the path, through the front gate, down the street and to the bank, where I ordered a cheque for Carmen. I then walked along the high street to the Post Office to pick up my passport forms. I stopped in at Marriott and Son's for a box of Breakfast Teabags and two packets of biscuits. Tonight was going to be a celebration.

33

A Big Celebration

Three months later, my now rather pregnant mum, Bryn, and my siblings were around at Mrs Marton's house for a double celebration. The first was the wedding of DI Marton to his fiancée, the former 'fuckwit from the office' who was actually the sweetest woman you could ever wish to meet and a perfect match for her new husband. Their ceremony had been held in the afternoon in the gardens of the house; although autumnal, the day had been warm, with a clear, cloudless sky.

After their wedding celebrations came the 'going away' party. This was for the newlyweds, who were to be honeymooning on a cruise around the Mediterranean, but also for the youngsters heading off to Spain.

The DI's son, Thomas, had recently turned nineteen. We had met the week after the initial plans had been worked out for us to travel to Teruel together. We had gotten along really well, as though we had known one another for a lifetime. Actually it was a different lifetime, but I'll tell you about that later!

Thomas had the same colouring as his father but was taller. Not quite as handsome, but with promise. He was intelligent, some might say nerdy and always dressed in jeans, jumpers and trainers. He had an intuitive ability to put people at ease, which reminded me of my elder brother. Being brought up with the Marton name, he was inclined toward the spiritual side of life. Although he didn't have the gift of clairvoyance – the ability to see – he was able to feel energies and was very perceptive to people's emotions; in spiritual circles, he would be called an empath. He understood a lot of my gifts – he'd been around people like me all his life; his father's sister, it turned out, was in the same spiritualist group as Bryn and did the 'circuit' of spiritualist churches. This made it a lot easier to persuade my mum that I would be travelling with Thomas for at least a week in a VW campervan. A campervan that he'd picked up for one hundred and fifty quid from a hippy in the car park of the local pub!

Although I was too young to drive and didn't yet hold a driving licence, Thomas had started to teach me. In the new hypermarket car park just out of town, on an evening after they had closed, he would show me how to put the van into first gear by putting my foot on the clutch and then slowly lifting my foot until it reached biting point. That was where the engine sound changed a bit and you could feel a slight lurch in the van. I slowly learned how to release the handbrake and slowly move away from our standing point before dipping the clutch and changing into second and third gear. I learnt quickly, although initially I had almost crashed into a tree as I'd let the clutch come up and put my foot to the floor on the accelerator pedal.

We had become firm friends and had begun to spend more time together – initially in order to organise and make arrangements for our trip but once all our arrangements had been organised, re-organised and then re-re-organised we would just hang out together.

I liked him. A lot. Not in a boyfriend kind of way. I'm not sure I was Thomas's type, but that sort of thing wasn't talked about when I was 16 years old. I knew a few people who were like Thomas, but some of the older kids and most adults would make unkind comments about them – to their faces and behind their backs. I didn't understand it. I thought love was love, whoever you felt it for. Arrien said that people were afraid of things they didn't understand and that I would learn about it with Carmen.

I think Thomas was the first person I'd met that I wanted to be friends with. Most of my friends from school were friends of convenience. I would hang around with them because we were in the same classes. But I always found them to be 'lacking'. I don't know what they were lacking, but I was never completely comfortable in their presence. Again, Arrien said I would find out why when I got to Spain. Thomas and I weren't judgemental with one another; we laughed all the time and we could have deep conversations about any subject you could throw at us. We weren't afraid to rebuke each other, either, if we thought the other was being silly or judgemental about other people or situations that we didn't have enough evidence to criticise. I liked the feeling of safety and comfort that I felt around him.

Whilst we were practising driving the van in the car park, Thomas also showed me some basic mechanics – just in case he would tell me – and we looked at the space in which we would be sleeping and decided who would sleep where. We went shopping together to the Army and Navy Store in town where we bought a small tent and a couple of sleeping bags. The van had come with a set of camping pans, a kettle and a little camping stove, but we needed a new gas bottle, cutlery and crockery.

"It's like we're setting up home together," Thomas giggled while passing me a large plastic bottle for holding water. And it hit me that, yes, we would be living together in a very small space for twenty-four hours a day for about two weeks. *That's enough to test any relationship,* I thought, smiling.

But, right now we were celebrating in The Manor House, as I preferred to call it. It was lovely to see my family and siblings, apart from my brother, who was somewhere overseas, looking so happy and relaxed. I don't think I had ever seen any of them looking so 'at peace' if I can use a phrase we normally reserve for the dead. But they looked so happy it filled my heart with joy beyond any I had ever felt before.

"Keep that feeling in mind. And your heart," said a voice I

didn't recognise. I looked behind me and saw a figure of light walking toward the library. I followed, curious as to who it was. I knew it wasn't a ghost, but it didn't feel like a spirit guide or one of the light beings from The Light House. She – I felt it was female, even though you can't distinguish between the sexes on the other side – opened the library door and walked in, leaving the door slightly ajar.

I followed and closed the door behind me. There was a small lamp on the table. This was the only earthly light in the room, but by the bookshelf that had held Mrs Marton's mother's diaries were two bright lights. One was the figure of Mrs Marton's mother. Within the light, I could see the shadowy image of her, partially obscured by the brightness of the light surrounding her. She was in conversation with the figure that had come through the door. I couldn't see her face. She was facing the other being. After a few moments, they stopped talking – I couldn't hear what they were saying. I could only hear a buzzing sound so highly pitched it was hardly apparent.

The second figure turned to face me. *This is odd*, I thought. She was of the light. I could see that. She was shining like the Higher-Level Beings from The Light House.

Hmm! *Higher-Level Beings*, I thought, wondering where that idea had come from.

But she had a physicalness, an aliveness, that I had never witnessed before. I was fascinated. Enchanted. She had very dark wavy hair reaching her shoulders and a dark complexion, with dark, beautiful eyes. Kind. Ancient. Aboriginal. But I was having a lot of difficulty reading anything else from her. Arrien wasn't around. I called her to see if she could help with this perplexing being. But she didn't appear. The Being began to move toward me with purpose. Floating. Gliding. Moving so gracefully and gently, I couldn't take my eyes off her.

"What you looking at?" She said pleasantly but with a hint of mischievousness and disappeared. The only light left was that of the lamp on the table. I giggled. A little embarrassed at being caught staring. A little confused as to what had just happened. I called to Arrien and she appeared with her arm through mine.

"You'll find out in Spain," she said.

I don't know if you can imagine how excited I was to get to Spain!

34

Green Onions

We had spent the final few weeks before setting off making up music cassette tapes for the van. The radio wouldn't work, but the cassette player had an amazing sound, so we compiled some of our favourite tracks onto five C120 cassette tapes. They held sixty minutes of music on each side, so we would have ten hours of different tracks. We thought that would be enough different music to get us through the long trip. The first track we chose was 'Green Onions' by a band called Hooker T and the MGs. It was quite old, but it was a tune that was playing on the radio the first day we met, and it inspired a happy feeling in us both. We even made up a dance for the song as we were recording it onto our first tape. It was basically stomping around his bedroom at Mrs Marton's, where he was staying during his final week before departure, nodding our heads and waving our arms. It made us feel good, and we'd burst into laughter at the first note. We'd then walk around the room, moving our heads back and forth like Egyptians on bad television programmes. I'm sure anyone watching would think us crazy.

    We set off from outside Mrs Marton's house two weeks before I was due to be with Carmen. We had worked out that it should take us about one and a half weeks to get there but gave ourselves extra time in case of any incidents or in case we came across somewhere beautiful we'd like to spend a little more time.

    Mrs Marton, Bryn, Thomas's aunty, and a few more people

they knew from the spiritualist community had surrounded the van whilst we were in it to send love and blessings to us and the van! There were also quite a few Higher-Level Beings with them. I had noticed that there was a difference between ghosts (the Soul of someone who had passed over, usually looking as they did, at their best, when they were alive) and spirit guides (usually human-shaped but with less definition and more light around them) and the Higher-Level Beings, these were completely made of light although they would have a shape similar to a human. Occasionally, you could see a face or several faces overlapping, showing the appearances they had when they were incarnated on earth. These were the beings that may have been to earth in the past but had completed the lessons they were here to achieve and had moved higher on the other side. They mostly helped the human race to achieve their lessons – they were the managers, if that makes it easier to understand. Although the hierarchy on the other side is not like here on earth. On the other side, we have an autonomy that so few have here. But I'll share more about that later.

With an atlas on my lap and a large map of England in my hand, we waved goodbye to our friends and family. Thomas put Bessie into gear (that is the name we gave the van) and we smoothly moved off from Mrs Marton's drive and headed toward town as 'Green Onions' played quietly on the cassette player. Once we reached town, we needed to take a right-hand turn that would take us to a newly completed stretch of motorway, which joined the main route to the south coast, where we were to catch a ferry over to France.

35

Holiday (Away From Home)

The journey down was smooth, our excitement and trepidation mixing together and cancelling one another out. We sang along to our mix tapes and stopped off at motorway rests for fuel, food and visits to the toilet. We had arranged to stay overnight, in the van, at the holiday home of one of Thomas's dad's police friends. This was just south of Cambridge and we had written instructions on how to get there from the motorway, so we arrived without a hiccup just before eight o'clock that evening. Mart's friend wasn't staying at the cottage, but the couple in the neighbouring house had prepared a lasagne for their tea and, having chatted with us about who we were and what we were doing, gave us a huge portion to share as we were too late to go to the supermarket. Carolanne, the wife, asked if we'd like to use their phone to contact our parents to let them know we were okay, and Robert, the husband, suggested we use their toilet before going back to the van for the night. How romantic it was for us to be going on such a big adventure, they said, hugging each other and smiling.

There have been times in my life when I looked at human beings and thought what a waste of time we were, that there was no hope for us, and that we would be so much better off if we were completely erased from the face of the earth. Then there were other times, like today, when other human beings did something so kind and unexpected. It made my heart fill with joy, so I hugged them both tightly and told them they were wonderful.

Our first night in the van, and alone together, was a little bit weird. Not between us. We were friends and would remain friends for life, of that I was sure. But the space was limited, closing curtains, preparing the beds, brushing our teeth, and getting changed into nightwear. How long should we leave the light on? Did you want to read? Did you want to listen to music? Should we plan the next part of the trip? There were things you just didn't think of when you were planning a journey like this. And it was cold. And it rained. Heavily. And at 3am, I desperately needed the toilet.

Trying to find the light switch in the pitch black and cold when you were desperate for a wee was another hurdle we hadn't considered. Although the van had a toilet, it didn't work as it should, so we had said we'd only use it in real emergencies, so it was a trip outside. Peeing in the cold and the rain in the garden of strangers was not one of my finest life moments, either.

We decided to get up at four-thirty. We had ended up both sleeping on the bench bed, sharing our body heat and the sleeping bags. We were both cold, slightly damp from going outside in the rain and neither of us could sleep. It was a mix of excitement, fear and a bit of stress. But we had managed our first night in the van and were really pleased with ourselves. It was too early to say thank you and goodbye to our neighbours, who were probably still asleep, so we wrote down their address and promised ourselves we would send them postcards, as we travelled, as a thank you.

We arrived at the ferry port in Dover several hours earlier than we had planned but were very weary. We went to see if we could find something to eat, asking directions from a friendly port worker. He asked us where we were going and where we had come from, then suggested we ask if we could travel earlier. Sometimes, there were spaces available on the ferry as they didn't always sell, he told us. We followed his advice and were told there was a space on the ferry that was currently loading. If we were quick, we could get on that and we would be in France half a day ahead of schedule!

I had never seen the sea. We lived inland at home and had never been on a proper holiday. Well, I had never been on a holiday, full stop! I was excited to see the sea in person. So as soon as we were parked up on the ferry and were allowed up on deck, I ran to the side of the ship and gripped the rail. We were in a port, so there were lots of other boats and buildings surrounding us. The water below us was a murky grey colour. The sky above threatened more rain. It felt cold. I could smell rotting fish and foodstuff, mingling with oils and petroleum and other scents I couldn't identify.

"This isn't the greatest introduction to the oceans," Thomas said beside me, also holding onto the cold white rails that surrounded the deck. "We should grab some breakfast and come back out when we've left the port. That's when you'll see the real sea!"

Thirty minutes later we had eaten a full English breakfast from the onboard café. It wasn't the best meal I had ever eaten; it was certainly the most expensive. But it did what it needed to do, which was fill my belly, empty my hunger and calm my nerves. The engines had started up whilst we were eating, sending a low hum and vibration across the whole of the vessel. Then a horn sounded, the hum became deeper and the vibration increased. We were setting off!

Thomas and I ran the best that we could; the movement of the ferry made our feet move too far forward and then a little bit back. I burst out laughing suddenly and when Thomas looked at me quizzically, I started to sing, "What shall we do with a drunken sailor, what shall we do with a drunken sailor...?" He joined in with the rest of the verse as we staggered up the steps and toward the same railing we had held earlier.

It was drizzling again. The sort of rain that is almost a mist but very wet. Thomas stood behind me with his hands on the rails either side of mine. Protective. Sheltering. He was telling me to look further out and not too close to the boat as that would help me not to feel seasick. I looked as far away as I could. To the horizon. I could see a slight curve where the sky and sea embraced. The grey of the English sky breaking and showing a hint of blue in the far distance. The boat rose up and then fell down rhythmically. But out of tune. The rising waves were responsible for the rise in the vessel we were aboard, but the waves were not marching to a beat, so the boat would rise and fall. Rise and fall. … Rise … and fall. Stay low. Then rise. It was fairly disconcerting if I am honest. Not knowing when the rise or the fall would hit affected my stability. I would try to take a step forward and the vessel would rise, so I would lift my foot higher, thinking I would meet the deck of the boat, only for it to fall again and my foot not knowing exactly where it was going to land.

As we left the English shores, we ran around to the back of the boat to wave goodbye to England. I would be back to my home in a few months if everything went to plan, but Thomas would never live in England again, so I knew I would have to make the most of the time I had with my best friend.

As the vessel moved out into the open sea, I marvelled at the beauty and power of Mother Nature. This was not a gentle crossing; as we moved out of the safety of the harbour, the waves buffeted the sides of the ferry, making it lurch this way and that. Rising up at the front and then dipping down. I was mesmerised by the water. It seemed to contain a thousand shades of blue, turquoise, green and grey – each colour had its own multiple shades of white. A body of water would rise up from the rest as if to challenge the ship, crashing into it with a mighty roar and then falling dramatically into the murky froth on the surface. Further away, large waves would rise up and curl forward, with the white foam teasing its edges forward. Suddenly, a patch of water would sink into a deep bowl shape, wider than a housing estate and deeper than hell. It seemed impossible and almost unnatural for the water to behave in this way. I was hypnotised by its beauty and ferocity. And for a moment I felt like throwing myself into the swirling maelstrom of ocean. Being swallowed. To be a part of this moving, swelling, beautiful piece of art. I felt a longing, an urge, to be part of something so much bigger, so much more than me.

Thomas placed a hand on my shoulder, jolting me out of my spellbound state. He rubbed my shoulder, warming me up, and suggested we go inside out of the rain. I think he felt the power of nature surging through him, too. A dangerous power. So we took one last look and went inside.

As we neared the French port of Calais, we chose to stay inside, where it was marginally warmer than outside but definitely drier. We huddled at the window to watch as the port welcomed us in. These images are etched deeply into my memory banks. If you were to cut me open, you wouldn't see bones and organs and muscles and bodily fluids; you would see a looping film of this journey from leaving the English port to arriving at the French port. I had never experienced anything like this in my life so far, and I had been introduced to a power so great it took my breath away. Physically and metaphorically. I was in love with the ocean. Deeply, dangerously and unconditionally. And I felt a moment of sadness that, once we were evicted from the ferry, we would be going inland and far from the sea.

36

Lost in France

Arrien, my spirit guide, had slowly visited me less and less over the preceding six months, telling me it was time for her to move on. She "had a job to do in the higher-up", she laughed. But I would have a new guide, Kaleb. She pronounced it Car-Lev, but I imagined it written down with a 'b' rather than the 'v'. He was quieter than Arrien, wouldn't stand so close to me, and would rock the top half of his body in a sort of bow when he had finished a sentence. He reminded me a little of myself when I was younger. Very quiet around others, always watching and learning from their behaviours. He was very old. Not the vision that I had of him. I saw a man aged about thirty, maybe forty years old. He wore a long, light-coloured robe with a darker scarf wrapped several times around his neck. He smelled clean. Not shower-fresh clean, just not of anything bad or putrid or body odour. Arrien had smelled of meadow. He had the air of one who had seen a lot. Been involved in a lot. Seen bloodshed and war. Seen famine and peace. I felt that he had known humanity and was weary of our behaviours as though we have had all this time on earth and still haven't learned from our past mistakes. I liked him. He was very respectable and respectful. I had come to understand that the characteristics of my guides were the characteristics I was to learn at that time. Arrien had been outgoing, talkative and interested in other people at a time when I was introverted and kept very much to myself. Without her influence, I know I would not be in a campervan with another human who I had met only a few short months previously, travelling to foreign countries to learn about my gifts when I didn't really know what they were or what I would be learning!

But now my time had come to calm down a little and be respectful of the people and places I would come into contact with. Not that I wasn't normally respectful!

Our first meeting with a non-English person in France was two hours after leaving the port; we decided we should stop to eat, fuel up, use the toilets and double-check our travel plans. The weather was still very cold and the heater in the van was beginning to play up, so we didn't have consistent heat. Both our moods were a little low.

The roads were fairly straight and quiet, so we saw the petrol station ahead of us with plenty of time to decide we were going in. It looked family-owned rather than a petroleum company-owned station, a little ramshackle and in need of love. A couple of earlier petrol stations had given us both a bad feeling, so we drove past without slowing down. When we pulled in beside the fuel pumps, Thomas jumped out, opened the fuel cap and struggled with the nozzle ... but couldn't work out how to make it dispense fuel, so I went inside to ask for help.

"*Oui, je peux t'aider?*" the gruff voice of a scruffy-looking man called out as I entered. He had his back to me, rummaging through a drawer beside a door which opened onto the garage where a battered old car stood with its bonnet open. A dirty, limp rag sagging over one wing.

"*Rauol, tu es un idiot! Ne perds pas mon tem.*" He turned, scowling, and stopped in his tracks when he saw that I was not Raoul. He smiled, showing that he had only two brown teeth. His smile lit up his face and his voice softened. "*Bonjour ma belle, comment puis-je t'aider?*"

I realised I had no idea what he was saying. Although the sound was lovely. His voice was almost a purr, contrasting drastically with his appearance.

"Erm, er ... fuel?" I mimed, filling up the van, and pointed outside, where I could see Thomas peering over the fuel pump, nozzle in one hand and fuel cap in the other.

The scruffy mechanic chuckled warmly, "*Laisse-moi allumer la pompe a carburant.*" Walking behind the service desk, he reached beneath it and I heard the clunk of a switch being pressed.

"You English?" He asked, still smiling. I nodded. "You no speak Francais?" I felt ashamed that I was in his country and couldn't speak his language. My face turned pink. I shook my head and looked at my toes.

"Sorry," I said.

He roared with laughter and came toward me, reaching out his hand and giving my shoulder a gentle shake.

"Is polite to help people, yes?" he said, looking at me. I said yes and thank you. But he had turned away and was walking back to the open door. He grabbed the frame with one hand and yelled,

"*Mon Coeur, Viens maider, s'il te plait! J'ai trouve un chaton.*"

As Thomas came through the door from the forecourt, a rather tall and round woman entered from the garage. She was also in scruffy overalls but with all her teeth. Unkempt, dark hair piled atop her head and the warmest aura I think I had ever seen. I grinned widely.

"Oh, are you English?" she asked in an English accent that reminded me of farmers. "Oh, my! Come through, I'll put the kettle on. I haven't spoken English for over a year. I'm afraid I'm going to spoil you and keep you here, forever, with tea and cakes."

After the two males nodded and grunted slightly to one another, she took us through the garage and into a room beyond. It was rustic but beautiful and warm – a large open fire, stacked high with burning logs, dominated the room. A small kitchen area to one side held a tin kettle, which she filled at the ceramic sink. The room smelled homely, of baking, dogs, bodies, sweat, and light perfume. They were Elizabeth and Alain Babin, she told us as we sat on the mish-mash furniture. There were five armchairs in varying states of oldness, but all looked a lot more comfortable than the seats of the van, which would begin to numb your bottom and upper thighs after an hour of driving.

They had been married for a year, Elizabeth told us. She had come travelling in a van like ours with three other friends three years earlier, but when they had arrived here, she fell in love with Alain. And possibly the space, she loud-whispered so her husband could hear. He had more teeth then, she told us as she passed us sweet tea in delicate mugs; he was the most beautiful human being she had known. She brought a large sponge cake to the low table enclosed by the chairs, cutting large slices and passing them to each of us in turn on mismatched plates. The cake was deliciously moist and sweet with a taste like marzipan. And more-ish. I could have eaten the rest of the cake right there by myself!

Alain's mother was alive then, she continued, and she told Alain to marry Elizabeth on the spot. They both giggled. There was love in their eyes and a tenderness for one another that made my eyes fill up.

"She was right," I said. "She would be very happy to see you together like this. And proud." Alain's mother stood between their chairs with a hand resting on the back of each. I could see that she loved Elizabeth as much as she loved her son. She spoke to me in French, but I understood her in English. I wasn't sure I would be able to understand spirits abroad, but I was cheered up immensely to know that I could.

Alain's mother suggested I tell them how cold it was in the van. So, I mentioned how warm it was in their room compared to the van. They looked at one another knowingly and asked if we would like to stay here overnight as the weather would be awful but would improve tomorrow. Elizabeth remembered how awful the van that she travelled in was, how cold it was, how small it was for her height, and how there were no facilities! She offered us a couple of her jumpers that she'd outgrown – one was a perfect fit for Thomas and the other just a bit big for me but perfect with another jumper beneath.

We fetched our nightwear and toiletries from the van and Elizabeth took us up to Alain's mother's old room, suggesting we get comfy and then if I'd like to help prepare tea, I was more than welcome. I put my pyjamas on the bed and my bag of toiletries on the dresser. There was a pack of large cards with beautifully patterned backs. Very old. The rounded edges were split and yellow. But I was drawn to them.

"They are mine." Alain's mother said in two voices – one French, her mother tongue, and one English that her Soul was speaking for my benefit. Both at the same time and yet very separate. "Take them," she said, "Elizabeth will be glad."

I took the cards downstairs and into the living kitchen, where Elizabeth was peeling potatoes. She laughed when she saw the cards in my hand and asked why I'd brought them downstairs. I felt awkward, not sure if I should tell her that her mother-in-law was still in the house. Some people don't want to know, you see. Then Alain came through into the house, having shut the garage for lunch. He looked at Elizabeth. He looked at me. He looked at the cards. He looked slightly perplexed and then said in broken English and a very heavy but soothing French accent,

"Please take them with you when you go! They were my mother's. I'm sure she is still in this house, and as much as I love her, I'd be quite happy for her to leave. Hint. Hint, Mother." He and Elizabeth started laughing.

His mother told me it was because she wanted them to have a baby, but they were in no rush. I blushed slightly as she showed me what she meant – an image of the couple the night before making love. Then she told me that they felt they didn't have enough money to bring a child into the world. But if they found the necklace.

"The necklace?" I said out loud without thinking. Sometimes I forgot that I was having a conversation with someone who no one else could see or hear! Three sets of eyes were staring at me. Four, if you count Alain's mother.

Alain asked me what I knew about the necklace, smiling an odd smile that I couldn't quite place, but I knew it wasn't bad. I felt anxious. We had been offered a warm place to stay for the night and a hot meal. If I told them about the necklace, they might have chucked us out. I felt the warmth of Kaleb at my side. It was a feeling of safety and truth, so I sent a mental apology to Thomas, who was looking forward to home-cooked food that wasn't from a tin or a service station and told them.

Alain burst into laughter. His mother had always told him about this necklace that had belonged to Marie Antoinette. She had given it as payment for one of Alain's ancestors to release her from the conciergerie the day before her execution, he told us, but something had gone wrong and he had been unable to fulfil his promise. The necklace had been hidden and the ancestor himself was tried and executed as a traitor.

"That is the story she always told, anyway," Alain said, then asked how I knew about it. I quickly stated that I had a gift of being able to speak with our departed loved ones, then told him his mother had been waiting for a pregnancy before she was going to tell him the location. Unfortunately, she had passed over before she could tell him. But she thought it was time now. But no one knows where it is, or even if it does exist, Alain and Elizabeth protested.

I looked toward his mother standing beside the fire, warming her backside, a look of disbelief on her face. She kept tutting and shaking her head and making noises through her closed lips. *Should ... Should I get it?* I stuttered in my head to his mother.

"Yes. But first tell him his middle name is the same as your friend's surname. They might find they are distantly related!" She chuckled as a look of shock passed my face. Thomas ran to my side and grabbed my arm.

"Are you okay? Here, sit down." He sidestepped me to one of

the chairs closest to the fire, and the heat warmed the chill in my bones. I asked Thomas to show his passport to Alain. Your middle name is the same as his surname, I told Alain, then suggested we go out to the *'pwee deuh'* before it got dark.

"What well? We have a well?" Alain had lived in this house all his life and was unaware there was an ancient well at the bottom of the garden!

Behind the garage and house was a soil and gravelled yard, dried and hard from many years of footfall. It was currently turning to mush from the recent rains. At the very end of the yard were piled bits of old cars, bicycles, an old oven and other bits and pieces of junk.

Following Alain's mum's instructions, I moved a few of the smaller pieces, then asked Alain and Thomas to move what looked like the rotting body of a Clement Bayard car. It was partially stuck in the ground – years of heavy rain had caused it to sink into the mud, which then dried hard when baked by the sun. An axe was brought out to hack at the ground and the vehicle body was removed in three separate rotting parts. Several rotting and moulded tree trunks fell apart in our hands. Then, beneath that, what looked like a cement paving slab. Elizabeth went off to put the kettle on, deciding we would take a quick break, as we were all sweating and covered in muck and debris at this point. The clouds chose to open slightly at this particular time, and dampness surrounded us in the air and beneath our feet. Alain muttered something very quickly, in French, under his breath, which I think meant that 'this had better be worth the effort.'

Thomas found a large metal bar in the garage that was slightly bent at the end. I think it was for putting tyres onto wheels or taking them off, but after we'd had a cup of tea and a few minutes' break, Thomas and Alain used the bar to lever up and push aside the manhole cover. Beneath it was a perfectly symmetrical, round cavity built of white stone blocks. Alain dropped a coin that he'd pulled from his trouser pocket down the well, but we couldn't hear a splash. It was either very dry or very deep, he said, but he wasn't smiling. He asked if he had to climb down inside. It wasn't very wide, so I thought if the necklace was at the bottom of the well, it would be me climbing down and I really did not fancy that! I looked towards his mum who had moved across and straddled the well. She reached for one of the stones and slowly and purposefully slid it out, placing it on top of the well. Of course, only I could see this, so I went to stand in the same place and reached down. My foot slipped on the now-damp earth, and I fell forward straight onto my face. Three pairs of hands reached for me and lifted me simultaneously over the hole and back toward solid ground. I told Alain what I had seen and he knelt down at the side of the hole and began testing the rocks … a bit further round, I told him, the next row up, a bit further round. We were all about to give up when one stone fell out of its own accord. Well, Alain's mum had pulled it out, but it takes a huge amount of energy for a spirit to do that kind of thing; she lost her vibrancy and became transparent. The stone hit the wall across from it and then ricocheted down the well. We all took a deep breath and held it as Alain went flat onto his tummy and pushed his hand into the hole left by the disappeared stone.

After what felt like an eternity, he gasped and shot up onto his knees. Clutching something to his chest. His eyes were wide and tears were clinging to his eyelashes. His face had gone a strange pasty pale colour. His lips began to move wordlessly. A puzzled look passed across his face, and then he threw himself back onto his belly and used his other hand to search inside the hole. He gasped again, bringing up a second larger package. He placed both packages onto the mud and went back for a third try. This time, he came up empty. He picked up both packages, stood up and handed them to me, asking,

"S'il te plait, peux-tu tenir ca?"

Then he grabbed Elizabeth's two hands and began jumping and shouting as the clouds ripped open. So infectious was his joy that

Elizabeth joined in. Then both Thomas and I began to laugh and jump around like demented chickens, impervious to the cold and wet of the French countryside.

We took turns to shower and change into clean clothes whilst Elizabeth – too late now to start a fresh meal – heated up the leftovers from their previous evening meal along with some bread she had warmed in the oven and a selection of meats and cheeses from the fridge. It was by far the best meal I had eaten in my whole life and I had no idea what it was!

All cleaned, fed and watered, we returned to the comfortable chairs by the fire. Alain placed two large logs onto the fire and listened for a while to their cracks and snaps before picking up the two packages we had found in the well. Apprehensively, he began to unwrap the decaying fabric wrapped around the first one. As a group, we hadn't properly spoken since returning from the well, and conversation was not high on anyone's agenda right now. It was as though we were waiting for a miracle to occur or for a badly organised practical joke to go off. I hoped for one and prayed it wasn't the other.

Alain's hands were shaking as he fully removed the cloth from the treasure, which he lifted up to show us. Three strings of beautiful pearls, all held together by a large diamond-laden clasp. Dirty. But still stunningly beautiful. We all made quiet noises that sounded like 'wow'. He passed it to Elizabeth, who looked it over and pressed one of the pearls to her teeth.

Elizabeth passed it to me – I flew instantly back to 1793; in tears, the woman was pleading for her life. For news of her child. 'Please help me. Please help me. As God is my witness, I will be better. I will do better.' A man nodded his head and took the jewels from her hand. 'Tomorrow. I will come for you tomorrow.' He ran out of the building and out of the town. He didn't stop running until nightfall when he arrived at a small farmstead. He took the jewels to the kitchen and wrapped them in the handkerchief she had given him the day before. 'Hide them', he told his wife. 'Don't tell me where. I'll need two good horses. Can you bring them to the city?' And he left again. Running. Back the way he had come.

I passed the necklace to Thomas and described what I had seen. There were some pearl earrings too, I said, that had been passed to the man from the queen and from the man to his wife.

Alain looked at the second package in his lap but waited till Thomas had returned the necklace before he opened it. There was tension in the room. Not a Beastman kind of tension. That was a type of tension that sat all alone in the middle of a desert on another planet. This tension was excitement and anxiety – good anxiety – a bit like Christmas Eve when you know you've been good and there are going to be presents, but you're not sure what they will be or how many there'll be or if you will like them when you open them. That kind of anxiety.

He pursed his lips and blew out a long, loud breath. Then another. And another.

"Come on, Alain," ushered Elizabeth. *"Faisons Cela! Faisons Cela!"* Let's do this.

He quickly swept away the corners of the cloth covering to reveal a leather-bound book about the size of Alain's large palm. Expensive. From the look of it. Old, too. There was a gold cross stamped into the front of the black leather cover, along with a swirling gold border surrounding it. On the spine were the words 'La Sainte Bible' in gold capitals. The cover and the gold were well-worn and well-loved but beautiful. We were all in awe and wondering whether it also belonged to the queen. Alain flicked through the pages and gulped loudly, making a strange, strangled sound. His eyes widened and narrowed as he tried to make out what he was looking at.

"What is it?" Elizabeth, Thomas and I asked in unison. Alain tilted the book so we could see and flipped through the pages. It wasn't a bible at all. The pages were handwritten in a beautiful old script, and the top of some pages were dated. It was a diary!

"How very clever!" I said to Alain's mum as she slowly began to fade. I told Alain that his mum was leaving now. He burst into tears and began talking very fast. I heard *'Merci'* and *'j'aime ta mere'* – we had learned that in French lessons at school and I was pleased that I had learned something. She had a final message for him and Elizabeth before she disappeared completely, leaving only a scent of jasmine and warm bread.

"Why did you say it was clever?" Elizabeth asked whilst pouring everyone a glass of red wine. I told her that everyone had bibles, so no one would look inside a bible. So, it was very clever to use a bible cover to hide the diary. Especially if the diary contained information the writer did not want anyone else to read!

Alain passed it to me, asking if I could do the same as I did with the necklace. He meant could I pick up the story from the vibrations of the book's energy. I took a deep breath and then, as I whooshed it out, I took the book from Alain. Immediately, the story began to flood in.

The diary began in August 1792, the time that the palace was stormed and her life changed forever. She talked a lot about how her beautiful friend Yolande had deserted her, the safety of her child and her regrets about not being a better person. It mentioned the man who was going to help her escape and their conversations over the last two months of her life. There were then two pages written by another hand – the wife of the man who took the necklace – stating how she had come into possession of both the book and the jewellery. She had sold the earrings for two fast, well-bred horses which she rode into the city looking for her husband. The news that the queen had been executed that very morning was all over the city, so she was not surprised to find her husband had already been captured and his execution was imminent. She had managed to visit him in his cell, where he passed her 'his bible' and instructed her to get as far away as possible and keep the queen's belongings safe until it was appropriate to return them to her family. She rode back to their farmstead and packed up her children and their belongings with the intention of travelling to England, where she had family. She got as far as this very place before she was struck with a fever which, over the following month, killed her and her youngest children. The elder child hid the book and the necklace after writing the last page. It was dated December 24th, 1793.

"I have a voice that I don't recognise saying the book should go to Hedwig?" I said, puzzled. "I think it is a direct descendant of the queen's friend, Duchess Poly-nac?" I was hearing the names and as they were not English names, I felt bad that I might be saying them wrong. Everyone smiled. Elizabeth asked what we were to do with the necklace. "That's yours," I said. The voice that I couldn't place was very determined about both those things.

It was very late when we finally got to bed, and Thomas and I fell asleep very quickly. The sound of the heavy rain was like a lullaby. We woke late the next morning to find Alain fixing the heating in the van as a thank you for our help in finding the artefacts. He also did something to the engine, which made it run better; we would be able to get a top speed of maybe fifty miles an hour as opposed to the thirty miles we'd been doing up until this point. Alain refused to accept payment for the fuel we filled up yesterday. They asked if we would stay longer, but we wanted to see more of France before we headed to Spain. I bought and posted postcards for mine and Thomas's families and friends in England – and for Carolanne and Robert - then we said our goodbyes. Elizabeth gave us the leftover cake and loads of cheese and suggested which bread would keep the longest if we weren't able to buy it fresh every day. She also gave us two bottles of the red wine from the evening before. Neither Thomas nor I liked alcohol, so we decided we'd give it to the next nice person we met. We hugged for what seemed like an eternity. Both Alain's and Elizabeth's eyes filled with tears as they waved us goodbye and we set off on our next adventure.

We decided we couldn't visit France without paying a visit to Paris. It was a straight road, according to the map, so we should have been there in a couple of hours, but we had to keep stopping at quaint small villages along the way, amazed at the architecture of the old buildings and the beauty of their histories.

We finally arrived on the outskirts of Paris at nightfall, so we parked up and went in search of somewhere to eat. We took our toothbrushes too, so that after eating, we could brush our teeth, use the facilities and go straight to sleep on our return to the van.

Our fourth day was spent in Paris – it was far too busy and not quite as romantic as you see in the movies – where Thomas was spat at by a man in a beret who smelled of cigarettes and failure. We decided to visit Marie Antoinette's old home at Versailles, but I became extremely anxious and had a panic attack for no apparent reason, which didn't stop until we had passed Versailles and headed toward Limoges.

When we were on a straight road away from towns and villages, we would swap seats and I would drive for an hour to give Thomas a break. Just before we got to Limoges, there was a large beautiful lake visible from the road, so we drove down to it and set up our camp for the evening. Settled on the shore of the lake with a small crop of trees to the side, we were able to make a cup of tea on our little stove, and we ate cheese and bread while watching the sun go down on the lake.

"It was a marvellous thing you did for them," Thomas said after we had eaten in that comfortable silence that two people can have. I looked at him, not sure what I should say.

"Your gift is amazing!" He turned to look at me and his face showed an admiration I had never seen before. I was used to people telling me off or getting upset if I told them what I was seeing or hearing. I wasn't used to people accepting what I was saying. And I had never before experienced an actual physical finish – nobody ever came back to me and said, 'you were right', or 'I found it where you said it would be'. I read about Mark and his grandma in the paper, and I'd told the police about the ladies from the care home. But I had never fully witnessed the truth of my 'gift', as Thomas called it. I felt emotional again and wasn't sure if it was because of this, because I was missing my family or because I was living in a sardine tin without a proper toilet. Thomas shuffled closer and put his arm around me, rubbing my arm to take out a little chill that had begun to settle in the air.

I thought about the tarot cards I had received from Alain's mum.

"Can you read tarot cards?" Thomas asked as if reading my thoughts.

I smiled and told him I didn't know. I'd only ever seen the cards that Miss Dougal, the English teacher, had been using. I stood up and reached into the van for my backpack – an item on Carmen's shopping list, which was the nearest I would ever get to owning a handbag and contained just about everything I owned that was small enough to fit in it. My arm disappeared up to my elbow. I didn't have a lot of belongings. I fished around and then brought out the pack surrounded by the scarf. I unwrapped the cards and began to shuffle them in the way that I'd seen Miss Dougal shuffling them. Then I split the cards into two piles and picked the card from the top of the lower pile.

I turned it over and placed it on the ground between us. The image showed a naked man and woman, their bodies entwined. Twisted together, almost like a candy cane. They seemed to be melting together into one being. The word beneath said *Les Armoureux*. The Lovers.

"Erm ..." Thomas started to speak. "Is that supposed to be us? Because ..."

"No," I said really fast. "Well, yes, but not lovers." I calmed down as the meaning began to swell through me – I began to feel the meaning of the card. "This card means two people who are on a journey together. Not just literally. But we are on another journey too. Our current situation means we are entwined. We were meant to be here. Today. Together."

I flicked over the next card, *Le Fou* – The Fool. A man in bright clothing, with a bundle tied to the end of a stick across his shoulder, was standing atop a mountain. Behind him was an evening dusk. He had one foot on the rock and the other in front as though he were about to take a stroll off the mountain. As I looked at the card, his face changed from that of a young boy into that of a man and he took the step forward into sunlight.

"This card means taking a leap of faith," I said. "It is about the journey we take from childhood into adulthood. Being afraid but taking that step forward anyway."

I flicked over the next card, *Le Monde*. The World. A beautiful woman dressed only in a scarf, dancing within a clear turning globe of the world.

"When you take that leap of faith you will achieve greatness. This card is an ending, sort of. But also a new beginning. Like this one." I pointed to the fool. "They are both saying that you can't start something new without finishing something first. But in order for that something to end, you need to be clear where you are going." I looked at Thomas and he looked sad.

"Are you okay?" I reached out a hand to him. "Does it make sense?"

He nodded. There was a tear in his eye. But I couldn't read him. *Part of his Marton stock*, I thought, they are able to block out others from their energy. I wondered if I did that too.

"Let's get some sleep. We can set off early in the morning." He began to pack away the cooking stove and utensils. I wrapped the cards back up and put them into my bag, then took the cups, plates and cutlery down to the lake edge where I gave them a swish in the water in an attempt to clean them. I was sure that if we died of food poisoning on our journey it wouldn't be down to the food, but my poor attempts at washing up.

The following day Thomas was awake at seven o'clock. That is the earliest either of us had been awake since we started this journey. I looked at him carefully, trying to look at his aura, as I could sense he was upset but couldn't understand why. Had I done something? Said something?

"Stop doing that!" he barked, venomously. Throwing a pan he'd left under the bed into the back of the van.

"Doing wh…?" I started to ask.

"You know what! You look at people like you can see inside them. Like you know what is going on inside them. Like you are judging them." He spat the word 'judging'. He was angry. Not at me, but at that moment I felt like he was. And I felt angry too. Angry that he thought I would judge him. Angry that he thought I would think less of him for any reason. Angry that he thought I was that shallow.

"I'm sorry." I didn't know what else to say.

"No you aren't. You're never sorry. This was a stupid idea taking a little girl with me. What on earth was I thinking?" He continued throwing things and muttering to himself. I didn't like this side of Thomas. My energy was depleting quickly. I was feeling sad and tearful. Weak. I wasn't sure what I should say or do. Or if I could make it better.

I climbed into the passenger seat whilst he finished throwing things around in the back. When he finished he slammed the door closed. Opened it and slammed it again. He opened it again and slammed it shut a third time making an irritated noise then stormed around to the driver's side. He pulled open the door threw himself in and slammed this door really hard too with an added tutting noise to make it clear that he was not happy.

I tried to think what it was that I had done to make him so angry. I turned my body away from him and curled up with my head on the passenger door window. I had turned the music on quietly as I climbed in to the van but Thomas now switched it off, muttering under his breath.

"Do you think you might get your lazy arse into gear and tell me where we are supposed to go?" he said, punching the map into my back with a force that was uncalled for. I sat upright and opened the map. My eyes filled with tears and spilt down my cheeks. I wiped them away absently keeping my eyes on the map and not looking at Thomas. I gave him the first instruction and he set off, grinding the gears as he did so.

We drove toward Toulouse in silence. By the time we stopped to refuel I was desperate for the toilet but had decided I wouldn't bother him or give him any excuse to be unhappy with me. I wasn't sure what I had done to cause him to be this upset. But I didn't like it. When I went to the bathroom at the fuel stop, I took my backpack with my passport and purse. Just in case!

The bathroom was behind the service area. It was small and dirty and smelled disgusting. I did my business as quickly as I could; hovering over the dirty toilet seat instead of sitting on it. There was something dry smeared across it and I really didn't want to touch it with any part of my body. I then brushed my teeth but couldn't rinse as the water was a strange orangey colour and I wasn't sure if it was poisonous!

I left the bathroom without washing my hands, which made me feel dirty, and returned to the front of the service area, where I had left Thomas and the van at pump number two. There were four fuel pumps with three vehicles in front of them. None of them were the van. I walked around the other side of the fuel station to where the gents toilets were, thinking Thomas may have parked up and gone to the toilet. I followed two large trucks that were just arriving and parking up at the rear. No van. I walked to the door of the gents' toilet and called out Thomas's name. No response.

I walked back round to the front and toward the road. The road was long and straight. If he had driven off I would have seen it, I'm sure. I could see a long distance both ahead and the way we had driven in, so I was sure he hadn't driven off without me.

The fuel station had now emptied of vehicles, a vehicle was driving toward the fuel station, and had indicated to pull in, then changed its mind and carried on to where I was standing. A rusty Crew Cab pickup truck with four men inside. Dirty. Scruffy. Smelled of harm. My whole body prickled with fear but I was unable to move.

"Est-ce tu vas, ma jolie?" the driver asked greasily through his open window, as the rear door opened and the two passengers slid out.

"No parlez francais." I responded. As one, their lips parted into what I can only describe as grimaces, but I think it was supposed to be smiles. The driver and front passenger now stepped out of their vehicle so the four men were stood in a line in front of me. I had a memory of something similar and part of me thought 'not again' and another part said 'this isn't for you silly, it's for the others'. But I didn't understand then.

I felt Kaleb at my side. 'May I?" he said as I felt the warmth of his Soul pour in beside my Soul. He began to speak – through my mouth – a language I didn't know or recognise. Except it was familiar. Warm. It could be Hebrew, Arabic, it felt like I'd heard it before in another life. One of the men looked at me, then lifted his eyes upwards – I think Kaleb's Soul had grown exponentially and this man could see or sense it. My Soul was sitting quietly inside. The other men were staring open-mouthed at me, this little girl with the powerful voice of a man. It felt as though Kaleb was saying that they could not harm me. That I was not there for them, but that I was there for the girls, and I would take them now. If I didn't take the girls now, I would take the Souls of every man here. This was a choice that they could make, and I would do nothing to stop them whatever choice they made. The sensitive man, the one who could see Kaleb's form, began to whimper and dropped to his knees, the fear of what he saw equal to the fear he had of his fellow travellers visible on his face. The passenger flung open the cab door to retrieve the keys and ran to the back of the pickup truck. The other two stood still as though unable to move. I heard a sound in the distance like sirens, but I felt like I was under a spell and unable to break it.

The man in the back of the pickup truck was crying – he couldn't find the right key but he was trying. "I will find it. I will do it", he repeated again and again in a language I couldn't figure out. I walked to the back of the truck at the same time that the lock was finally opened. I saw Thomas running toward me in one vision and three small girls cowering in the box in another.

The world seemed to slow down as I climbed onto the flatbed of the truck. The man who opened the lock appeared to fly backwards from the vehicle. The siren became louder, and tyres screeched as a vehicle with blue flashing lights came to a halt. Thomas's face etched with distress looming closer. Two men in uniforms holding guns. Shouting. More sirens. I moved toward the three girls and spoke in three different languages at once in both my own and Kaleb's voices.

"You are safe now." We both reached out our arms to the girls. "Come with us. You are safe. You are in no more danger." As they reached their hands to us, I felt Kaleb reduce and remove his Soul body from mine. In turn each girl stood up, moved toward me and threw their arms around my neck. My heart broke as the last one stood. Her pain spanned a thousand galaxies. Her skirt covered in blood. Her eyes empty. Her existence numb.

It is so hard to feel both hatred and anger in the same breath as love and compassion.

I cannot tell you how much I wanted to rip apart those sad excuses for human beings whilst holding on to the children whose lives they had ripped apart for their own amusement.

How these creatures are allowed to live in the same world as love, beauty and innocence still alludes me.

I felt Thomas's arms around me, and he spoke softly and gently to the young girls and me. An ambulance appeared, along with more police vehicles. I was still in a daze. Feeling numb. *I must be in shock*, I told myself. Then as one girl was lifted from my arms, I noticed I had placed a metre-wide shield of my energy around her. And around each of the other two. It was my own personal energy and not that of the universal field, so it was weakening me. I was glad. I would happily give up every inch of my energy and every part of my life if I could just take back the last few days and weeks of these girls' lives. I cannot ... dare not ... share the details with you, my lovely friend . Those horrors are for me and those children alone.

And I can tell you now that those vile creatures who call themselves men will suffer in their afterlife. I know this. I can promise you this, dear friend, because I am the one who gives them their justice. And I promise. Right here. Right now. I will not be kind.

37

A Word From Thomas

Thomas didn't tell me any of what follows. I managed to get hold of a copy of his witness statement from the French Police. He had spoken in English to the police whilst a translator put his words into French. I had them translated back into English, so these are as near as you will find to his actual memories from that day.

Oh! I should also mention that this is the original version before they took out a few of the more challenging parts of the statement. You'll understand why they had to take them out as you read.

"My name is Thomas Marton. I am a British citizen travelling from my home in England to Spain, where I will be taking up a place at university in Madrid starting in January. I am to be staying with my aunt, Carmen Sahira, in Teruel over the Christmas period prior to starting my course.

I am travelling with a friend of my great aunt, Emily Marton, who lives in the same English town as I do. My aunt is a mentor and neighbour to the young girl with whom I am travelling.

We are travelling in a 1957 VW Campervan. I am driving her to Teruel where she will be studying with my Aunt Carmen. I don't know what she will be studying. I think Spanish or spiritual stuff.

We had driven from the UK to Calais and have been staying in the campervan as we travelled. We had gone through Abbeville to Paris and from Paris to Limoges.

We both have money for our journeys and purchased food from supermarkets, petrol stations and cafes on route.

We had stopped at a petrol station on the A20 just outside of Montauban to fill up with fuel, use the toilets and get some food. She had gone to the toilet while I filled up with fuel. A queue was forming for the fuel, so I moved the van forward before going to pay. I realised there was a café attached to the station, so I then drove round to the back to the car park and went into the café to check the food and order us both a coffee. I had just finished ordering the coffee when I saw her come round the side of the building and walk toward the road. I put the coffee on a table near the window and banged on the window to let her know where I was, but she was too far away. I saw a pickup stop in front of her and two men got out.

The pickup was old. I didn't see the number plate. It was green and orange. I think the orange was rust. It had a double cab at the front with four men altogether, I think, inside. I couldn't see anything in the back of the pickup.

She spoke and two more men got out and stood in front of her. I was worried at this point because she looked scared, so I ran out of the café.

I was worried because she is very small for her age. She is sixteen but looks like she is fourteen. The men were very large and I had a bad feeling about them.

As I ran toward them she started to glow and it looked like she had grown ten feet. Ten feet is approximately 3 metres. I could hear a voice speaking in a different language. I don't know what language. It wasn't English, or French. I speak a little French. I have an 'O' level school certificate in French. I don't know if it was an Eastern European voice. It appeared to be coming from her. Her mouth was moving, but it was a man's voice and it seemed to be everywhere around me.

It looked like she had a giant pair of white wings. I know that sounds mad. I am telling you what I saw.

One of the men fell down and started to scream. Another went into the cab of his vehicle. No I can't say it was the driver. I don't know who it was. It was one of the men who hadn't fallen over. There were two still stood there. The one who went into the cab was now in the back of the pickup. He had keys in his hand and was trying to open a wooden box that had three separate locks on it.

I could now see there was a box on the back of the pickup, because the man had dropped the tailgate in order to climb into the back and I was running toward it. The box fitted the width of the pickup and was about two foot high and two foot deep. Two foot is about sixty centimetres. It was that size as far as I could tell, but I didn't have a tape measure so couldn't be more precise.

The man opened all three locks then she seemed to fly across the side of the truck and onto the flat bed. She was standing up and didn't seem to exert any effort. It didn't look like she had moved at all, she was on the roadside one minute, then on the back of the van the next. The man who was there rose up into the air about six foot, or two metres and it looked to me as if he was thrown – but she hadn't touched him and there was no one else there on the back of the van. He appeared to float away for another two to three metres before he fell to the floor. I don't know if he sustained any injuries. I was too far away to see.

The wood on the box seemed to just splinter. Like, loads of tiny pieces of wood just flew up into the air and straight at the man who had opened the locks. She wasn't close enough to it to touch it or to have smashed it with anything.

This all happened really quickly. I felt like it had happened in a dream. I ran over to the pickup and saw three little girls getting out of the box that had had the locks on.

I feel really stupid saying this but I screamed. I could see horror in their eyes and it felt like it burnt my heart.

No. They weren't scared of her. They hadn't seen her then. She had kind of disappeared and there was just a man like from the bible. It wasn't Jesus. I just know it wasn't Jesus. Because according to the bible that I read Jesus has blonde hair and blue eyes and this chap was most definitely not blonde!

The girls' faces lit up as they saw him, and then he started to disappear and she began to reappear. She held out her arms and they fell into her and a gigantic bubble seemed to surround them. I had reached her and tried to touch her and put my arm around her to make sure she was alright but I couldn't move. It felt like there was a glass dome over them all.

Then the ambulance stopped at the side of the pickup and she ushered the girls toward the ambulance people. What do I think happened? I think she was protecting them. I think she was making sure they were safe until they really were safe. That's all that I can say. And I'm sorry if you think I'm mad. I don't care if you think I'm crazy. That is what I saw. And if it wasn't for her, those girls could be anywhere now. So don't go trying to pin any blame on her.

38

Purple Teardrops

I was interviewed by the police five times that day. I was held in a police cell in Toulouse until a stray photojournalist managed to sneak in and take a photo. It was in all the French newspapers.

'ANGEL DETENU DANS UNE PRISON POUR ADULTES' was the headline in one, 'Angel held in adult prison', with my tiny, fragile, terrified face splashed across it.

"SAUVEUR RETENU PRISONNIER" – 'Saviour Held Prisoner', ran another.

The parents of one of the girls went on television demanding my release. Insisting that I needed hospital care along with the other girls as I was a victim and not an abuser.

I was taken to the same hospital as the three girls and allowed to visit each one. I think the police were hoping the girls would scream or look scared and they could then feel satisfied – or perhaps a little smug – that they were right to arrest me. In turn they broke down in tears and grabbed tight hold of me when they saw me, *"merci pour ma vie"* the first girl repeated time and time again till my heart broke. I kept getting snippets of vision of what each child had suffered as I held them and I had to block it out. It tore my heart apart.

The eldest girl. She was thirteen years old. She was the one who had suffered most. The doctors were keeping visitors to a minimum as they didn't want to traumatise her any further. Her parents insisted I be allowed in. I wasn't sure I could cope but didn't want to not see her. Didn't want to single her out for any reason.

As the door opened I saw a light behind the curtain surrounding the bed. Her mother was talking to me as we walked in, her voice calm but strained, broken English. Not French. As she pulled back the curtain to reveal the bed and her daughter, I noticed her Soul was trying to leave. Her mother stood stock still as she could see that her daughter was dying. This woman had witnessed a lot of death. I sat beside the bed and reached for her hand.

"I don't want to live," her Soul said. "I don't like this world." Tears were falling down her human face. Silent. Rivers. Her human self was hanging on. She wanted to say goodbye to her family. But her Soul was desperate for a peace she hadn't felt on this earth.

"Can we have a few moments?" I asked her mother, knowing I had no right to ask anything from a woman whose daughter was ready to leave this world. Yet she nodded. Tears falling silently down her face, too. She turned and left the room.

I don't know what happened next, but as the door closed we were both standing in The Light House. But this wasn't my Light House. It was similar. But different. This was her place. She smiled. The whole universe lit up with love and joy.

What is your name, I asked, without speaking.

My earth name is Talia, she replied.

That is an Angel, isn't it? I asked.

Yes, I am an Angel. I was sent to earth, like you, to do a special job.

Who will do your job if you leave your body? I asked.

I know I need to go back, she said, the light dimming ever so slightly. *But it really hurts, you know?*

I know. But we can hurt together. Okay? We can keep in touch and you can tell me what you can't say to anybody else. Okay? We can share our secrets with each other. We can heal the world together. We can help each oth....

We were back in the hospital room before I could finish a sentence that I hadn't really understood. There were raised voices on the other side of the door. The door burst open and a bearded man with the weight of the world pressing hard upon his shoulder stormed in flanked by two men in suits holding firearms. He grabbed at his daughter crying, the armed men reached for me grabbing my arms roughly, pushing them behind my back and my body against the wall. Talia's mother wept as she walked back through the door.

"Daaa-aad," Talia spoke her first words since entering the hospital. Both parents gasped. Their tears immediately stopped flowing. The whole room seemed to stop. The doctor, who had stood meekly at the door, pushed his way past the mother and through the two armed men till he reached the bed. He pulled the father away from his child and stared at her.

"She's alive!" he sounded shocked, as though it was a done deal that she was going to die. "She ... she's alive!" he smiled and did a little jig. Talia's parents moved to hold one another and look at their daughter.

"Thank you," she said to me. "I owe you my life. Twice!" Her father roughly pushed his armed guards away from me and grabbed me in a bear hug, so tight I thought I would lose consciousness.

"She needs rest!" I blurted out. "And quiet." I started to walk toward the door, then added, "And lots of love." I smiled at her mum as I walked out, thinking, that was a reeeeaaally cheesy line.

I had a full health check at the hospital and was given my own, private, room for the night. Courtesy of Talia's father, who was some high-ranking politician from Israel. He and her mother took turns to visit me so I wouldn't be alone, bringing flowers, food and gifts. None of which were expected. But they needed to show their gratitude and their apology. He had thought I wanted to kill their daughter, they had been told this by the police. In the early hours of the morning, he sat beside me and cried. He was trying to make a difference in the world and there were people who didn't want change. Didn't want peace. Money, he said, came quicker and easier when there was promise of war and fighting. He had been threatened several times to change his stance and to change the minds of those who followed and believed in him. It was common knowledge that he would rather die than reject his beliefs. So, they had kidnapped his daughter and the daughters of supporters of his political party.

"I don't mind giving my life for my people's freedom. But my daughter is my life, too, and I never wanted her to be hurt in this process. I cannot carry on putting her life in danger."

"Don't give up," I took his hand, he was shaking uncontrollably. Within him roiled anger, fear, desperation, joy, and a thousand other emotions that would be too boring to list. "She will be okay. She needs your love and your support. She doesn't need you to give up on the world in which her children will live. Her grandchildren. They need a safe world. A world of love. Not fear and anger."

"You have the upper hand now," I told him. The perpetrators of the kidnapping were in custody. The world knew who they were and why they harmed these very young girls. The world will not stand for that. The world will take a second look at what is happening, and allegiances will change. Good will overcome evil. "It won't be today," I told him. "But your heart is good and kind. You believe in life and good and that change can happen. You believe that love is the way forward, not war and anger, and for that you can expect changes to start happening."

"Are you really an Angel?" he asked smiling for the first time since his daughter had been found, tears still pouring down his face. "I heard rumours from the police officers at the scene about…" he trailed off, looking at his feet, not sure to believe that which is unbelievable. "The doctors told us Talia would not survive the night."

"Talia is the Angel," I smiled. "I would expect great things from her in the future. I've told her we'll keep in touch if that is okay with you and her mum." He grabbed me in another bear hug and sobbed again.

After he left, I managed to get a few hours sleep. I was mentally and emotionally drained. My energy was low and I really wanted to just disappear somewhere quiet. By myself. On my own. I tried to return to The Light House. My Light House. But I was too exhausted. I wondered what had happened to Thomas. I had seen him briefly, but he had been put into a vehicle by a uniformed man and taken straight to the station where I was questioned. It was a case of high importance; someone there had said. I needed to give them all the information I had, including where the pickup truck had travelled from that day. They thought that I was with those men initially. But slowly the witness statements came in – from Thomas and the truckers and the workers in the cafe and fuel station. And of course, the two girls who were able to speak talked of being rescued by an Angel. That was Kaleb.

I tried to call on Kaleb several times during the later part of the day. But I guess the energy required to do what he did that morning was enough to require a full spiritual reboot. I couldn't see or hear anyone or anything else either. Exhaustion can do that to you. It can make you feel alone even though you are surrounded by people and spirits and Angels. Although I wasn't aware of them, my room was filled with the light of Angels, spirit guides and the ancestors of the girls and their families. I wish I could have seen it because it would have looked beautiful.

Early next morning, I awoke to a feeling of home. My brain had woken up, so I could hear and sense my surroundings. But my body felt like a stone. Heavy. Immoveable. I could hear rustling sounds and whispered voices. I thought I recognised them but was still too 'asleep' to work out who or what I was hearing. I heard the door open and a nurse entered – I recognised the squeak of her shoe from the night before; the nurses were working double shifts so the girls would not have too many different faces around them and so a sneaky photojournalist or terrorist didn't have any access to the floor we were all on. She spoke quietly and a man answered, equally quietly. Both voices were French. But I recognised his voice. I pushed myself out of my sleep state – curiosity can do that – and opened my eyes. My mum was sat in the chair next to the bed, asleep, a little drool had escaped the corner of her mouth and sat like dew on an early morning petal. My heart filled with joy to see her. Bryn was stood at the bottom of the bed looking at me.

I sat up and whispered, "I didn't know you spoke French."

He smiled and whispered back, "I didn't know you had superpowers!" He came around the bed and hugged me – like a father. A tear escaped from my eye, so I reached out to touch my mum's hair to take the attention away from my eye. As she woke up, she sobbed loudly, shot out of the chair so fast she could have won an Olympic medal – if jumping out of chairs was a sport – and grabbed me in a tight hold that literally took my breath away and forced a strange sound from my lips. Bryn laughed, my mum cried and I told her how much I loved her.

Breakfast was provided by Talia's parents – a giant gift basket of croissants and other pastries (I particularly liked the chocolatey ones, with the oozing centres – I dipped them into a cup of thick hot chocolate and enjoyed the feel of the warm oozing chocolate in my mouth. I was definitely taking this home). As we ate, Mum and Bryn recounted how they had arrived.

Thomas had called Mrs Marton in a panic when I was 'arrested'; she contacted Mum and Bryn and arranged a flight for them to come across to France to help and support me. Initially the police wouldn't let them into the hospital, but Talia's parents had intervened and said how shocking the French police service was! I think he was in shock and still frightened as I think they did a marvellous job with the information they had.

Hindsight is always a marvellous thing! We can all make judgements 'after' the facts are known. The hardest thing is to make a judgement about a situation 'before' it happens. Would

Talia's parents have allowed their daughter to walk, unchaperoned, across the street to her friend's house had they known that she would be ripped from the pavement and come to such harm?

Of course, they wouldn't.

If I had known the consequences of the tarot cards that evening, would I have still read them?

Hmm!

Well, that's the thing, isn't it? Hindsight.

Would I want Thomas to be upset at me? No.

Would I want to sit for almost three hours in a van in uncomfortable silence? No.

Would I want to come face to face with four bad men? No.

Would I want to assist in the release of kidnapped children? Absolutely!

You see, hindsight is a marvellous thing, but EVERY choice we make has a consequence. EVERY CHOICE. Not making a choice, by the way, IS a choice. How you live your life every day affects the people around you. The choices you make affect everyone, not just you. Your decision to throw a sicky at work means that someone else has to work twice as hard to complete not only their work but yours as well. Or maybe lowered production because of your absence means the company doesn't get that contract it so desperately needs to keep you in employment. Of course, when you are handed your redundancy notice and they lock the gates for the last time, you are the one saying how useless management was. And all this while it was you, taking a sicky here and popping a few products into your pocket there.

Hindsight is a wonderful thing if you take the time to look properly!

Anyway ... I'm making you feel guilty. I apologise. But perhaps you can have a think about your actions next time?

Talia's father had offered Mum and Bryn their apartment in

Barcelona for my recuperation. I only had a few days left before I was due in Teruel. We were to leave as soon as possible – the story of me having wings and superpowers had spread and the hospital was surrounded by journalists and television news crews. It was, apparently, a modern-day miracle. A twelve-year-old girl (me, hah!) had stopped a gang of international kidnappers and released their victims. There were another four girls found in an abandoned farmstead near a place I can't help but call Villa Mustachio. Sometimes all you have left is a sense of humour and it can become quite dark. Please don't judge me for finding humour in the pain.

39

Viva L'Espana

Talia's father had procured a luxury coach for myself, Mum and Bryn to travel to Barcelona in. He said it would be more comfortable than a car and the paparazzi wouldn't be expecting me to travel in something like that, so I should be able to travel peacefully. I visited the other two girls and gave them my address in Teruel and England. I said I would love to hear how they were getting on but would understand if they didn't want to contact me. The choice was theirs, and they would always be in my heart, I told them.

My farewell with Talia was longer. She was alive, but very poorly. I can't tell you what she went through. Although her emotional and psychological scars will never fade, physically she will recover. She was in and out of consciousness. When she managed to sleep she would awake screaming. Then she would be afraid to close her eyes. With Bryn's help I had managed to increase my energy enough to reconnect with Kaleb, but I had to go to the hospital chapel, the quietest place in order to speak with him. We organised several Angel Healers and with Bryn and myself as human channels we sent her an enormous amount of healing energy. Her parents, who were in Talia's room with us, both said they felt a sense of peace and could see flashes of different coloured light flying around the room. That was the energy of the Angels. Whilst the healing was occurring, Talia's Soul spoke with me. She said we would meet again and work toward building a more peaceful world filled with love and not fear. That was her life journey. That is why she was here. Although she had suffered at the hands of those men, she told me, it had given her a platform. She would be able to share her story with the world.

Farewells done, we slipped out of the hospital via the morgue. I know, ironic, isn't it? There were lots of spirits down there, but none of them spoke to me. Or Bryn. They were lined up against the walls as we walked down the corridor. Silent. Not what I have ever experienced from the dead before. But I wasn't worried. I was concerned for my mum. She was fatigued from the journey and the stress of the situation. Her pregnancy was going well, but she was carrying twins and we didn't want a repeat of the last twin fiasco. I don't know why I just said that. Why did I just say that? I have a memory tickling the back of my memory but, hey. If it's important it will come forward!

The luxury coach was shiny and smelt brand new. The leather upholstery felt as soft as it smelt and Mum was practically asleep before she sat down. There were two men and a woman onboard already, as well as the driver – a man to serve us and two bodyguards. This was a luxury we had never had before. The man who served us, Aaron, was British and from Scotland but worked as a top-class butler to high-paying foreign businessmen who wanted a little bit of Olde English elegance. He was marvellous and I would employ him myself if I had the money. He didn't have a bad bone in his body and was all about 'service'. He believed that serving others was a way of serving mankind itself. Each act of service he provided was an act of love which spread to the person or people he was serving.

"Although some of them are absolute pigs," he loud-whispered with a giggle.

The bodyguards were also wonderful. One sat toward the back of the coach, and one to the front. Every twenty minutes or so, whoever was at the front would stand up and walk to the back, stopping for a quick chat. 'Everything okay?', 'How are you feeling?' the woman asked. She was very intuitive and believed that people knew when danger to themselves was imminent. She always checked how her charges were feeling so she could be prepared to take any necessary action. This woman had seen firsthand the destruction one human could force onto another. Through war. One man's instruction – because it is usually a man at the top of the war pole – could be the difference between life and death for hundreds or thousands of men, women and children in one moment. Those who lived often wished they had not. She was one of those. She lived in the hope that death would take her. Would remove from her head the images of battle. Remove the decisions she had made that could have been better. But until that time, she would make sure that no one died that didn't need to. No one would be harmed that wasn't deserving. She was a good Soul and passionate about life. I wanted to hug her, but she wasn't the hugging type.

Her colleague would then walk to the front of the coach. Silently. He had come from a military background too. His mind, though, was darker. He had killed for pleasure as a youth. Forced into the military as cannon fodder, he'd risen through the ranks quickly. He loved the routine, the discipline and the camaraderie. He knew how to get a job done. Quickly. He had been offered work as an assassin – a paid killer – but his Soul wasn't that dark. He believed that some people deserved to die more than others and he wanted to be in control of that. I want to say he was a nice man. Because he was, but there was a side to him that I knew I wouldn't like if I saw it face-on.

The bodyguards were a wonderful luxury that wasn't needed. I understood Talia's father's concerns and knew that he had to do this for himself rather than for us. I was okay with that. Aaron was a luxury I could get used to. He said that 'anything you want I have got' so mischievously, I had to test him. I had the thick hot chocolate drink to dip the warm, oozing chocolate croissants into.

I asked for tomato soup (I don't actually like tomato soup!) which Mum had with some fresh, warm bread. Apparently, the coach was equipped to sustain a family of four for up to four weeks without stopping. But he couldn't tell me if that included fuel. Thomas and I had had to fill up the van at least once a day and this vehicle would fit about ten VW campers inside, so I think it would take a lot more fuel!

When we crossed the border From France into Spain, Aaron started to march up and down the coach waving a Spanish flamenco fan, with a pretty lace edging, in one hand and twirling the other whilst singing,

"Oh! This year, I'm off to Sunny Spain, Y Viva Espana
I'm taking the Costa Brava 'plane, Y Viva Espana
If you'd like to chat a matador in some cool cabana
And meet senoritas by the score, Espana por favor …."

We all joined in with the 'viva Espana' bit – the only bit we knew. Even the bodyguards cracked a smile and I felt the energy of all the occupants of the bus lift higher and shine a little brighter.

"It only takes the action of one person to change the entire world." Talia had said.

And I knew what she meant. And I also knew what my path was now. It wasn't going to be easy. Being a girl. And small. In a world full of men who were full of themselves and who glorified money above everything else. But hey, Rome wasn't built in a day. It actually took one thousand two hundred and thirty years. And one thing I have in abundance is time.

40

Barcelona

The day before I was due in Teruel to begin my training with Carmen, I had an argument with my Mum. I don't think we had ever argued before. She was afraid for my safety and wanted me to go home with her and Bryn. I knew I had to go to Teruel. After many raised voices and petulant pouts – both mine and my mum's – Bryn intervened. He said that I was an adult now and had to make my own choices. Mum's job was to support any decisions I made, although she was allowed to tell me what she thought of those decisions.

It made my final day in Barcelona feel rather sad. We had spent time as a family on holiday, visiting all the places families on holiday in Barcelona visited. And the apartment we were staying in was also pretty amazing. It was as though the universe had said, 'thank you for putting yourself in harm's way to save other human beings. Here is your reward'; although it wasn't that simple, obviously. I had mental scars from the last few days in France and no amount of fully serviced penthouse holiday could take that away.

Yes! Fully serviced! The penthouse apartment had about eight bedrooms – I didn't go in them all – and an outdoor swimming pool that had a 'wardrobe' of different swimwear available for guest use along with the warmest, fluffiest towels ever in the history of the world; my opinion, but I'm sure it's true. A beautifully wrapped box appeared in my room the following morning. A rather expensive watch. A gift from Talia, it was inscribed 'because time is precious'.

There was a live-in chef and housekeeper, so if I had wanted to, I could have just left everything for the housekeeper to clean up. Obviously, I didn't, but I could have! The housekeeper and chef were a married couple who lived there permanently. They would have the place to themselves for most of the year, but the family would visit once or twice a year and they would have guests visiting in between times, too. The paying guests were the worst, Valerie told me. She was the housekeeper. French. She spoke five languages. Her husband Jean, also French, also spoke five languages. They were lovely, and like Aaron believed that serving others was their life duty. I was puzzled as to why they would serve people as servants.

"No, it isn't like that," Valerie responded. "The majority of people who come here have extremely high-powered jobs. Or, like yourselves, need an escape. The family are responsible for saving thousands, if not millions of lives in their political careers. If I can give them a moment of time where they can show love, togetherness and relaxation to one another and they leave here feeling rested and relaxed, that means they can have more focus on their career. Family is so important. But it is only a small part of our life in this world." She had become animated, alive, alight and I was able to see her purpose. She was here to make life easier for those people who had the power to change the world. As a poor person from a poor family, I found it difficult to understand why rich people needed servants or staff. I used to think that it was part of their self-indulgent lifestyles. But actually, these staff were their equals. They weren't 'lesser than' their employers, but an integral part of their lives. The staff were paid to make life away from work less harsh. It was a mutually beneficial swapping of resources. Valerie and her husband could live comfortably in a city and a home that they would not otherwise be able to live in, for a wage they would not otherwise be able to earn. In return they made the place warm, welcoming and relaxing. Providing everything the family or guests needed to make their break away from the difficulties of their day-to-day life just that – a break away from the mental complications of their daily life.

It made me realise also, that people with a lot of money don't necessarily have an easy life. Yes, we see people on the television and in the magazines, wearing expensive clothes and living in expensive houses and we idolise them in one breath and abhor them in the next. They are so beautiful; but they have too much! They are so talented; but they are so rude! We hate them for having so much without realising that we are the very people pushing them into seclusion and depression and desperation. We see their beauty, their talent, their ability to make changes to the world and we want a piece of that. But we don't want to do the work. And actually there is far more work than the petty public ever see. Take Talia's parents for example. Her mother started out in a poor family in Hungary. She was talent spotted by a model agency scout and was thrown into a world of money, drugs and sex at the same age her daughter is now.

She was pushed, pulled and manipulated by every person she came into contact with. Every published photograph of her shows her smiling – a beautiful smile that makes you feel that she is smiling just at you – but you don't see her being punched in the face by a photographer for crying because she hasn't slept for two days. You don't see the makeup artists telling her she is ugly and just a phase that will pass before she gets her first period. You don't see her clothes ripped off by a jealous rival in the middle of winter in a city shoot where her naked teenage body was seen by hundreds of onlookers. You don't see the agents and aides offering her special jobs if she repays the favour. You don't see the work she does for drug-addicted former teenage models. You don't see that seventy percent of her financial earnings always go to charities. Because of course, you don't want to see that. You just want to think that she is smiling for you. Just you. And then when she announced that she was giving up her modelling career to marry and support her politician fiancé? Were you aware that her house in Paris was burnt down? That her mother's home in Hungary was broken into and the walls smeared with human faeces? Were you aware that she was kidnapped, beaten and left for dead by her 'biggest fan'? Nope! I didn't think you did. You probably thought that she was some bimbo marrying a rich politician for money and fame. But she works with her husband. She shares his workload alongside his dreams and fears. In such a modern world we are still so judgemental. When a rich politician or celebrity is rude, we take it personally. Perhaps we should stop, take a breath and ask ourselves why they are being rude. Perhaps today is the day that you will not be so judgemental of others?

41

And So It Begins

Talia had telephoned me the morning I was due to travel to Teruel. Her dad was sending me a car so that I could get there safely and he had arranged for Mum and Bryn to take a private jet back to Britain. I started to protest, but she had told him I was the reason she was alive and he would feel indebted to me for life; that was his way she said. I told her that I had done nothing, to which she snorted down the phone, her living to carry out her Soul purpose was as much payment as I needed.

"I know," she said, still weak, her voice timid, "but perhaps you can enjoy his gratitude for a little while. Just until he knows I'm okay." *She is such a lovely human being*, I thought to myself, then saw her face in the room with me. Except it wasn't her face, but a spirit.

"Talia?" I spoke into the phone loudly, a touch of fear in my voice. Had she gone? I couldn't bear it if she had passed over. I knew I should be glad for her, but I felt a deep sadness that I couldn't explain.

"Yes, I'm here," she replied. "Are you okay?" Then Kaleb appeared in front of me. Clearly. As though he were physically in the room with me. Talia – or the girl that looked like Talia, stood next to him. Also looking like she were physically in the room.

"Did you have a sister?" I spoke gently into the phone, my eyes bubbling with a warm liquid that would not spill over. Suddenly understanding.

"She is with me now," I told her when she said yes. "You lost her two years ago in the bombings. She was the same age as you are now. It wasn't publicised. No one outside the family knew." I heard sobbing and realised that the whole family could hear me. But knew I had to continue.

"Her name is Abigail and she wants you all to know that she loves you. She's telling me that you don't need to mourn for her. She is happy. She is grateful for the teddy bear she has named him Growly." There was a sound of laughter on the other end of the phone and their father spoke with a gentle laugh.

"She talked about that bloody bear for weeks and I told her she couldn't have it. Too European with its noise box, I said. Of course, it was the first thing I did afterwards. I bought her the bloody bear. Too late, though."

"The timing was perfect," I repeated what Abigail was saying to me. "But you need to remain in Europe for a few more weeks. She won't say why." She began to lose her vibrancy so I told the family. They said, "I love yous" and Abigail said them too. She said hers in two languages and I passed that on to her family. Then she completely disappeared and just Kaleb stood there. Looking happy! He bowed gently from his waist; his eyes never leaving my face.

The trip to Teruel was uneventful. Thankfully. I had had enough excitement for a while. Enough fear too. There is only so much a girl can take. And a few days in a posh penthouse in Barcelona, although extremely grateful, wasn't exactly an hour in The Light House!

We took the coastal route, and the views to the sea were spectacular in places. I asked the driver to stop every so often, so I could hear the ocean, smell the salt and feel the wind on my face. He showed me a bay just below the town of Tarragona that was empty of humans, beautiful and peaceful. Standing barefoot on the beach, digging my toes into the warm sand and hearing the sound of the sea as it stretched out infinitely toward the sunset has to be one of the most perfect moments in my life. In that moment I was so grateful to Talia's family. They had the ability to choose intuitive staff who knew exactly what you needed.

Being November, the light faded early in the evening. It was almost six o'clock as Jerome, the driver, pulled up at the address I had for Carmen. It was in the old part of the town, the houses were very traditional-looking. He opened the car door for me and I climbed out. Jerome was already knocking on the house door. It had been a long day for him, too and I think he was desperate to finish for the evening, get some food and relax. There was no response, so I knocked louder this time with the side of my fist.

A woman in the house opposite stuck her head out of the window and shouted something in Spanish. Jerome answered in Spanish and asked a question. I don't know what it was, but she responded and laughed then pulled her head back inside and slammed the window closed.

"She doesn't know who lives here," he said in perfect English. His Spanish sounded perfect, too. "Apparently there is a woman who comes here occasionally but doesn't stay long. She called her a bruja. A witch."

"Sounds about right," I responded. "It's late and I'm tired, and you are probably desperate to finish for the evening," I continued. "So I will leave her a note and we can go find somewhere to stay for the night." I was a little worried that she wasn't here, it was the fifteenth of the month and she had specified arrival after lunch and before full darkness. It wasn't fully dark, but it was certainly getting darker. And the temperature was decreasing as we stood there. I ripped a page out of the notebook I kept in my rucksack and borrowed a pen from Jerome. I wrote a quick message saying I had arrived but she wasn't in, so I was going to find a hotel for the evening. Then we got back in the car and drove away.

Jerome contacted his employer, while we drove to his hotel, and it was suggested that Jerome booked an extra room, for me, at the hotel he was staying at in the centre of the town. We drove there in silence and I wondered where Carmen was. I closed my eyes and took a few deep breaths. I called for Kaleb and felt his presence immediately. I asked for his advice on the situation. He told me to wait till tomorrow and then vanished.

The hotel was posh. But I was getting used to that. Jerome booked us both in and suggested we settle into our rooms, then meet at seven thirty for dinner. He was meeting some friends later, he said, and asked if I would be okay on my own. I was actually looking forward to some time alone, as I hadn't had any proper alone time since leaving England. And I'm not counting the time I spent in the police cell!

Dinner was delicious, six courses, but all really small. One course was what appeared to be a lettuce leaf on top of a smear of something vegetable. Another was a sliver of some type of meat with an emaciated slice of potato and a yellow flower. *No wonder rich women are skinny*, I thought, judgementally, if this is what they consider food they can keep it. I'd stick to my corned beef hash and Lancashire hotpot, thank you very much! After dinner, Jerome and I said goodbye and arranged to meet for breakfast the following morning. Apparently, he had been instructed to stay with me until my new guardian had appeared. I hoped that would be sooner rather than later.

I retired to my room and telephoned Mum. They had arrived home an hour earlier and were really pleased to hear that I had arrived safely in Teruel, but worried that Carmen was nowhere to be found. I promised that I would catch a plane home tomorrow if I hadn't found her by lunchtime.

I then tried to call Mrs Marton, but there was no reply. It was Monday, though, and I know she prepared the church on Mondays, although it was quite late. I hoped she was okay.

I decided to have a bath. There were all kinds of luxury products in the bathroom, and gentle music piped through invisible speakers when the light came on. I pressed a button that put a plug into the plughole, then touched the tap with the red button. I poured in half the contents of one of the complementary bottles then turned on the cold tap. I would spend an hour or so luxuriating in warm, soothing suds. There was a bookshelf of brand new books in the living area of the suite – books in different languages – so I took the first nice-looking book with an English title and took it into the bathroom with me. The complementary bathrobe was huge – meant to fit both men and women from medium to extra large – I was size tiny, but it was really soft and felt warm, so I wasn't complaining. I suddenly thought how lovely it would have been to have this as a blanket when we were kids.

I shrugged off the bathrobe and dived into the bath, turning off the taps as I did so. I hadn't realised how deep the bath actually was until I got in. The water came right up to my chin. The bubbles reached my ears. *I may have overdone this a bit,* I thought and giggled. I picked up a handful of bubbles and blew them, a few bubbles escaped and rode up to the ceiling before popping, the rest flopped back and disappeared into the sea of bubbles. I laid back and closed my eyes.

"That looks lovely," said a voice beside the bath. I shot upright and opened my eyes expecting water and bubbles to escape over the side of the bath and across the floor.

Instead, I was in The Light House.

"Erm, isn't that dangerous? Me being in the bath," I said to myself. I couldn't sense any other beings. I felt calm but also a little anxious. I wanted to know how I got here. And I wanted to know who had spoken to me in the bathroom. I turned around, looking for someone. Anyone who would help me. I was in my Soul form. So that was good. I called for Kaleb but had no response. I called for Arrien. She used to be with me before I finished thinking that I would need her. But no Arrien either.

I wondered if I had drowned in the bath. It was very deep and I was very tired. But I wouldn't be alone here. I was sure of that. My Soul group would be here to welcome me. So, what was going on? I tried to concentrate. I looked at the walls of my room. They looked almost solid. That wasn't right. I took a deep breath. Well, I didn't have lungs in this world, but I imagined I had taken a deep breath. In human form, taking a deep breath settles you. Focuses you. And it worked. The walls began to shimmer and lighten until I could almost see through them. And there was the door. I walked toward it, but before I could walk through, a voice spoke.

"Another lesson complete. You are good."

I jolted at the sound of the voice. I realised I was back in the bath, water and bubbles sloshing all over the floor. The water was still hot, so I was pleased about that. I recognised the voice. But I don't know where I'd heard it before. I closed my eyes again and for the first time in a while, felt all my muscles relax and my mind felt tranquil.

I awoke next morning at seven thirty. Early. I lounged in the overly large but tremendously comfortable bed for another ten minutes before wandering into the bathroom to brush my teeth. I felt refreshed. I felt happy. I felt eager to get on with my day. I dressed in a clean pair of jeans that I'd bought in Barcelona. My suitcase was still in Thomas's van, so I'd had to go shopping with Mum and Bryn in Barcelona.

By eight fifteen I was waiting for the lift on my way to breakfast when I suddenly decided to turn back and fetch my rucksack from the room. It had my passport, purse, tarot cards and a lip salve alongside a notebook and a few other bits that randomly find their way into bags, so it was definitely not a breakfast necessity. It was eight twenty-one when the lift doors opened onto the reception area of the hotel. A spacious area with lots of mirrors and columns, making cosy seating areas. Real potted plants were dotted around and a uniformed janitor was trimming leaves and watering each one lovingly. The only other people around were the male receptionist, busily tapping at a keyboard, and two people leaning on the reception desk. The desk spanned the whole of the back wall and was underlit – just in case the huge lump of stone that practically hit you in the face as you walked in through the six large glass panelled front doors, didn't scream 'reception' loudly enough!

I recognised Jerome, the driver from yesterday, as one of the people leant on the desk. He was tall and wearing a fitted polo neck sweater (that showed off his previously hidden muscular torso) and elegant belted trousers. Casual. *Quietly handsome*, I thought, unlike his professional persona yesterday in black suit, tie and white shirt. Although he was kind to me yesterday, today he looked friendly. There is a difference, you know! He wasn't looking at me but at the other person leaning against the desk. Very casual. They were in conversation, and I took a peek at their auras. They were both flaring with pink! *So this is who he was meeting last night*, I thought, smiling to myself. The second person was shorter than Jerome. She ... I assumed it was a she because of her shape ... had shiny, tightly curled dark hair, falling just below her shoulders. She had a large bottom restrained in black tight-fitting trousers, a cream-coloured jumper and chunky boots covered in mud. I hoped the receptionist hadn't seen that, or she might be made to clean up the clumps that were strewn about her feet.

Jerome looked up, saw me, smiled and waved his hand. Just before his companion turned, I knew who she was!

"Carmen?" I asked as she turned. There was surprise in my voice because she was older than I had expected. But this was the woman, the spirity light being from Mrs Marton's library!

"Oh! Darling child. You are everything I expected! It is like we have met already," she said with a cheeky wink as she grabbed my arms and kissed my cheeks. A proper lip-to-skin kiss. Not like the French who made 'mwah' sounds into the air as they put their faces next to each other and kept their arms and bodies as far apart as possible. I immediately felt an affection for her. I felt like we were family.

"People come into our lives for a reason, a season or a lifetime," she said. "Sometimes many lifetimes," she added as a correction. "When we meet the people who should be with us for any of those moments, we can sometimes feel a connection." She was smiling. She could do what Mrs Marton could – she could read my mind.

The three of us went through to breakfast, Carmen speaking with Jerome in Spanish. Very quickly. I was trying to place her accent. Her English was very good, but she wasn't English. Her Spanish sounded excellent, but there was a hint of something else, too, that I couldn't quite place. Occasionally, she would say, "We just said ..." as though this was including me in their conversation. The waiter came across to take our orders and each adult took turns to order theirs. I began to order mine, but Carmen put her hand on my arm and said something in Spanish – I wanted chocolate croissants and hot chocolate, but the waiter brought me a glass of freshly squeezed orange juice from oranges picked this morning, Carmen told me, along with a bowl of fresh fruits – some of which I had never seen before but were bloody lovely! Again, local produce, Carmen said proudly.

After breakfast, which I ate in silence, Carmen and Jerome said their goodbyes in English. I thanked Jerome for all his help and told him I was grateful and appreciative of all the help I had received from him and his boss and to please pass on my regards. I was about to fetch my holdall from the hotel room, when Carmen took my arm and began to lead me outside.

"You won't need it." She told me as she took a pair of dirt encrusted hiking boots from her backpack. "You will need to put these on. Your other belongings will be brought out later. Don't worry."

The hiking boots fit me perfectly. But I did wonder who else had worn them and whether they may have had verrucas or athlete's foot.

"You get very judgemental when your energy has been hacked." She said looking at me seriously as she pushed me gently down an alley between the hotel and the neighbouring buildings.

"What do you mean? I asked, and then "Where are we going?"

We arrived at the end of the alley and into a wilderness. That is the only way I know how I can explain it. I looked behind as we stepped out of the alley and the hotel and town seemed to be miles behind us. Ahead were rows of small trees, fruit trees, perhaps, or olives, I told myself. But I didn't know what an olive was. Beyond the trees, in the distance, mountains loomed up in hazy shades of grey, lilac, purple and black. I could feel the heat of the sun on my face, but my hands were cold.

Carmen was digging into her backpack again. It seemed to be full to bursting and very heavy; each time she swung it up onto or from her back she made a huffing noise.

"You will need these," she handed me a bottle of water and a pair of gloves. I put the water into an external pocket on my backpack, so I could reach it easily. Then as I started to put on the gloves, I realised that these were mine!

"Thomas is here already." She said matter-of-factly, and I bristled slightly at the sound of his name. "I hope you didn't mind me going into your suitcase, but I knew you'd need the gloves. It gets colder the nearer the mountains we get."

I asked where we were going; she responded, 'you'll see'. I asked her how Thomas was – hoping she'd say he was rotting in hell for leaving me at the fuel stop, but she replied, 'you'll see'.

I wanted to ask her more questions, but she was keeping up quite a pace and, not knowing where I was, I really didn't want to get left behind. I had already started to sweat, and the gloves were put away in my jacket pocket. I was grateful I hadn't put on a thicker jumper. My breathing was getting faster and I could feel my heart thumping inside my chest.

We exited the fruit tree grove and began to climb a rocky hill. It didn't look steep but I could feel my calves burning and the cheeks of my bottom were also hurting.

"You are unfit for one so young," were Carmen's only words for the next hour or so.

Another hour later, according to my new watch, that I couldn't stop looking at – I'd never had a watch before and I was quietly pleased to have one now – Carmen pointed to a rock with a flat top, the height of a table.

"We'll stop there," she said, slightly out of breath. I was gasping for air at this point, my body was screaming for a rest, my feet burned inside my boots and felt wet. *Perhaps I now had verrucas and athlete's foot*, I thought, horrified!

Carmen put her pack on top of the rock, tapped with her hand and said, "Sit,' whilst reaching behind the rock. I removed my backpack and placed it on the rock with Carmen's, then jumped up and sat on the rock. It was cold. And damp. The cold dampness went straight through my body and to my bones. I wanted to stand back up, but my feet were throbbing. I thought they deserved a little rest. So, I took a gulp of the water from my now near-empty bottle. Just as I was thinking I wouldn't have enough water for the rest of the journey, Carmen swung a string bag up onto the flat stone surface and handed me a fresh bottle of water. Then she handed me a paper-wrapped parcel. I opened it to find a sandwich of chunky bread with soft vegetable filling. I don't know what the vegetables were, but it tasted delicious. She passed me another bottle, this time with orange juice, freshly squeezed that morning with locally produced oranges.

"Thomas had left this for us," Carmen told me. He had gone on ahead with supplies. I asked where we were going, and she pointed ahead to the mountain range. Not the first mountain, but the one behind it, she said. Not the big one, but a smaller one that was hidden behind the first one. I asked how long it would take to get there and she said,

"You'll see," then began to pack up her bag.

We had been walking for almost four hours before we got to the base of the first mountain. We stopped for another break. This time, hidden behind a rock were two plastic boxes filled with large sliced tomatoes sprinkled with salt and pepper. I could smell lemon. I wanted to hate it. I wanted to throw it down and demand some proper food – I had, after all, paid a small fortune to this woman for food and lodgings alongside the training. I mean, I wasn't training for a mountain climbing expedition or anything.

The truth is the tomatoes were delicious. The best tomatoes I have ever tasted; I even lifted the empty tub to my lips to get the last drops of the intermingled juice of the tomato and lemon. Carmen smiled. I wondered if she was trying to convert me to vegetarianism or veganism. I'd always found meat to be either chewy, stringy or tasteless, depending on the cook and the piece of meat. So, it wouldn't be a great wrench to stop eating it all together, but I'd like to have a say in the matter and not be forced into it.

I suddenly realised I needed to pee. But I didn't want to pee in front of Carmen and I didn't want to pee on the ground. I was worried that I might upset the wildlife. But Carmen, mind reader that she was, pulled two plastic-lidded containers from behind the rock and handed one to me.

"I'm just going to go around this rock to relieve myself of all this water," she said, smiling diplomatically and pointing to a rocky outcrop a little higher up. "I suggest you go around that one." She pointed to a larger outcrop to our left. As I rounded the corner, I noticed that it was shaped so that I was hidden on both sides. A large boulder above would hide me from the view of any onlookers – although there hadn't been another being since we left the hotel. I was beginning to warm to Carmen.

"Make sure the lid is on tight and put it into your backpack," she called. "You might need it again before we get there."

After another four hours of walking in some of the most stunning scenery I had ever witnessed, we were at the base of the second mountain. I'd been wearing the gloves for over an hour now. As the sun melted behind the mountain, so did the heat it brought with it. I could see my breath in the fading light and was about to give up hope of ever reaching our destination. But then I saw, about a metre from the ground and accessed by age-worn steps, a wooden façade looking like it had been stuck onto the side of the mountain. Approximately three metres wide and three metres tall, this wooden boarding held a rough window and had a doorway cut into the wood, with a proper wooden door, making it look like a house. A dull light shone through the window. Carmen strode up and through the door without a backward glance, so I followed tentatively. I hadn't known what to expect, but it wasn't this.

Inside the door, a small table covered in an old lace fabric held a gas lamp. This is what we could see from outside. We were in what appeared to be a large cave naturally hewn out of the mountain above us. As we moved inside, it opened up to reveal rooms. There was a small kitchen area with a sink and an old cooking stove, a mismatched set of chairs around an equally mismatched table. On the opposite wall was what appeared to be a fireplace – logs were lit, crackling gently in the light of more gas lamps, and the smoke wound its way up to a small hole in the roof. Two old chairs with shrunken, faded upholstery were placed in front of the fire. Thomas was sat in one. Head down. Not looking at us. Not greeting us. The sound of a whistle made me turn my head back to the kitchen. A tin kettle was boiling on the wood-powered stove. Carmen brought three cups to the rickety table and started to spoon something dark and powdery into a silver-coloured metal pot with a spout, which she then filled with the water from the boiling kettle and placed a badly fitting lid on top.

"I'm not a relationship counsellor, so sort your shit out so we can eat," Carmen said to us both as she disappeared into the back of the cave. It seemed to go deep into the mountain. I was curious as to how far back it went, but I thought I'd better 'sort out my shit' because I was very hungry and rather exhausted.

"How long have you been here?" I started at the same time as Thomas said,

"They wouldn't let me talk to you." There was a sadness in his eyes that I couldn't fathom. I sat in the chair opposite him and encouraged him to speak. I had collapsed on the back of the pickup truck, he told me. A policeman had lifted me out and put me into a police car, which sped off. They wouldn't tell him where and he couldn't understand what they were saying. Fortunately, one of the diner staff spoke English and offered to find out where I had been taken, but the police station had been heavily guarded. He was searched and questioned without legal support and they wouldn't allow anyone to speak to me.

He had contacted our families in England and a French solicitor was engaged, but he wasn't allowed access to me either. The next thing they knew, I was in hospital and being guarded along with the other girls as the terrorist organisation responsible for the kidnappings had made further threats. One of the men in the truck had confessed to a further four girls being held nearby. They had been rescued, but one had already died of starvation and the others were in a serious state as they had been left there, alone, for over a week.

My heart began to ache all over again for the girls, their families, for Thomas and for my family – who had told me none of this. I reached out my hand and Thomas took it, bursting into tears and apologising for not being with me. I moved across and sat on the arm of his chair, putting my arm around his shoulder. He turned his head into my chest and sobbed. I rested my chin on the top of his head and stroked his hair. I told him everything was okay. We would be fine. It was over now. But Thomas was not me. Thomas had not seen the things I had seen in my life. This would remain with him for a long time as a failure on his part. I just hoped he would find enough happiness for this not to hurt so much as he continued on the path of his current existence.

A smell of fresh coffee filled the air and Carmen appeared with what looked like a pan of hot stew! She placed the steaming pot on the table and began to fill the cups with coffee and the bowls that had appeared miraculously with the stew. She didn't need to call us to the table – the smell of food did that. We sat and ate in silence. A friendly silence. A silence of hunger being satisfied and friendships renewed. A tiredness overtook me as I took the last mouthful of food. Carmen held my arm, helped me to my feet and guided me through a curtain where she sat me on a bed. She removed my boots while talking soothingly and I fell asleep, fully dressed, as my head touched the pillow.

I awoke to the sound of laughter and chatter through the curtain. English. Happy. Relaxed. Mrs Marton?

I pulled the bedclothes aside and realised I was in pyjamas. I didn't remember putting my 'jamas on! There was a pair of slippers – not mine – on the floor next to the boots, also not mine, that I had worn yesterday. Above, on a hook screwed into the rock wall, was the warm, cosy bathrobe I wore last night. I think it was last night. I slid my feet into the slippers and my arms into the robe, wrapping it tightly around my body before peering tentatively around the curtain.

Four women were sat at the kitchen table, drinking out of mismatched cups. Chatting amiably with smiles on their faces were Carmen, Mrs Marton and two other women I didn't recognise. As one, they placed their cups on the table and turned to look at me.

Okay, I thought, *this isn't freaky, even a tiny bit*. Perhaps I'm dreaming. As one, their lips curled into a smile and they let out a giggle. Yes, I said a giggle – singular. Although they all made the sound, it appeared to be a single tone. *Witches!* I thought. Then smiled. Quite sure I wasn't dreaming.

"Bathroom is through there," Carmen pointed to another curtain a little beyond my curtained room. All the curtains were mismatched as though they had all arrived in different periods of time and trends. But I liked it. It felt really homely. I realised that I actually needed to pee really urgently, so I made a quick shuffle walk to the specified curtain dipped behind it quickly to find a modern rose-coloured bathroom properly plumbed in! I dashed to the toilet and sat down just in time, then took a moment to look around whilst I was otherwise engaged! There was a half-sized bath with a shower above and a pretty floral shower curtain on a modern oval chrome rail fixed to the rock ceiling. The walls were all rock, and they curved gently into the ceiling. Opposite the bath and toilet was a ceramic sink on a pedestal with a pink-painted chair next to it piled up with mismatched towels. Above the sink was a small shelf with my toiletry bag on it.

"Paper goes in the bin, please and not down the bowl," a voice shouted from the kitchen, and I realised they had stopped talking whilst I was sitting there and they could probably hear every sound I was making! *How embarrassing that could have been*, I thought and giggled. The group around the table guffawed loudly and continued with their chatter, leaving me to finish off my ablutions. The towels were a little bit scratchy – *not the quality I had recently become used to*, I thought, smiling to myself.

I dashed back into my curtained quarters unnoticed. Well, the quartet were fully aware of what I was doing but were giving me space to get dressed. I threw on clean jeans from my suitcase, which had been left on the floor partially opened, and a thin jumper, put on socks and lace-up plimsolls – my normal daily wear – before exiting through the curtain to join the group in the kitchen.

As I reached the table, I looked across to the fire, expecting to see Thomas. But to my surprise, my sister was sitting in Thomas's chair, with her feet up on a small, torn leather pouffe that hadn't been there the night before.

"Hello, Titchy," she smiled, getting to her feet and wrapping me in a big hug as I ran toward her.

She was supposed to be in Scotland for Christmas with her college friend. What on earth was she doing here?

"That was just for Mum," she replied sheepishly, responding to my thoughts. "You're not the only one with talents, you know." She pulled a face and stuck out her tongue, then grabbed me in another hug, telling me she had missed me.

Water, orange juice (freshly squeezed from local fruit!) and a bowl of fruit appeared next to the two fireside chairs on the small table that previously held the lamp near the door. The four women were silently making their way through to the back of the cave dwelling, so we were alone.

"I don't have time to tell you everything right now," she told me, "but I have been working with Em and Celia for the last couple of years."

"But I've sent you two postcards to Scotland!" I said upset that she hadn't told me this sooner.

"Titch, are you listening?" she said with an urgency that was quite unlike her. I nodded, wondering why she was working with the other two women. Then I realised that Em was Mrs Marton.

"You've been working with Mrs Marton?" I asked. "Not for her. But *with* her, like I do?" A thousand questions began to fall into my head and I felt weak and a little confused. She took my arms and sat me down into the armchair by the still burning fire and looked me in the eyes.

"You are here to learn about everything. You aren't like me. You are your own person. Your talents are unique to you. I can't tell you anything else because the learning has to be done in a kind of set order." She furrowed her brows and looked at me seriously. "I'm so sorry about France. You did a brilliant job. You are amazing, you know that, right?"

Then she passed me juice and fruit telling me I had to eat as the others had gone upstairs to prepare. My first thought was, *there's an upstairs in a cave*, and then *what are they preparing for?*

42

Lessons

After finishing breakfast, my sister and I walked to the back of the cave – it went quite far back. I realised it looked smaller because of the darkness as we moved further in where no natural light from the window and open door could project. Carrying an antique oil lamp to light the way, we walked for several minutes, passing curtained-off sections every so often until we reached a final curtain, which my sister pulled aside to reveal steps roughly cut into the rock but worn smooth in the centre. *This cave must have been in use for hundreds of years*, I thought as we began to climb. Each step was a different height and depth to the one above and below it; some steps dug further into the sides making pockets where random items were stored. A dried posy of twigs, here. An animal skull there. A leather-bound book not dissimilar to those in the Light Room. A large stone bowl with a pestle of the same material sat beside it.

The stairway twisted like a serpent, back and forth, back and forth, as though the builder was chipping away at the softest parts of the rock with no idea of where he was going to end up.

"She!" said Carmen as we reached the top. The room opened up into a gigantic echoing space. Natural light shone in through windows improved by the weather in the far wall. Each window a different size and shape; some low to the floor of the cave and some reaching high above and into the ceiling of the cave.

"These caves were carved out by women over ten thousand

years ago. Using just the materials they had to hand," Carmen began. "These caves were built by women, for women. And not just any woman! But the women of the spirit," she continued. She told the story of women who had visions of the true spirit and were shunned by their clans and families. They found their way here. Were called to this place. And together they built a home and a place of learning. To teach the younger women, who were also called here, to ready the world for the return of The One. A being so strong and powerful that it could end death and destruction, hate and despair, anger and fear.

"Why women?" I asked. "Why not men and women?"

"Because man began the descent into earth as a living Hell," began the woman I would come to know as Celia, my sister's mentor. "Man and woman should be equal," she continued, "but slowly, over the millennia, men have reduced women's roles to that of a shackled domestic servant. They have found ways of silencing the woman's voice and making her 'less'."

"Not every man is responsible," continued Em Marton, my mentor. "We are talking about more than twenty thousand years ago. So many women leading clans and tribes and whole cities, in fact. But power leads to fear and fear leads to anger. A woman in power is great until she has to give birth. If she doesn't have children, she is not a woman. If she has children, she becomes weak and a liability."

I frowned and opened my mouth to speak, upset at this last comment, but the woman (whom I soon learned was Jacinta) continued,

"You know as well as we do, and you are still a child, that that is nonsense. But a man wanting power will manipulate anyone and anything in order to get that power. Again, not all men. And these days there are as many women who abuse their place on this earth to gain a modicum of something akin to power that is actually detrimental not only to themselves but to every living being on this planet."

Carmen took on the story. "Power is not about how much money you can make. It is not about how big your house or your car is. Power is about how you treat people. This meaning has been lost over time. It has been altered from its original meaning to be more masculine, more about authority over people and exerting physical force. But the original meaning is 'to be able'. This meaning is more feminine in its root because it is about giving rather than taking. It isn't about being 'more than' but making everyone 'able'."

My sister continued. "Women, historically, like really long ago, were the people in the tribes who kept everyone together. They were the ones who organised and took part in the hunting, they cared for the children and the sick. They decided where the tribes would travel to and where they would stop and make camp. They made decisions about what the children would learn and who would teach them. They handed out the roles to each family or tribe member. And for millennia this was accepted as the norm. If one woman went into labour her daughter or sister would take on her role as leader."

"But then," Jacinta took up the verbal baton, "tribes became bigger. The men's role became very physical; the more men were available, the less women needed to go hunting. They would stay behind and teach the children to hunt, prepare the animal skins for clothing and shelter and make the food. They were still big decision-makers until a bad winter meant there was a shortage of food. The decision was made by the women that the men should eat more so they were strong enough to hunt. The rest of the tribe would conserve their energy and eat less."

This was fine for a while - the group continued taking turns to recount the tale - until one day the hunters found game far from their tribal home. They ate their meal and hunted again. For several days, they hunted, ate, and were thrilled with their success in such a time of lack and forgetting their families at home. When they had several carcasses and no one to comfort them, they returned to their village where they found several of the women and children dead. Starved of food and water that they had promised to bring. The rest of the women and children were very weak. The hunters – upset at not having the usual celebration upon their return and angry at themselves for not returning sooner – gave only the most meagre of portions to the survivors. To make themselves feel better, they blamed and killed the leading tribal woman for not having protected her tribe well enough and the remaining adult women were beaten for not caring for the children.

For months after, the blame was put upon the remaining women for not caring for their families. Too weak to fight them off, many were beaten and humiliated regularly by the hunters. The men attributed the anger and fear at their own misconduct to the women. And so a vicious circle was begun. The women were not good enough. The men were the saviours. The women were not good enough. The men were capable. The women were weak. The men were strong. And within a very short space of time many of the women began to believe this story. And many similar stories were made in other tribes and other parts of the world. Except a few women knew the truth. And they believed the truth could be fought for.

"It isn't a story of men versus women. Or this sex is better than that sex. Or I am better than you. Or she is better than he," Jacinta finished their story. "It is that we are all capable of different things and we are all able to provide for the society in which we live. Each in different ways at different times in our lives."

"But it has been ingrained into society," I added, thinking about my experiences in life, so far, "about power. What it is and how it should be used."

Five faces smiled at me. In harmony all five women nodded and made a 'hmm' noise. They were satisfied that I understood.

"True power comes not from your abilities and strengths as a human on earth, but from your connection to your Soul and to your eternal home," they said together, as one, and I realised it was not their human voice that I could hear, but their Soul voices. For their Souls were all connected, as was mine.

"As are all the Souls of mankind. They have mostly forgotten, though." This was my lovely sister. I loved my sister in that moment more than I have ever loved anyone on this earth plane. Because suddenly something clicked in my brain. A knowledge I knew but had forgotten. I smiled and a drop of liquid pooled at the end of my nose. I sniffed it back in then wiped it with the sleeve of my jumper. Jacinta made a balking sound and passed me a paper tissue. I looked at my sister knowingly and we all smiled.

The group of women had come together to teach each other the forgotten powers. Because the males were not as intuitive as women so were less capable of certain powers. The power of guidance. The power of healing. The power of influence. The power life giving. The power of life taking. The power of kindness. The power of the unconditional. The power of being able. The power of en-able-ing.

Your first job is to be cleansed I was told. Energetically. The past few weeks had taken a toll on my energy and although I knew how I could replenish my energy I wasn't currently refreshing it often enough or full enough.

"That's why I'm struggling to see my guides and spirits," I suddenly realised.

"Urgh!" My sister pulled a face but smiled, "I wish I could do that." She had only just started to connect with her guides, she told me. My talents were very rare and usually took many years to learn with the aid of experienced teachers.

"Usually very old!" Jacinta mentioned. She was probably the youngest of the four women here, but much older than our mother. So to my young human eyes she was very old. Celia scowled at her saying she wasn't that old thank you very much. We all laughed, but then the air became serious.

Carmen came across the room toward me, she was barefoot. I

noticed the others were too. She led me to the centre of the room where she pointed to a blanket on the ground and asked me to lay down. Around the blanket were four low stools, all identical made of wood, but with individual evidence of wear. There was also a thick cushion at the head of the blanket which Mrs Marton, or Em as she was called here, knelt on. It looked like the rug in her parlour and I wondered if it had once been part of it. The other four ladies headed toward their stools, crossing each other, so I guessed they each had their own particular stool.

I felt someone lifting my foot so I raised my head to see Carmen removing my shoes. She smiled, placed them behind her stool then placed another blanket across my feet. My sister knelt beside me and gently lifted my head, placing a hard pillow beneath my head. She smiled, ruffled my hair lightly then returned to her seat.

I closed my eyes, took a deep breath, and then heard chattering voices. I opened my eyes to find the room was really dark with a chill in the air. Puzzled, I turned my head this way and that and looked up, to where Mrs Marton was sitting. Except she wasn't. I looked again side to side again but there was no one else here. I sat upright. I felt confused. I went to stand up and found that I almost floated to my feet. My body felt so light and refreshed. No aches and pains from the day before. My head felt really clear. Almost empty if that doesn't sound silly. All the roiling memories of the last week had calmed down. My head felt peaceful.

I don't think I mentioned what it felt like to be in the situation at the fuel station near Toulouse. I don't really want to relive it if I'm honest. It felt awful. Then as Kaleb joined me, I saw everything about these men in front of me. Every part of their current lives. Every one of their past lives. And they weren't nice. The images. Not the men. Those images had been churning around inside my head. They had started off this life with great hopes and expectations, as we all do, but circumstances manufactured the men that I was with that day. Not a single one of them would have wanted to be in the position they found themselves that day. But fear. There is that word again! Fear. They were shown fear as children and they lived with it for almost every day of their lives as they grew up. Yes, they could have chosen different paths, but sometimes we choose the worst path because it is the easiest path. To break the spell of generational abuse, torment and torture is not an easy choice. It leaves you alone. It leaves you grieving for the people you have left behind. You are mentally unprepared to start again with a different mindset to the one you grew up with. With people who don't know you. You make mistakes. The new people laugh at you or misunderstand you or, worse, they fear you. And then you are back where you started but with out the support network you once had.

Am I siding with those men? After what they did to those girls? Absolutely not! But I ask you not to judge them too harshly. You were not born in their shoes. You have no right to judge them for who they are. You have no right to pass judgement on any being.

That is my job.

And I'm just about to start my apprenticeship!

43

An Introduction

There was a lit oil lamp by the stairs. My slippers were there too. I'm not sure where my shoes were! I pushed my feet into the slippers as I picked up the lamp and began to carefully make my way down the stairs. Shadows cast by the light made interesting shapes on the dark walls. I held my hand against the wall to keep my balance and to guide me round the corners. The air was warm. The stone was warm. Being November I thought it would be colder. Even Spain has bad weather in the winter. Then I remembered something from a science class about rocks – that lesson had fascinated me for some strange reason – apparently caves keep the heat year-round so even in winter it will be warm. I remembered, with a smile, that I'd thought how cool it would be to actually live in a cave.

I arrived at the bottom step and swept aside the curtain to reveal the main cave, oil lamps had been lined up against the flat wall – the one without any curtains or rooms coming off it, so I could see clearly all the way to the kitchen area. There were several people that I could see, but also voices of living people I couldn't see. The whole space was also filled with spirits, guides and light beings. The space in my chest felt like it had expanded to fill the universe. The corners of my mouth stretched so far across my face I could feel it in my ears.

My sister came forward to greet me and took me to the fireplace where Thomas stood up and offered me his seat. I felt a kind of numbness that is difficult to describe. It wasn't numb of feeling like your mouth after a visit to the dentist to have a tooth out. It wasn't that numbness of emotion when you've had some really bad news and are unable to process it. It wasn't a spiritual numbness when you have lost your faith in everything. It was more a feeling of such utter calmness that nothing can shake you. Nothing can put a dent into the armour that surrounds you. Yes! That is it! It is like wearing an armour of protection through which no bad 'ness' can penetrate.

People I had never met before came up and introduced themselves to me, but I felt like I was floating in a bubble. I was present and yet not present. I was here and yet separated from everything. Carmen came across with a glass of water.

"Con gas," she said handing it to me with one hand and poking me in the ribs with the other. The 'bubble' around me popped and I was suddenly very aware of my surroundings. I still felt light. I still felt protected. But I was very much 'here' and very much 'now'.

Everybody began to sit down facing the fireplace. I wondered where all the chairs had come from because there weren't so many before. I also wondered where all the people had come from. Some of them were pretty old and I couldn't quite imagine them having walked here the way that Carmen and I had.

Celia stood up and walked to the side of the chair I was sitting on. She welcomed everyone to this evening's meeting and introduced me as the newest member – of what she didn't say – she hoped everyone would make me welcome and asked that they all share with me anything they felt compelled to.

A gentleman with dark skin, very short, greying hair and beard, wearing a suit and tie, asked, "*Hal hi min khati maykilz?*" His guide, standing at his right shoulder, translated it in several languages all at once. "Is she of Michael's line?"

"Yes." Celia nodded as a few people made 'ooh' sounds. "She is also a direct descendent of Mary's." To which there was a loud gasp. One woman touched her forehead, her chest then both shoulders whilst muttering something under her breath.

I was puzzled at the time, as I'm sure you are too, as to what they meant and who they meant. But it will be my first lesson. And I will share that with you shortly. I just wanted to show you that although this was supposed to be a space for women there were men here too. Initially I thought that perhaps these women – Em, Carmen, Jacinta and Celia – were anti-men. And as you know by now, my experience of men has not shown them in the best light. Hasn't been particularly positive. I thought, perhaps they were part of a group of … I don't know … man-haters or something. But none of the women felt like they hated men or had any issues like that showing in their auras. So when I saw the group containing men as well, I think that made me happy because we are all born equal. No matter our gender, our skin colour, our religious beliefs, our place of birth, our family of birth. We are the same.

We become unequal when we grow to believe that which we are told without question. When our parents share their venomous dislikes with us and we carry that torch of venom. When our governments or community leaders share their version of battles and wars and we accept without looking at the version of our 'enemy'. THAT is when inequality creeps in. Because with those stories of 'others' we are also being told stories of self. We are told that we are better than them. Or they are better than us. We are different to them. And they are different to us. And we begin to judge. But it is not your place to judge. It is your place to 'be'. It is your place to 'be able'. And mostly we are 'unable' because we cannot see clearly with the tainted eyes we are handed.

The meeting was a bit like the spiritual church back home. Except everyone here had the gift of clairvoyance or clairaudience. That's being able to see or hear beyond the human plane. There are lots of other talents, most people stood up and gave messages to me using their specific talent: you have four guides beside you; you have suffered much in your short life; you will do great things in your life; your ancestors are proud of how far you have come. And many more like that. I smiled and nodded and thanked each person and their guides while wondering when I could eat something because I was getting a bit hungry. But there were about sixty people in this deceptively large space and they each wanted to say something.

After what felt like two hundred years, but was probably two hours, the gentleman who spoke originally stood up. He had an air of a leader about him. An air of power in all its meanings; old and new. I liked him. I recognised him. But I wasn't sure why, because I also felt a twinge of fear.

"On a daily basis," he began, "the people you see here today vibrate to a frequency of over five hundred hertz." I nodded my head but had no idea what he meant. Except there was a little something tapping at the back of my conscience that said I knew exactly what he meant.

"The general population of most countries vibrate at a frequency below two hundred and fifty. With many of those below one hundred and fifty." I continued nodding my head. He continued talking.

"Five hundred and above is the vibration of the healer, the intuitive, the higher level pacifist, the people who 'affect' others to change and to become able without force of will or strength." Ah! I was beginning to understand.

"The lower the vibration the less creative and therefore the less 'able' we become. The people who feel anger, fear, shame and guilt are vibrating at the lowest levels. They are kept there by social media. By their peers. By their governments wanting to keep them dis-abled."

He was looking at me intently. I felt like the only person in the room, as though he was speaking to me and me alone. And it suddenly hit me like a force of ice-cold water on a stormy sea. I felt it like a physical punch to my abdomen. The breath vacuumed out of me.

"You cannot properly lead your people whilst in a low vibrational state," I said with surprise as my own thought processes started to unwind like a tightly coiled spring. "You don't have the ability to give yourself strength, never mind your people. By keeping the majority in a general state of fear, anger, despair, guilt and shame they will not rise up and try to overthrow your regime that you have built on fear and anger. They are un-abled. Our society is built on un-abling the many. The most powerful!"

The room erupted in applause. I fell back into my chair, unaware that I had been standing. I felt a surge of power burst through my being and for a moment I saw the highest level aura of every being in the room. The living and the non-living. It was such a beautiful sight of whites, purples, blues and pinks. Rainbows of colours dancing and swooping like a firework display but without the noise and the cold. I felt an energy so powerful rise up within me and flow out to each and every other being in the room. Intermingling, swirling and twirling. Becoming one and yet totally separate all at the same time.

And I realised that I was stood with the truly most powerful people on the planet.

In a cave!

I chuckled. And then I bent double as laughter burst out, not only through my mouth, but through my whole being. And the whole room joined in. Not because any of this was funny. But because this was a revelation that even the highest paid and most 'powerful' of politicians in their offices and generals in their war tents weren't even microscopically aware. They had learned the wrong things from the wrong people for hundreds and thousands of years. And they thought they were right!

44

The Apprenticeship

The service was brought to an end and soft drinks were handed out – alcohol lowers your vibration. Personally, I have never liked the taste of it and saw the negative effects first-hand, with Beastman. So, although I have tasted alcohol and will probably do so in the future, it isn't my drink of choice.

This evening was becoming a party. There weren't any party games and nobody fell over drunk or got into a slanging match with Deirdre, the slag, at number fifteen. But music started playing and people started swaying. I was introduced to everybody in attendance that evening. There were spiritual people representing almost every country in the world. Some people representing more than one country or group of countries. And I lost count of the number of invitations I received to visit and speak at one convention or another. However, I'm not sure what I was supposed to speak about or how I was supposed to travel to these places.

"You'll see," Carmen and Em said together and hugged me tightly, then giggled like little girls. I promised myself I would check them for any alcoholic or chemical substances later.

Thomas found me as people began to say their goodbyes. A slow Spanish song was playing, he grabbed me round the waist and pulled me toward him then started to sway to the gentle music. I giggled. He twirled around lifting my feet off the floor then enveloped me in a tight hug, still swaying and nestling his chin into my hair. At that moment I felt happy. I felt peace. I felt calm.

I felt 'at home'. And I felt loved. Loved by Thomas. Loved by Em, Carmen, Celia and Jacinta. Loved by my sister. Loved by the crowd of strangers who were now my friends. But mostly, loved by me. I had never really felt any emotion for myself before. So this was a strange but satisfying feeling that I wanted to keep. Forever.

I don't know what time I went to bed, but when I awoke the first thing I noticed was the quiet. I got out of bed, wrapped myself in the over large hotel bathrobe that had lost some of its softness, slipped my feet into the slippers and peeked around the curtain. Steam was beginning to escape from the kettle on the stove and I could hear logs being placed onto the fire. I moved swiftly to the bathroom and behind the curtain thinking I would take a shower and brush my teeth.

I was sat at the kitchen table, fully dressed, before Carmen had finished preparing breakfast. Fresh fruit again. But this morning she had drizzled honey – fresh from local bees, I presumed – onto the fruit and sprinkled on some broken, toasted nuts. It was delicious!

My lessons would start properly today, she said. It would be just her and me. Thomas, who would be staying in the cave until the beginning of January, would be out running errands most of the days. After breakfast we went to the large room upstairs. Carmen had told me that yesterday, I had a super powerful healing session with four super powerful healers and my sister, who would be a super powerful healer one day. This healing had removed a lot of lower energies that I had picked up from being around the men in the pickup – who were struggling with the lower-level energies of fear, shame, anger and guilt. They had lower energy beings attached to their auras sucking out any higher-level energy that they had. The police officers were also struggling with the lower vibrational energies that always surround people who help others; quite often their good energy would be stolen by those they try to help. When your good energy is pulled away from you by others it encourages more lower energy to sneak into your aura, Carmen continued. It was the same with the journalists, medical staff and parents, she said. Each one feels a level of guilt, shame and anger at what has happened in their town, their home, in their hospital. They internalise those feelings and make them a part of their self. This lowers their energy, too.

"Instead of feeling those emotions and then using them as an energy source of their own to fight back and find justice, people like to wallow in those emotions and become the victim. The moment you allow yourself to feel like a victim, the darker energies and entities win!" Carmen was alight with passion for this concept.

"I'm not saying that you cannot grieve the death of a loved one or feel guilty for causing another being harmed or hurt. But you cannot live in that grief and that hurt." She beckoned me over to the centre of the room, sat down cross-legged on the floor, and then continued.

"When the vibration of your energy is low, imagine that your energy is a shield, okay? It protects you, yes? If a real shield, a shield made of metal, were constantly bombarded with tiny metal pellets, day in, day out, raining, shining, whatever, it would eventually start to wear thin. Okay? It would become rusty in places. And maybe it would even get holes in it. It would still be able to protect you for a while, but there would be places where the little pellets and soon bigger pellets would be able to get through, yes?" She kept looking at me to make sure I understood, so I kept nodding. I understood exactly what she was trying to say and I didn't need the analogy of a real metal shield to help me.

When I was about seven years old I was in the town centre with my mother and my elder siblings. We had been to a supermarket which was selling potatoes really cheaply - there had been a glut of potatoes that year and they had started to go soft. Potatoes were a great filler food. They were cheap, versatile – you could have baked potatoes, roast potatoes, mashed potatoes, chipped potatoes

– and you needed only a small amount of protein with them to provide a meal which filled a starving belly. Anyway, we all had carrier bags full of food, mine were two bags of potatoes. Heavy. Pulling on my shoulders. The plastic handles cutting uncomfortably into the palms of my hands.

The supermarket was at the far end of town, so we had to walk there and back through the centre of town. There was an old train bridge that we had to walk through and on this particular day there was a figure in black hunched up hugging his knees and rocking back and forward. He was mumbling "spare some change," over and over and over again.

"Walk quickly," Mum had hissed quietly at us, stepping into the road to avoid him. Just as I was walking past him, a car came speeding past so I had to quick step up onto the pavement. No mean feat when you feel like your knuckles are dragging on the ground. As I did so the man reached out with both hands and grabbed one of the bags and my coat. I stopped mid breath. I could see the man's aura. At first glance it looked normal. It was normal. But there was a dulling of the light surrounding him – it wasn't grey like the being's that hung around Karen. He smelt like he had given up on life. But he wasn't ready to die. There were spots of blackness at the very edges of his aura and what looked like burn holes around his heart. I don't know if you've ever seen someone put a lit cigarette onto a piece of paper and watched as it smouldered into the page until a small circular hole was formed with ragged burnt brown edges. Well it was a bit like that. Except these edges were more ragged and the burnt parts were black like tar. Hanging onto the aura close to these small holes were little black beings like misshapen Rorscach ink splats. Not human. Not animal. Not spirit. Something in between. They scared me. They sent a block of ice far down into my heart and lowered the temperature of my body till I could see my breath. I could feel the ice-cold air on the inside of my mouth and nose as it was inhaled, like freezing fingers pushing down into my lungs.

So, yes. I told her. I understand.

"Eventually your aura is taken over by the darkness, and whatever is in your aura slowly makes it's way into your body. So the dark spots can become life threatening illnesses – like your pneumonia." She continued. "Your energy became weakened by the experiences you had as a child."

"But I visited The Light House," I countered, puzzled. "Didn't my energy get replenished and cleansed there?"

"Your Soul energy, yes! But you can't take your body there, and whatever is on your physical body shield will stay there until you have it properly removed."

"So ..." I was feeling a little puzzled, "my Soul isn't the same as the aura?"

"No." She smiled warmly and looked at me with understanding. "It isn't very simple at all, otherwise the whole world would know. Most people who are born remembering these things disengage with the knowledge when they realise there is more to learn." She looked sad for a moment before smiling and continuing, "One of our jobs," she swept her hand around the room, suggesting all the people who were here yesterday and all the people like us who weren't, "is to help to remind people who they are and from where they have travelled. Our job is hard. But if we can reach one Soul at a time, we will succeed."

I huffed out a large sigh, blowing out my cheeks, and raised my eyes to the roof.

"What happens if we fail?" I asked. "What happens if we can't reach them?" I was thinking of Beastman, Tony Davenport, Marguerite Paxton, the men at the pickup van.

"But, my dear child," she looked at me with a look I couldn't quite comprehend, then took my face in both her hands, a tear spilling from her left eye, "you have already affected them in so many ways that it has already changed the world!"

She stood up and beckoned me to the back wall of the upper room, where etched into the floor was what looked like a hexagram; it had six points, two identical triangles one pointing up, the other down, overlapping. It was encircled, each point touching the circle and each point joined to the next point on the inside of the circle by a concave line. These lines weren't etched as deeply as the others but were very clear.

"Unlike you, I need this to get there," Carmen said, sitting in the centre of the carved shape. "Come on, I'll explain as we go." She tapped the floor in front of her and, still puzzled, I sat down facing her.

"Close your eyes and take a deep breath," she said, so I took a deep breath, without closing my eyes and found myself in The Light House! I was alone.

"Carmen?" I called out. I could see other light beings milling about and felt Kaleb behind me. I turned and he bowed from his waist, hands together at his heart as though he was praying.

"She requires help to get here," he said, bowing again. "Reach out with your mind, to find her," he sighed an almost imperceptible sigh. "You know where she is. Imagine she is here."

I pictured Carmen sitting on the warm stone floor and me stood next to her in my Soul form. I stretched out, my light shape shifting and expanding to reach her. As my light form touched her aura I felt a shift in the energy and she, her light form, was stood in the Light Room with me.

"There, you go," she smiled. "It's easy when you know how!" Her light was bright but not as bright as mine. Her light form also quite small. Her light form suddenly shifted into her earthly body shape, but almost clear, still glowing, and I realised that mine had shifted too. I wasn't judging her, by the way. I was noticing. I am, at this point, still learning, and in order to learn you have to notice both the similarities and differences of the people, places and things around you, not to judge whether they are better or worse than you. But when you are able to see, to truly see, who or what something is, there is no need for judgement because you see what that person, place or thing is here on the earth for. And generally, it has very little to do with you!

Carmen looked around, I could see her light shimmer brighter as she entered this space. A feeling of rapturous joy overtook her and she floated around for a few moments until she 'found' herself again.

"I have only been here once before," she told me conspiratorially the light at her heart centre dazzlingly bright, "when I did my training. But I wish I could travel here whenever I wanted, like you." I smiled, not wanting to make her feel less.

The Light House had changed into the upper cave but with clear walls, floor and ceiling. All shimmering lightly. Carmen pointed to the shape on the floor of the cave image in The Light House, tracing it with her human fingers. This shape is based on a hexagram, she began to tell me. Throughout history this star shape has been used as a symbol for countless tribes, countries and religions. Wrapped in a circle like this also has historic symbolism. But ours is special because we have these additional lines. She traced her finger around the concave line from the top point of the star to the right-hand point. "This star shape symbolises many things; the masculine and the feminine; the earth and the sky; tribal friendships; reconciliation; the six known dimensions – although there are probably more being discovered now. The circle shows that these things are all connected – wherever you travel on the star, you can follow the lines to return to where you started. The inner lines, well, I don't know much about them, but they are more about what you do and I believe it is about travelling between the dimensions."

Although I didn't understand a word of what she was saying it all made perfect sense. Has that ever happened to you? My physical brain still needed to catch up with what my Soul body already knew.

"It will come to you," Carmen was saying, "but let's continue where we left off."

Mist began to swirl around The Light Room and the invisible

cave walls suddenly became a room. A bedroom. All pink. Really pretty. A door slammed, I turned to see, but the door was closed. I turned back to the room. Beside me were Kaleb and Carmen in their ghostly human forms. In front of me, a small child in jeans and a jumper, trembling, liquid appearing to seep from between her legs and soak into the denim, down the inside of the trousers and into her shoes. A man walked toward her and touched her hair. She was unable to move, but the trembling increased until she was almost vibrating. Almost. But not. I remembered this scene as though it was yesterday. I saw the dark, lower level energy beings, laughing like pack dogs around him. Sucking at his energy. Beginning to wrap their darkness around her. But then a strange thing happened. The girl remained in the exact same position, but her light expanded and she called out, silently, words I couldn't make out. A language I hadn't yet learned. The room began to fill with light beings as I stood watching my current observer-being expand with joy and love as I saw all my old friends appear. One at a time. Ten at a time. And they all looked with such love at this little girl, quaking in her piss-soaked shoes. Then another thing happened. Although I don't remember this, I also do with such clarity and yet forgetfulness.

A brighter, larger, more intense light seemed to pour into the room. If I say it turned and smiled at me, you would think I was totally crazy. Because we, Carmen and I, weren't there. We were looking back on a part of my past life. A part of my life before Kaleb and before Carmen. But, as you know, I am trying to share my story as honestly as I can.

This light – so huge it must have been the size of the moon – seemed to flow inside the little girl. As it flowed inside it also flowed outside and grew to fill the room, along with the little girl's inner energy. Their joined light energy flowed around the room, encompassing all of my spirit friends. Swallowing them up but they were all still there. Individual and yet a mass. The collective light energy then touched each of the dark energies, spirits, whatevers, and they exploded! Literally exploded! With a bang! Like a nuclear bomb! And like a nuclear bomb the explosion shook the very foundations of the building we were in. Not only the building that the human me was in, but wherever it was that Carmen, Kaleb and the grown-up-in-The-Light-House-me were! The explosions took the breath from my light body.

There were five explosions. Then silence.

The little girl began to talk to the man whose hand was still in her hair. She told him he was not a nice man. Her voice was coming out of her human body and her light body which was so tall it touched the ceiling. His light body oozed out of his body, smirking. Not quite so tall as the little girl's energy.

"You don't scare me," he said. "You have no power over me. You can't make me change. I like who I am. I like what I do."

The child's light body took the hand of the man's light body – there were no hands, but I am trying to explain it to you so you can understand – and the room they were in suddenly changed. It was a view of the human man, older, happier. In love. With children around him and joy in his heart.

"That's bollocks," the spirit of the man said. "No one will ever love me like that, and you know it. You're full of fucking lies." His energy darkened, he was angry and he was frightened. He didn't feel that he deserved that kind of life. That kind of happiness. He tried to pull away, but the child's energy was strong. Very strong.

"This can happen for you," she said. "I can help you. We can help you. If you ask for help I can give it to you, but I can't force you to choose happiness."

Breathing out a dark, tar-like substance, he spoke again. "I'm going to a better place than what you can give me." He laughed. "A place I can do what I like with out being judged by little cunts like you." He spat the words venomously.

"Show me," she said. And he twisted. The room began to change again. I could feel an icy coldness wrapping around me. I knew that Carmen and Kaleb were still with me, but they felt far away. I reached out for Carmen and pulled her close to me. I could cope with what we were about to see, I suddenly realised, but Carmen maybe couldn't.

The darkness and cold was overwhelming. We were in a room very similar to The Light House room, but I can only describe this as the Dark Room. The walls were clear, with darkness running in every direction. No light. Not even a star. The walls felt like they were oozing like an open sore. The only light was coming from our little group, and that was diminished greatly by the weight of the blackness surrounding us.

Seeing the beings here was like looking through a photographic negative. It was all exactly the same but without life. Without warmth. Without love. There was a feeling of desperation here. Fear. But not the fear I have ever witnessed before. This was deeper. Darker. More frightening. Harsher. A sense of dread that no human has ever felt began to creep into the atmosphere. Something was coming. Something ... The larger light – the light the size of the moon – shifted slightly and wrapped itself around the three of us observers. Protective. The interlopers in this moment of the little girl's life cocooned by something bigger, warmer, stronger. Safer.

But then it lifted me from the cocoon and brought me to stand with, beside, my child self. I looked behind to see Carmen enveloped. She was not going to want to see this part. I had a tiny nagging feeling at the back of my mind that I probably didn't either. Tony, in his physical form, opened his eyes wide. I have never seen eyes open so wide. This was not what he was expecting. This is not what he had been promised. His mouth opened and closed like a guppy fish in a giant aquarium. His body began to wriggle as though he were trying to escape.

"This is not the lowest level, Tony," the moon-sized light said, its voice soothing. Loving. Both male and female. Old and young. From before the world began to far after it ends. "But this is the best level that she will choose for you." He pointed to the little girl. The historical me. "She is the one who will bring you here. Or wherever is appropriate."

"I don't belong here." Tony's Soul was writhing. "Fuck off and take me home." He could feel this place more than I. I was cocooned. In love and in light. And in an energy far more power full than I had ever felt before. Except I must have felt it when I was here before. Had I chosen to forget?

Tony's Soul body was beginning to darken further. It began to crack. Tiny crackles like aged paint on antique furniture. Little pieces beginning to peel. He looked at his hands with panic and fear.

A rasping sound came from a doorway to the left. A dark oozing mass contracting and pulsating moved rhythmically into the space we were in. It saw our group and scowled, spitting out a dreadful tarry substance which seemed to eat through the floor like acid. Then it seemed to sense – for it didn't have eyes or ears that I could see – Tony. It was attracted to his darkness. His low energy. And his fear. It appeared to smile an awful, lopsided, open-mouthed smile, seeping the black tarry goo.

"Oh!" it spoke without words. Dark. Menacing. Yet needy like a petulant child. The voice feeling like an icy hand gripping my body and trying to rip out my heart.

"I have one!" it said, moving toward Tony. "I do need it. I do need more." Tony began to shake and make a strange sound in his throat.

Everything stopped. The walls began to clear and everyone but the girl, me and the enormous energy had disappeared. The room became brighter. It wasn't the dark place or the Light Room anymore. It was very square. Like a cube. Sharp corners. Very precise. The light was brighter than any I had ever seen.

"Are you God?" the little girl asked.

"No," the light being responded.

"Thank you," she said.

"Thank you," it replied.

"Who are you, then?" she asked. "I imagined this is where God would live. I thought God would be really huge."

"Ah!" the voice was soft and sweet, a hint of feminine. Because it knew this girl had suffered at the hands of man. "God is a man-made concept, you know?" it said. "God is an excuse, sometimes, too." It seemed a little sad.

But I'm getting ahead of myself. I'll tell you more about this later. Let's get back to Tony and the Dark Room.

"Help!" he said quietly, barely perceptible. "Please, help me! I won't. Ever again. I won't," he shouted in between strange gurgling noises.

The darkness began to melt away, and we were stood back in the pretty pink bedroom where Tony began to blink rapidly, then realised where he was.

"You fucking liar," Tony said and tried to pull his hand out of the little girl's hair, but he had clenched his fists, in his moment of fear, and held tight to the hair. The girl was still out of her body. The gigantic light being was still in the room. Tony had changed his mind now that he was back on safe soil. The little girl reached down with her spirit hand and pushed it into the crown of his head. She picked out a small black moving object, not an animal, but stirring. She passed it to the larger light being and it instantly exploded. Louder than the other explosions. Causing my spiritual ears to hear a high-pitched ringing noise. Tony screamed, thinking he was being held by something, not realising his hands were wrapped around her hair and he pushed her away.

At that moment her spirit being snapped back into her body and the girl dashed for the door. Too late he reached for her and instead headbutted the door. Anger rose up in him.

"Fucking bitch!" he said. She'd done something to him, he thought. Drugged him probably. Made him see this shit. She was going to pay. She was like his mother. Fucking women. They were all going to pay.

The room began to swirl back into the light room. Carmen looked depleted. Five light beings flocked into the room and stood around her. Their light pulsating. Building her energy back up.

I looked for Kaleb. "How did that help the world?" I asked him. "It made him angry."

Kaleb smiled and described how his usual calm and charismatic character had hidden his true self and would have continued to do so, destroying life after life of not just the family he was involved with, but every other human with whom both him and those he abused came into contact with.

"The kind of pain a man like him hands out doesn't disappear with him. It hangs around like a rotten smell and farts out when his victims least expect it, usually the people they don't want to hurt. And it becomes a never-ending cycle of the abused innocently becoming abuser. It was the same with Marguerite."

The swirling wall thing began again and I thought this was like one of those movies where they don't have enough money for proper special effects. But this was real and not a movie.

I was standing in a kitchen, Kaleb beside me. Observing. There was a little girl. Very pretty, even features and long blonde hair that would soon darken. She was hungry. She was also dirty. I suddenly recognised this place as one I'd visited before. It was the place where Marguerite had hidden the bodies. Before there were any bodies to bury. Before she was hurt. Except she had been hurt. She turned around as a pan clattered behind me. For a moment, I thought she was looking directly at me. But then she said,

"Mum, I'm hungry."

I turned to see a painfully thin woman at the sink, trying to wash a pan, but struggling to stand and to breathe. She had a metal ring around her ankle. It had once been very tight and had worn away at her skin leaving what looked like a raised circular welt around her ankle. It was this welt that was keeping the ring in place. A chain was attached to the ring by a worn and rusted padlock. This too had rubbed against the ankle causing old swelling and bruising that hadn't lessened over time.

"Mum!" little Marguerite called out in frustration.

"Ignore the old tart." A male voice came from outside. A thin man. I could smell him. Anger. Fear. Rejection. Desperation. The usual suspects. But also, Entitlement. Proprietorship.

He believed he owned this woman.

She had never wanted him, so he had taken her. Kept her against her will. Forced himself upon her. The children who survived without medical care were alive. Those who didn't were buried in the grounds. Those who were weak and dying he would abuse. Take his anger toward the world out on the dying bodies of his own flesh. He taught his living children to do the same. No point having kids if you couldn't blame them when things went sideways, he would tell them. Laughing.

"Are you hungry poppet?" he asked Marguerite. She nodded. His smile, as he walked toward her, made my stomach twist so tight I could feel all my internal organs squeezing.

I pulled myself out of the kitchen and back into The Light House. The dread and fear I felt suddenly diminished.

"Why are you showing me this?" I asked both Kaleb and Carmen. She was now shining brightly, "How have I changed the world?"

Change does not happen overnight. A voice so loud, yet whispered, sounded from within. Without. Above. Below. Beyond. It was in my ears and in my heart and in every atom of my body. All my bodies.

The room swooshed away again to a living room that I didn't recognise, to a young woman, about my age, who I did! It was Karen. She was sat on a beige sofa with her knees tucked under her, a large paper-backed book in one hand, a coloured pen in the other, and a pencil case on her lap.

"Hiya, love," a woman's voice from the hallway. A door clicking shut. Her mum walked into the living room wearing a coat and carrying a bulging shopping bag. "How was therapy?" she asked, bending down and kissing her daughter's head.

"Great. I can get through at least half a session without crying now," they shared a knowing smile, "You?"

"Guilt!" her mum said. "I can't help thinking …"

Karen stood up and threw her arms around her mum. They sobbed and held each other tight.

"We're gonna be fine," Karen said, rubbing her mum's back.

It still surprises me how strong young people are, how they are the ones supporting their parents through situations like this. But Kaleb was right. Because of what I did, Karen and her mum are going to be safe. They will never lose the pain but they won't inflict it upon anybody else.

We HAD made a difference. But what about Marguerite? How had we made changes there?

Carmen's form began to pale and suddenly she was no longer present in the Light Room. Kaleb beckoned me forward through a door, and we went back to the library. A large book appeared on a table in the centre of the room and flipped open to a living moving scene. Her mother. Young. Beautiful. Free. With a family who loved her. Parents. Brother and sisters. A husband and a daughter! Their fears that she was dead. Guilt. Anger.

But the knowledge that her body would now be brought to rest and her grandchildren finally able to have answers. The bodies of her own babies given the burials they deserved.

"The Soul does not rest," Kaleb's voice was sad. "Until the story is completed, there is always disturbance on a spiritual level."

When I returned home to England, Kaleb continued, DI Marton would tell me there had been further bodies found at Marguerite's former home. I would be able to suggest where he might look to help his investigation. He reminded me that there were also the children and babies that Marguerite and Denise Benton had murdered, whose families would finally have closure. Along with the innocence of Jason Benton that this situation had brought to light. History would be rewritten.

"Don't ever think that what you do has no effect. That what you achieve makes no difference. Your actions are like a pebble tossed into a calm pond. You may be able to see a few ripples on the surface, but there is so much more going on that you will never see and never understand. It doesn't mean that you are not responsible. It doesn't mean that your actions were for nothing. It means that you have succeeded in so many ways that you will never be given credit for. But we don't do this job for the credit do we?" He smiled, bowing from the waist and I'm not sure, but I think he winked at me!

45

Connections

I returned to the cave room at the same time as Carmen. She hadn't been witness to the information about Marguerite and her family. *It isn't part of her knowledge,* I told myself. We each have a part to play and the part I played was not the same as Carmen's.

The following day, we returned to the upper cave, but this time, Carmen wanted to talk about connections, how all things are connected.

"Have you ever noticed that historically there are usually two or three people who 'invent' something at the same time?" she started, pouring two large glasses of water from a large, shapely glass jug. The morning light, streaming in through the holes in the cave wall sent rainbow-coloured strips of light flaring around the walls. "For example, Alexander Graham Bell, Johann Phillip Reis and Antonio Meuci," she passed me a glass of water and indicated I should drink, "all worked on the idea of the telephone in the 1850s. Around the same time there were several people trying to make flying machines, but we always say it was the Wright brothers in the 1900s who invented the aeroplane. Leonardo Da Vinci was drawing machines for flight four hundred years earlier and their designs are very similar, in my opinion!" she raised her eyebrows knowingly, and I smiled.

"What I'm saying is," she paused and took a deep breath, "throughout history the idea of something becomes available to all mankind at the same time. But not everyone is interested in building houses with blocks of stone when they already have a cave or a tent in which to live. Not everybody is interested in the wheel or moving vehicles when they are happy to be in the place they live. Only when the need arises do people show much interest in the things that are available to them. Some people – like Da Vinci, like Bell, like the Wrights, like us," she moved her hand back and forth between us to show that she meant me and her, "realise that there is something there and we go in search of it. We want to know 'is it possible?' and if it is, 'how can we make it real?' and then, usually, 'how can I make money from it?'" she pulled a face as though wanting to earn money was a bad thing.

"So!" she said loudly, making me jump and the water in my glass spill over the side and onto my jeans. She smiled whilst I wiped the water into the denim, then continued, "How do they all get this tidbit of knowledge at the same time?"

I stared at her for a moment, like a rabbit caught in headlights. I hadn't realised I would be tested! I thought she might continue, but she kept looking at me.

"Erm..." I began. Then I realised something. "We are all connected!"

She smiled, then nodded, indicating I should go on.

"Well, you and Em know what I'm thinking or what I'm going to say," I began.

She blinked her eyes and nodded.

"When I touch certain items or speak with certain spirits I can see their histories. Their whole lives. I know them as well as I know myself."

"And you?" she asked. "What can you do that most other humans cannot?"

"Erm." She really was testing me. "I can eat fresh fruit three times a day and not fart like a trooper?" I asked, jokingly.

She laughed, then looked at me sternly. I was going to have to do the work now!

"Okay," I tried to think, then realised. "Well, I can talk to dead people. I can see auras, Souls and people's spirit guides. I can unhook Souls from dead bodies. I can move to the other side." I started to run out of things I could do, and I didn't think reading, baking, and sleeping were on her to-do list!

"Super!" she said, smiling. "How do you communicate with dead people?"

I pushed air out of my mouth making my lips quiver and a farty sound. I didn't like having to answer questions.

"How do I talk to dead people?" I returned the question. Because in reality I didn't know. I just did it. I had no idea what I did that made me different to other living people and if I had known, well, if there had been a set of rules, like, number one take a deep breath. Number two, say 'Om' thirty-two times. Number three... well, I just wouldn't have done it. I think I have very little patience, I decided in that moment.

"You connect to the web," she said, noticing my childish obstinacy but overlooking it.

Historically, she began, science and religion were separate things. Religion hadn't wanted science to start digging into its spiritual parts, and science hadn't wanted religion throwing holy water and crucifixes at it, so they kept themselves to themselves. But recently science had been looking at the interconnectedness of all things! In their search for God, they found that everything in the world, in the universe, vibrates within its own little atmosphere. Whether you are talking about a human being, an apple, an atom of water, everything is vibrating. Because of this it is possible to reach into the vibrational field and touch an apple on a tree in Berkshire yesterday whilst standing here today.

Although I wasn't one hundred percent sure her description made sense, I understood what she meant. I had, after all, just witnessed the very same thing yesterday. Standing in the pink room, visiting Marguerite's past, visiting Karen and her mum. Each time I had been told stories by my spirit friends they had taken me to their actual not-just-an-image deaths, so I could see firsthand their demise.

"Call in Kaleb," Carmen asked, and as soon as I thought about him he appeared by my side. "He can take you places that I will never be able to visit in this lifetime."

I asked what she meant. She smiled.

"This morning I sent Thomas back to Teruel." She looked a little nervous. "I want you to find him and tell me what he has in his hand." I must have looked puzzled, so she swept her hands in front of her to usher me backwards until I was standing on the etched stone image that we sat on yesterday.

She told me that I should close my eyes and imagine Thomas's face. Imagine that he was standing in front of me. I did. And I did.

His face was an arm's length away. I reached out to touch his face. He flinched and I opened my eyes. Shocked. And unnerved!

"Did you see him?" There was an eagerness in her voice. An excitement. But also a hint of fear.

"Why fear?" I asked her. She looked as though I had slapped her across the face! Her face darkened to a deep red as she looked away.

"I can't help you," she said honestly. "When you are elsewhere I can't reach you. I can't do anything but shake your body." But then she looked even more frightened. "But only if your body is here!"

Apparently, when I closed my eyes my whole body had disappeared for two or three seconds. Carmen had not believed it at first. She swooped her hand through the space where I had sat only moments earlier. Then I had reappeared as though I had been there all the time. Kaleb stood apart from us, smiling.

"You are truly your father's daughter," he said bowing, then disappeared.

We practiced searching for Thomas again. Carmen had instructed him to keep walking around the town so that neither myself or Carmen would know his exact whereabouts.

On my second attempt, I pictured his face and became aware

of the hustle and bustle of a busy area. I found myself in a narrow road beside a set of large brown doors with large plate glass shop windows opposite. Straight ahead I could see an old, tall brick tower with a pretty, Moorish tile decoration. At the base of the tower was a beautiful pointed top arch. My favourite. Leaning into the corner of an upright pier was Thomas, looking a little out of place and uncomfortable. He looked at his watch, then adjusted the sleeve of his jacket. It was cold. I moved toward him and as he looked up I could see recognition light up his face. Had he seen me? Was I visible? I looked down but could not see myself. *Was my body in the cave*, I wondered?

Although narrow, the street was busy. A young man with dark, wavy hair stopped beside Thomas and they smiled at each other. Dressed in loose jeans and a thick jacket, he grasped hold of Thomas's hand and gave it a quick squeeze. He said something that I could not hear and then walked away. Thomas turned his head and watched until the young man had disappeared from view. When he looked back toward me he was smiling and a slight shade of pink had crept up into his cheeks.

We practiced this several more times over the next few days. On Thomas's arrival back at the cave we would discuss what I had seen, where I had seen him. He would confirm that he had been in those places at the time I had seen him. I didn't mention everything I saw though. Thomas deserved some privacy, I thought. Carmen would keep an eye on the time in the cave. She would time when I 'left', when I 'returned' and the approximate time I 'saw' Thomas. She would also check my body, Soul and aura to check that I wasn't causing damage to any part of 'me'!

I would be ready soon, she told me, but when I asked what I would be ready for, she would just say "You'll see!"

One day we sat in the upper cave and Carmen looked nervous. Looking back, I think most of what we were doing was as new to her as it was to me. She knew all her spiritual stuff, I have no doubt about that at all. But I don't think she had met anyone with my gifts before. I was sure there was far more to this than I was being told, but I also knew that I was being given information a bit at a time for a specific reason, as though I was being tested for my attitude as well as my abilities.

Today, she said, we would be learning the incantation to open up the earth portal. Unsure of what that was I just nodded. She was nervous, I realised, because she had never done this before. *Perhaps now was the time to put her at ease*, I thought.

"What is the earth portal? Why do we need to open it?" I asked, genuinely interested.

"Portals are like doorways, you know. They allow you to go from one area of a house into another," she spoke fast, nervously.

"What? Like curtains in a cave?" I tried to lighten the mood.

She smiled a strained smile, "Yes, sort of." Then she continued.

"A portal is a doorway to another level or dimension. Early on in history we had doorways, or portals, to the spiritual realms and to heaven. There were also portals to the lower levels. Each portal had a key and each mortal had access to the keys. But when things began to change and the power dynamics began to shift, the keys were slowly lost. Power-hungry men did not want to pass on the keys but to keep them to themselves, so when they eventually died, there was no one who understood them. And even fewer people knew of their existence. Today there are only a handful of people who know about them. We are trying to recruit more people, like yourself and Thomas."

"Thomas?" I interrupted. Does he have …" I struggled for the right word "… gifts. Talents. Whatever they are called?"

"Yes. Not like yours." She fought for a moment to find the right words. "He is of the original line?" she said it as a question as if I should know. And I remembered something from the party about me being of a particular line.

"Michael's line?" I asked.

"Yes. How much do you know?"

I shook my head and raised my shoulders. Always happy to use symbolism where words failed me.

"Okay," she sighed a deep sigh. "Let me open the portal and I can explain it all through there."

46

Doorways

Carmen started by taking us to The Light House. Well, I took her. It was quicker for me to take her as her method was slow and boring! Although after being escorted a few times she did begin to find her way faster! I think it is like anything; the more you practice and the more confident you feel about the result, the easier it is to achieve that result. It's a bit like riding a bike; the first time you climb aboard, you try to lift both feet onto the pedals at once and typically fall off. Trying to balance on two wheels whilst making the pedals turn, holding the handlebars in a straight line and staying confident can take weeks or months of patience and practice. Some people jump on a bike and ride away without a second thought. Others struggle so much that they eventually give up.

    I digress. We're in The Light House. My Light House. Because I brought Carmen. I could have taken her to her Light House, but actually we had more access in mine. Think of it if you will as a secret government organisation – it absolutely is not, but it might help you to picture it that way! If you are working in the garage and only need spanners, wrenches and a grease gun to do your job the powers that be aren't going to let you wander around the penthouse office where they keep the nuclear codes – for obvious reasons. The Light House is different in that each person who accesses their area has access to ALL the information possible. You have access to your records, your history, your future, the history of the world, the possible futures of the world, the truth about alien races, the truth about immortals, fairies, unicorns and dragons and of course, the truth about mankind. But you are only able to access the information you are ready to access. In the beginning, mankind were all supposed to be able to access their own Light House.

The key, not an actual physical key, but an incantation or set of physical movements, would allow you access to your Soul group's 'suite'. That is a set of rooms specifically for your Soul family. Because even in the beginning there were groups who couldn't remember everything and were of a lower light. Not of the darkness – that came later. Once in your Light House, you can access as much learning as you need to. You can add to your own earth lessons or check where on your lesson journey you are. You can speak with your higher level Soul family to ask for help or support that you need when you are back in your body. But without the keys we are unable to reach here.

It is by accessing the portals that we access our Light House and our Soul Family. But some of us, particularly Michael's line, had a higher purpose and so we were able to access further portals, including other dimensions.

"Are we going into other dimensions today?" I asked Carmen.

"Well, I can't travel there," she said, sounding slightly relieved. "I'm not from your Soul Family. I trained with Corrine, Em's mum, whose ancestors researched for years to find the keys. So although I can teach you all you need to know, I haven't yet managed to access all the areas. And of those I have, I'm in no rush to return." She managed a weak smile. I wasn't sure what to make of it.

Apparently, this is why I had Kaleb as my guide, she told me, he was from one of the highest-bearing Soul families and, like me was able to travel anywhere, I think!

Carmen asked me to bring the book of keys. "Just imagine you are holding it in your hands or that it is on the table."

"What does it look like?" I asked, thinking about the shelves of books in the library that looked like Mrs Marton's.

"It doesn't matter," she said, "just ask for The Book of Keys. What you most need will come to you."

"Can I think of a McDonald's cheeseburger with salty fries?" I asked, suddenly feeling slightly hungry. She pulled a face. I'm not sure she agreed with me eating meat as I hadn't eaten a single portion since arriving here almost one month ago.

"Just concentr—" But she didn't finish as the book appeared in my hands.

I laid it on the table and asked it to show me where I needed to go today. The pages began to crackle and move of their own accord, as though some invisible being were lifting the top corner of each page and flipping it over to the left, scanning each page, then flipping to the next. About four pages were turned, then it settled down. Carmen and I both moved a little nearer, our heads bent, so that we could see what was on the page.

I could only see a small dot in the centre of the page, but Carmen had put a finger to the top of the left-hand page, tracing along an invisible line of writing.

"Okay, so we just have to say this out loud," Carmen began as I touched the dot in the middle of the page.

Ahead of us, the bright white, invisible wall seemed to melt apart. Beyond was space. Darkness. Dots of light. Then a giant mesh of silver threads began to appear in that space. Millions upon trillions upon ... I don't think we have numbers that big on earth! But all these microscopic, silver, silk-like threads were weaving up and down and across, like weft and warp, and also, diagonally both left and right. All separate and yet interwoven. I reached out to touch them and Carmen seized a loud, sharp breath. I pulled my hand back and looked at her.

"Go on," she encouraged, nodding her head vigorously.

I touched the first string, a warp thread running top to bottom of the image and felt myself in the presence of a small girl on a hot beach somewhere sunny. She was with her parents. They were a happy family. They had good jobs. Money. Friends. Happiness. Success. The smell of the sea. And suntan lotion. Expensive.

I moved across to the next warp thread. They were so fine it was hard to pick them out individually. This time, I was in the presence of a boy. Another hot country. This one an orphan. Living on the street. Alone. Hungry. I could feel the pain in his belly. The stench of his surroundings burnt my nose. I felt sad and uncomfortable and wanted to come away immediately. I wanted to be away from such poverty and pain and desperation. But I made myself look a little longer. He was dying. I felt that now. He knew it too. He was walking to a place where they left the dead to rot in the hot sun. They would just chuck his body on the pile anyway, so he may as well save them the trouble, he told himself silently. The stench increased and his eyes were watering. But he wasn't afraid. I gripped the string a little tighter and pulled. I found myself standing next to him. He looked at me.

"Are you here to take me to my family?" he asked in his language and mine.

I hope so, I spoke into his head.

"I'm tired now. I want to go."

My heart swelled for him. Emaciated. His lips pulled back from his teeth. He hadn't eaten or drunk anything in days. A light appeared beside him, and tears began to pour down his face as he cried for the mother he could see in the light. She called to him, but his body did not know how to let go of his Soul. He stood there crying. Her arms wrapped around him, waiting for him to be freed from his earthly body.

"Yes, you can." Kaleb was beside me, answering my thoughts. He bowed from the waist, his hands in prayer position and retreated to The Light House. I reached out to the boy and cut the cord that kept his body and Soul together. His emaciated shell dropped to the floor. His Soul whooped and flew around me twice shouting his thanks. Then his beautiful light flew toward his mother light. And they disappeared.

I released that thread and moved across to a weft thread. Now I was in a room. People were talking about retribution for some slight that had occurred in their family hundreds of years ago and was reoccurring now. They had the ability to end it once and for all. But it would be bloody and could start a bigger war. There were raised voices. Calls for peace. Calls for war. Fear on both sides for what would happen if they acted or if they didn't.

I moved to another thread. A man, sad and beaten by life, writing a novel of love and triumph against the odds. *It is going to be the bestselling book of all time,* I thought. And I knew that, although I was right, he might not live to see it published.

I picked up two threads and saw how those two lives interacted. Multimillionaire and prostitute. Equals for mere moments. Then as far apart as it was possible to be.

Another thread, another life. Another thread, another life. Another thread, another death.

"Put a thought in there," I heard Carmen's voice as if she were at the far end of a tunnel. Echoing. Distant.

I picked up the millionaire and prostitute thread again. *You really ought to get clean,* I thought.

"I should come off the drugs," the prostitute said to his roommate as the phone began to ring.

"I've been thinking," said the millionaire into his phone, "do you fancy doing rehab with me? My treat?"

I smiled. *You should give him a proper job*, I thought without thinking.

"There are a few graduate opportunities opening up next month and I know you would be brilliant." said the millionaire to the prostitute. "I could talk you through the process if you want?"

I smiled and dropped the threads. I felt playful. I wondered what else I could do. And then I wondered…

I stepped back into The Light House. "Why can't I just grab hold of them all and demand peace on earth? Or maybe just gently suggest it?" I asked Carmen as Kaleb appeared.

Carmen looked at Kaleb. "You say 'peace'," he began, "But what exactly is peace? To one person, peace is the quiet of a countryside walk. To another, it is the absence of war. To yet another, it means something completely different. Until everyone is on the same page of the book, you have to use different words and terminology."

"So, could I take hold of all the threads and suggest no war?" I asked, intrigued.

"Of course," he replied with a little bow, "and those who are not living in a warzone? How will they understand no war?" I looked perplexed, so he continued. "For some people, if you tell them they cannot have something that they do not have, they want to know why and they will do their utmost to get that thing that you have told them they cannot have."

"Finding the strings that only fit your criteria is a lengthy process and by the time you have found and passed on the message, new people have been brought into the war, new messages from the earth are brought into the war, so your initial message becomes obsolete. Alternatively, one side starts to lay down arms, while the other, unaware of the peace ready to be made, increases their fighting, killing the peacemakers and aggravating anger in the living." He spoke with an air of experience that I didn't want to go into today.

"So lineage and stuff," I shifted topic because I couldn't get the little boy out of my head and he wasn't in a warzone. There is so much more in the world to put right. War being one. Poverty another. Abuse another. I could go on, thinking of my personal experiences to date. But it is too much for a child to bear. I am still a sixteen-year-old girl at the end of the day – most girls my age are experimenting with makeup, high heels, sex, music, and other stuff I have no idea about because I'm in another dimension experiencing every kind of hatred, fear and depravity one human can hand to another.

Carmen smiled a huge smile, she was back in her comfort zone. She called for another book – it came in the form of a small scroll, but as it opened up it was obvious that it was actually humungous! As it unrolled, the nearest unrolled bit disappeared, but I could tell that if it hadn't disappeared, the un-scrolled parts would have taken over the whole of the room we were in.

47

Family History

Okay! Now this bit is a bit of a mindfuck! I know I'm still young and shouldn't be using that word. I also know that I have some sort of talent that I haven't yet fully discovered, but the next bit was a bit Greek Mythology.

I mean, in Greek Mythology, you have gorgons, medusas and cyclops. Gods marrying humans and having demi gods or semi gods or whatever, who had powers to overthrow the monsters.

Well, this is where it starts getting a bit freaky, because I'm sure you know all the ancient stories are based on real stuff, right? And the Greeks and the Romans and the Druids and the Jews and the Egyptians and every other tribe all over the world all had their stories? Okay. The truth is – and I'm not allowed to mention some bits at this stage, you will understand why later – the scroll was a record of the whole of the history of everything. That's right, EVERYTHING!

So it didn't unroll all the way to the beginning. But it went to the beginning of me. So hundreds of millions of years ago, I was a star. An actual planet! Made by the origin of everything! And for millions of years I shone my little heart out into a wilderness of other stars and nothingness. Because that was my job. And then one day, the origin of everything came to see me for a little chat!

"I want you to implode," said the origin of everything. We'll call him Jeff, just to make it easier for you to understand and easier for me to type.

"Okay!" I said, because I was still very young, even though I was millions of years old, and didn't know that I could ask why. So, I imploded. The light at the core of my being – my planet – collapsed with such immediacy and such force, as happens when a star explodes, that my body, my surface, broke into a million tiny pieces.

"Here," said Jeff, handing my light core several tiny pieces of my exploded body. "Can you make me a planet? I want to put tiny creatures on it. I want to see how they grow and what they will make of the life they are given."

"Okay," I said, because I didn't have anything else to do at that point as I didn't have a star to shine.

For the next two million years, I made planets. Gigantic ones and tiny ones. I enlarged the space that Jeff had given me to make ever bigger, ever better planets and stars. Some were able to sustain life and others weren't. But none were suitable for Jeff's needs. He had other beings that were working on similar projects in other parts of the universes. Each had succeeded in one part of Jeff's plan but not in everything. So after millions more years he brought us together.

Although we each governed our own system of planets, we worked together to find the best parts of each of our best planets. For me, I was amazing at making the solid parts, the rocks. I started with the core of the earth and built outward bringing gases and other substances from my colleagues' systems. They took over at certain points to bring in something that they had learned from making their systems. We discovered that putting a Soul at the centre of the planet helped stabilise all the other attributes beautifully and eventually, after millions of years, we had the solar system that we know today. We were still monitoring our own independent systems and bringing through any new findings for this joint project. But Jeff was really pleased. And had begun to make 'life' to go on this one particular planet.

Unfortunately, not everything was able to survive on this

planet. We tried life forms on our separate planets in our solar systems first to see which ones reacted to which gases. And eventually we found a set of species which were able to live on the earth planet. You call them animals, but you wouldn't recognise the word we used for them. One of the animals was humans. They were dim creatures who would just sit most of the day until they needed food. It was the lowest form of life on the planet, but Jeff and the Dominions (that's me and my planet-building colleagues) had become quite fond of them. One of the Angels suggested that we put a Soul into the humans, so Jeff started small, and put two in a small area that the four of us would monitor. He wanted to see how they would behave and if the Souls were distressed, we would be on hand to remove them.

It was a roaring success and they began to mate and make more humans, so we needed more Souls. Sometimes the human bodies were unable to survive so we would remove the Souls. The humans began making rituals for when they had food when another was born or died. For different types of weather. All kinds of rituals. But they all used to speak with us. We were their guardians and they asked us for help with their food production. They asked us for help with their families. They asked us for help with their shelters. They asked us for help with their feelings. As their tribe grew bigger, we expanded the garden. As the garden expanded, they became more inquisitive. Sometimes we would find a lone human crossing a desert plain, climbing a mountain or swimming in the large body of water that covered the planet.

Even later, after we stopped guarding the garden, it was decided that each human would have their own Angel to guide and to guard them. Some of the humans had taken to doing strange things that we could not recognise as something we had made. They would harm others for no reason. They would steal food even though they had plenty of their own, just so that someone else wouldn't have food. They began to split away from each other. What had been one large family had become two, then three, then four, separate groups. Each moving away from their previous family and setting up new tribes, new gardens. It was fascinating to see how each tribe grew and changed and how their basic needs were always the same. They needed love, most of all; to be with or near other humans. But food, water and shelter were also high priorities.

Alongside our jobs leading our own star systems, we also worked together ensuring that this system ran smoothly. If a planet became misaligned or fell out of its orbit – which many of them did in the early days – it would have catastrophic effects on the other planets and stars, causing deaths, famine and changes to the structure of the planet of earth.

At one point, a close ally of Jeff, we'll call him Stan for simplicity, began to experiment with the humans who were behaving differently. Meanly. He found that he could manipulate them to do bad things. Really bad things. He enjoyed it so much that Jeff gave him an ultimatum. Stop immediately or be cast out of his Light House. Unbeknown to Us and to Jeff, Stan had been working on his own version of The Light House, a place where he was able to continue manipulating the humans who were genetically predisposed to that type of behaviour.

One of our other jobs, apart from making and monitoring the world, was also to bring home the Souls – which were eternal living beings – when the physical body in which they were incarnated stopped working. The body would die – they had stopped seeing, hearing and believing in us at this point, so we couldn't tell them how to make their bodies work better and live longer – so we would go and remove the Soul. We would bring it home and then it would make arrangements for its next incarnation.

Again, unknown to us, Stan had started to recruit Souls with promises of never-ending glory and seats on the throne of heaven. They would return to earth in bodies that were meant to bring glory to humans and the earth – better lives, happier lives, more abundant lives – but these tainted Souls spread fear and horror instead. They instigated war, brother against brother. They brought about famine. They incited hatred and prejudice against people who once had loved each other. They sought to alter the structure of power and told lies to shame and dishonour those who spoke truths and love.

Our work had been undermined by one Soul. For what end we do not know. But now, when a Soul was ready to go home, we would have to check whether it was to return to the higher level. More levels were created to take the different levels of Souls we were retrieving. Once upon a time, when a Soul left this plane, it went to the place you called 'heaven'. There was only one place to go. Now how tainted a Soul is with lower frequency energy depends on where it actually ends up.

I had already witnessed a little of that with our visit with Tony. But that wasn't nearly the lowest level!

Because more and more Souls were being tainted and therefore fewer and fewer Souls were willing to come to the earth, Jeff decided his experiment would be over and he would just end it. Many from the Angelic quarters, though, still believed in the human animals and asked if we could take over the reins of their survival. He gave us a time limit, which was very short, but promised that he would not destroy our work if we were able to turn it around.

So, over the next one thousand years, actual Angels began to be incarnated into human bodies! This was very difficult at first. I was one of the first to be incarnated. I loved this world that I had been party to creating and wanted to see it succeed. But an Angel's being is far greater than that of a normal Soul so there were a lot of issues that caused widespread plagues and deaths. You can tell when there is an influx of Angelic births as worldwide diseases occur.

Unfortunately, during these pandemics the humans laid blame at the feet of other people, countries, or behaviours. Initially, plagues were blamed on the behaviours of Pharaohs, but the entrance of Angels into human bodies caused huge problems with the atmosphere as well as infecting the physicality of the Angels. This caused both Angelics and humans to die. Later on, a new influx of Angels caused a widespread disease, which was blamed on vermin and so on and so on for the whole of history. Plagues and diseases that wiped out whole villages were the result of Angelic intervention.

Those Angels who survived in their earth bodies were seen as different by their families and neighbours. They were less emotional and quite logical in their thinking but were seen as 'less than' by many of their human contacts. They were able to access the higher realms, speak with ancestors and treat illnesses. They became the village healers and wise people. They would pass on their knowledge and talents to as many human people as they could in the hope that this would allow the humans to return to their knowledge base.

All this while, Stan was attempting a similar experiment, bringing darker-level beings into human form. Stan's humans were responsible for some of the biggest wars, man-made disasters and, of course, the witch hunts. By hunting and killing the men and women who knew the Angelic ways, who worked for and through God, they sowed seeds of fear about these customs and many humans began to shun these ways, leaving mankind open to the negative and lower energies.

The scroll was arriving at the present time. A new plague was being brought to the earth at this period. Love would be blamed for this new plague. But the world needed love now more than ever. I could see my life in this timeline. Mine was a brighter light than many other Angelic lights on the earth. I could see those who I was to teach. Those who I was to help.

I also saw my personal lifeline. From my birth – a star, which is still visible from earth today so bright and so distant was my light – daughter of gods and Angels. My many incarnations. Man.

Woman. Good. Bad.

In one incarnation, I was lured to the darker side. My Soul spent time in the lower levels. A thousand years. But my Soul fought to return home. To the light. And the struggle to get there was real. But I made it. I grew stronger and afterwards, I vowed to help eradicate the negative and lower energies. That is why I am here today. It is also why I can enter the lower energy levels of the afterlife.

And this is also why I feel like I am being tested. The highest-level beings and Jeff know that I am of the light. They know that my intentions are pure. But they also know how deviant Stan can be. They are checking to make sure I don't show any lower-level behaviours. It is also why Archangel Michael is my chief Guardian Angel!

I felt my light shift. Expand. I began to grow. Light began to pour into me and around me and through me. My physical body, sitting in the upper cavern room, also began to expand. Grow. Become light. My whole being, physical and spiritual, increased in intensity and size until it filled the space. Then, it increased further until I was looking at the cave from above. Then again, until I could see the town of Teruel. The country of Spain. The continent of Europe and then the whole of the earth. My light shielded the whole planet and kept growing. I took in the moon, the sun, the whole Milky Way. And still I kept expanding. I saw the solar system of planets I had made millions of years ago and enveloped them in my light. I expanded further and took in more solar systems. Both ancient and new. And still I continued expanding.

And then.
Silence.
White.
Peace.
The Light House?
No.

Bigger.

Back in the place with the me as a little girl.

She had just asked, "Are you God?"

It had responded, "No."

If there were facial expressions here, the little girl would be placing her hands on her hips and staring with a little scowl at this being.

"It is difficult to describe what I am," it said eventually. "Because there are so many systems set up on the earth plane already to describe me." It paused. I could tell it was choosing its words carefully. Not because it was talking to a child. And not because it was trying to work out which 'faith' she was, but because this was a concept it had never had to discuss before. Its usual visitors were very aware of who or what it was. It had been here since the beginning.

Like me, I thought. Then I hoped the little girl version of me couldn't hear.

"She can't," the big spirit said to just me.

"I am ..." it began, "...human consciousness if you will. As each Soul is born out of me, I take a small part of myself back from you. This way, we are linked. We are a part of each other before, during and after your life on earth."

The girl, had she had an expression in this place, would have looked momentarily puzzled before saying, "But if that is true, why don't you help us? My mum ..."

"Oh! Sweet child. I cannot!" If you have ever heard someone with a huge amount of love in their heart telling someone they can't have something and it's for their own good, you will understand the sorrow, pain and confusion that person feels. And I felt that now. This being of light, human consciousness, wanted so much to help its creation. Its children. But it was unable.

"Why not?" the child said. You have to love the innocence of a child without boundaries. For she is the one who asks the questions we all want the answers to.

It let out a sigh and took on a human-like form. It was genderless, with neither male nor female body parts and no hair. It was very tall with long, slim limbs. It wasn't wearing clothing, so you could see the dark honey colour of its skin.

"When human life on earth first began," he swept out a hand, the walls began to disappear and they were on the earth, showing the world as it was back then, "the animals were given choices." He continued, "Initially they were happy with what they had, but then they wanted more. We asked them what they wanted and we gave them. They wanted even more. We tried to change them, but they got angry with us. We decided together that they would make their own choices and find their own ways of doing things. We said that we would always be here for them and that we wanted to help them. And so, if they needed help, they called upon us. We gave everyone their own guide, but as the tribes grew, they decided that only one person should speak with us. That way, everyone would have their place within the tribe.

"But the darkness made people stop listening to their own guidance. They said that in order to receive help, the people had to pay. At first it would be food, but then daughters, then land and then gold. And then they begat buildings to speak to us, but they had forgotten how to communicate. Even the people put in charge had forgotten how to hear us."

The little girl sent out a wave of loving energy to the being. Although still full of loving energy, it had diminished a little.

"We asked that they not worship us, but they did. All along, they were worshipping themselves without knowing it."

"And now?" asked the little girl. "What happens now?"

"Ah, my child," It turned toward me and began to shine so bright I could hardly see. A high-pitched buzzing sound crept gently into my very centre, vibrating every part of my being here and everywhere that I was.

"Now, you have to bring back their understanding."
(THE BEGINNING)

A Note From the Author

I would like to thank everyone who picks up this book and reads the words that fill these pages. As a first-time novelist, I have poured my heart and tears into this project (every time I read it, even though I know the story intimately, my eyes still prickle and my breath still catches)!

If you enjoyed reading it, please leave a review on Amazon (it helps other readers to find the book) and please pop across to my FB page (www.facebook.com/LynnMurrell.Books). If you 'Like' the page and message me your email address I can send you – for free – the first chapter of the second book in The Light House Series (or another piece that I am working on!).

I would like to send huge thank yous to:

Rachel Maria Bell (rachelmariabell.com) whose astrological reading opened up my mind and energy to allow this book to be birthed!

Sue Freer – as the first human to have a copy of the manuscript, her enthusiasm and feedback made me cry (happy tears, I have to add!) Thank you, lovely lady. x

Marina Beech the Soul Alchemist (marinabeech.co.uk) for her support throughout this process and to Faye Allen, Tracey Lawton, Lucia Klencakova , Kimberley Matwijiwskyj, Maria Jordan, Beverley Weaver, Mariska Van Seventer for your fabulous feedback on the unedited version of the manuscript. It is so scary to hand over your first literary baby, not knowing what others might actually think of it and being totally blown away by the responses. Thank you. xx

Special thanks also go to Kate Spencer (www.kate-spencer.com), author and expert in personal and spiritual development, for inspiring me to write from my heart and my soul! Also, for introducing me to the fabulous editor, Michelle Emerson (www.michelleemerson.co.uk), without whom this book would not be in your hands now.

Lastly, but most importantly, I would like to thank my husband, Graham, for his unwavering support throughout this process and my sister Tracy, whose constant and unconditional support is worthy of medals. THANK YOU.

Printed in Great Britain
by Amazon